HEALING FROM REPRODUCTIVE TRAUMA

If you have experienced trauma during your reproductive journey, from conception through your postpartum recovery, you are not alone. Pregnancy and new parenthood can be fraught with numerous potential distressing situations, such as infertility, pregnancy and postpartum complications, pregnancy losses, and childbirth.

It's no wonder that 1 out of 3 parents report their birth experiences were traumatic, and upwards of 40% of new parents can experience PTSD during the perinatal period. Perhaps it was what happened to you that was distressing, and maybe it was how you were treated that created or added to the distress. This can be a difficult time to navigate, particularly if you feel scared, overwhelmed by your symptoms, and isolated and alone. And yet, there is hope for healing! This workbook was written to help you build resilience and navigate difficult feelings. Drawing from empirically validated research and clinical experience, this book will help you educate yourself to further understand what you have experienced, and learn how to manage your trauma reactions. Written with sleep-deprived and traumatized parents and parents-to-be in mind, this book is divided into easy-to-read sections to help you manage your emotions and find validation and reassurance. Chapters begin by helping you identify what reproductive trauma is, what is happening "below the surface" with the brain and body's reactive responses, and the various emotional aspects of these events. The second section focuses on building tangible skills to manage the impact of trauma, including trauma reactions and the influence on relationships and attachment with the baby. The third section provides a map of the future, instills hope around healing, highlights professional treatment options, and explores the complicated decision about future pregnancies.

Whether you are preparing for trauma therapy, already working with a mental health therapist, or just starting to explore aspects of your experience, this workbook can provide support wherever you are on your healing journey. Filled with activities and gentle writing prompts, this comprehensive resource is essential for expecting or new parents who have experienced traumatic distress during this time, as well as mental health clinicians and birth providers.

Bethany Warren, LCSW, PMH-C, is an experienced psychotherapist certified in perinatal mental health and EMDR therapy. She has worked with reproductive trauma for over 20 years and is the co-author of *The Pregnancy and Postpartum Mood Workbook: The Guide to Surviving Your Emotions When Having a Baby* (Routledge, 2022). Find her at bethanywarrenlcsw.com and on IG @bethanywarrenlcsw.

T0347824

HEALING FROM REPRODUCTIVE TRAUMA

A Workbook for Survivors of Traumatic Infertility Journeys, Pregnancies, and Births

Bethany Warren, LCSW, PMH-C

Routledge
Taylor & Francis Group

NEW YORK AND LONDON

Designed cover image: © Getty Images

First published 2024
by Routledge
605 Third Avenue, New York, NY 10158

and by Routledge
4 Park Square, Milton Park, Abingdon, Oxon, OX14 4RN

Routledge is an imprint of the Taylor & Francis Group, an informa business

Library of Congress Cataloging-in-Publication Data
Names: Warren, Bethany, author.
Title: Healing from reproductive trauma : a workbook for survivors of traumatic infertility journeys, pregnancies, and births / Bethany Warren, LCSW, PMH-C.
Description: New York, NY : Routledge, 2024. | Includes bibliographical references and index.
Identifiers: LCCN 2023014620 (print) | LCCN 2023014621 (ebook) | ISBN 9781032460772 (hardback) | ISBN 9781032460765 (paperback) | ISBN 9781003379973 (ebook)
Subjects: LCSH: Pregnancy--Psychological aspects. | Childbirth--Psychological aspects. | Infertility--Psychological aspects. | Psychic trauma--Treatment.
Classification: LCC RG560 .W368 2024 (print) | LCC RG560 (ebook) | DDC 618.2--dc23/eng/20230705
LC record available at https://lccn.loc.gov/2023014620
LC ebook record available at https://lccn.loc.gov/2023014621

ISBN: 978-1-032-46077-2 (hbk)
ISBN: 978-1-032-46076-5 (pbk)
ISBN: 978-1-003-37997-3 (ebk)

DOI: 10.4324/9781003379973

Typeset in Stone Serif Std
by KnowledgeWorks Global Ltd.

I dedicate this book to all of my current and past clients. Thank you for trusting me with your stories. It's been an honor walking alongside you as you heal. You inspire me with your courage, for showing up through the messiness, and working through the muck. I'm so grateful for you.

CONTENTS

PREFACE

I started my career as a Licensed Clinical Social Worker in the '90s, working in a hospital on the maternity floor. I absolutely loved working with pregnant and new parents and supporting them in their transition to parenthood. I was inspired running a postpartum support group and working with the multidisciplinary team of doctors and nurses. I also saw incredibly difficult situations that shaped the trajectory of my career. I held space for parents with their babies in the NICU, navigating their pregnancy complications in the antepartum unit, experiencing traumatic births and devastating losses, and facing challenging and sometimes life-threatening postpartum complications. I also saw how my colleagues and I struggled with secondary and vicarious traumatization by what we saw at times, even though we might not have been able to fully articulate how we were impacted by what we were witnessing. Interestingly, just like "secondary traumatization" has been a newer term that is more recently being discussed, the terms "reproductive or birth trauma" were also not really widely used at the time to reflect what our patients were experiencing. I also noticed an important pattern that traumatized new parents weren't just the ones who had "overt" or medical trauma such as emergent cesarean sections, catastrophic outcomes, physical injuries, or losses. Sometimes people also had negative impacts on their mental health when seemingly on the surface things had gone relatively smoothly when viewed through a medical lens, but they were still suffering. They were sometimes minimizing their own experience in hopes of trying to make sense of why they felt the way they did, saying, "but other people had it so much worse; why am I feeling the way I am?" They were certainly dismissed and invalidated by others at times as well, often with good intentions of trying to make it better: "Focus on the positive, your baby is fine, it's all okay." And this is what I came to learn about the subjective nature about trauma, how trauma responses will show up even when there are "good outcomes," and that there are numerous contributors to trauma.

Trainings I received on non-perinatal PTSD and trauma did not always fully capture my patients' lived experiences, nor what they needed, so I was continually looking to piece together resources and ideas for how to support my patients. It was with connecting with colleagues and reading Cheryl Beck and other researchers' work in the early 2000s that I started seeing studies and terminology that reflected what I was seeing in my work. I was a sponge, eager to soak up more about perinatal trauma treatment and prevention to better help my patients.

I shifted into psychotherapy with a private practice in the early 2000s, connected with a local Perinatal Mental Health nonprofit organization, the Postpartum Health Alliance, and have found my niche, where I have thrived ever since. I trained in EMDR (Eye Movement Desensitization and Reprocessing Therapy, a specific type of trauma therapy), learned how to assess and address dissociation, and I now try to attend every perinatal or trauma conference that I can. I'm really thankful for the community I'm part of and am surrounded by so many skilled perinatal mental health clinicians. In the years since I started this work, I have seen a lot of change around how perinatal mental health and reproductive trauma is discussed. I'm encouraged that there is much more accurate and accessible information available for parents, less stigma around perinatal mental health, and more availability with resources and screening. How far we have come: there is such fantastic content on social media and podcasts making information and support more readily available! There is still a long way to go, unfortunately, for accessibility of safe and equitable mental healthcare for all, particularly for women of color. Continued public awareness and information is necessary around Perinatal Mood and Anxiety Disorders (PMADs) in general, but in particular about reproductive trauma and perinatal-onset post-traumatic stress disorder (PTSD). Social media does seem to help with spreading information, and I'm encouraged to see so many conversations now around birth trauma, infertility, and pregnancy loss.

Because reproductive trauma can be quite nuanced and complex, survivors often share with me the difficulty in finding their experiences captured in resources, yet are seeking information and skills to heal. I often hear from those who are craving meaning of their reproductive experiences and relief from their distress, and the refrain of "I wish someone had told me this could happen." I listened to these themes and let this wisdom from survivors shape this book. Similarly to why/how I wrote my first book with my colleague, *The Pregnancy and Postpartum Mood Workbook*, I recognize the vital importance of having easy access to resources, empowering ourselves with information, learning *why* we're feeling why we are, and building a roadmap to find our way through. I also recognize that not everyone has access to, or is connected to, quality and affordable mental health care, yet they still deserve resources and support. I was inspired to write a book to help connect the dots for traumatized parents who are suffering, and one that could be a thorough resource with numerous skills and tangible concepts to help ease suffering and promote change. I poured my heart and my years of experience into this book, and I hope that you find it a helpful companion in your healing.

ACKNOWLEDGMENTS

As they say, it takes a village to raise a baby, and I like to say it takes a village to raise and support the parents as well (that's a lot of villages for anyone counting at home). I'm super grateful for MY village, for which I couldn't continue to do the work of supporting parents, and this book certainly wouldn't exist without it.

I'm thankful first and foremost to my ever-supportive husband who cheered me on with my first book, and who believed in me writing this second one before even I did. Thank you for all of your support, editing, for putting up with my *really* long hours and catching my overuse of quotation marks. Thanks to all my friends and family who have cheered me on along the way, purchased my books, and girlfriends who have patiently listened to me talk *all* about the process of writing a book, and pretending to be riveted. That's true love.

I'm profoundly grateful for my first readers, dear friends and colleagues Dr. Beth Creager Berger, Susie Morgan, and Gretchen Mallios. This book wouldn't be nearly what it is without your incredible brains. I'm forever indebted to you for your edits and feedback and for rooting me on from the beginning. I'm thankful for my community of supportive readers who provided the next rounds of important feedback and helped me take my book to the finish line: Emily Remba, thank you for your time and attention to detail; your personal and professional lens was so needed! Dr. Daniel Singley, thank you for your help and your valuable input and research on dads and partners. Thank you to my roomie and work wife Kim Panganiban who helped me tremendously on the partners/relationship chapter. Your expertise in this field is admirable, and I'm lucky I get to work with you. Thank you to Julie from Integrate Network for your generous help with yoga resources and for all that you do in this space. Dr. Danielle Heistand, thank you for generously sharing your professional lens and lived experience, I'm thankful to know you. Dr. Annie Murray, what a gem you are, thank you for your insight and input. Jillian Early, thank you for your friendship and your edits; each suggestion you made was spot on and you saved my bacon! Dr. Katayune Kaeni, you are such a special person – thank you for your friendship and support of both of my books; you are the true embodiment of "women supporting women." #matchingcapes. Dr. Rebecca Moore, I so admire you and the work you do, and am honored you supported my project. Thank you. Dr. Alison Reminick, I feel so dang lucky to know you and am grateful for your support; thank you for uplifting this book. And Cheryl Beck, what a true honor to have you read and endorse my book. Your research and voice have changed this field and I'm very grateful for you.

Thank you to my incredible editor Heather Evans who has been with me through both books – I couldn't have done this without you. You are a fabulous teammate. And a big thank you to the rest of the Routledge team.

And finally, I thank and honor every one of my clients who has shared their reproductive trauma with me. Whether I saw you 25 years ago or last week, your story has left an indelible mark on my heart. Thank you for your bravery in showing up in therapy, for working so hard, and for trusting me with your story.

Part I

Reproductive trauma, PTSD, grief, and complex emotions: Why are you feeling this way?

Chapter 1

Introduction

Welcome! I am so glad you've picked up this book. Whether you have experienced distress around your birth experience, your fertility journey, pregnancy or postpartum complications, pregnancy losses, or other difficult events in the perinatal period, it's important that you are here. Maybe you've experienced your own reproductive trauma or are the partner of someone who has. Perhaps the term *trauma* does not even resonate with you when you think about your experience, and yet, you may be having a difficult time moving beyond what you went through and feel stuck. It's possible that what happened continues to linger in your mind and cause you grief. That experience is welcome here too. I will be using the term *trauma* throughout this book to reference the various emotions and body experiences that can be felt after a distressing situation. We will explore together how trauma is subjective in that each person can experience the same type of experience or even the exact same situation in completely differently ways (which might have happened to you if your partner or loved ones had a different perspective). Regardless of what you went through, your experience matters, and how you interpreted your experience matters. This book is written to help you on your healing journey.

You are not responsible for what you went through. Yet at the same time, you are left to pick up the pieces in the aftermath of your reproductive trauma. You are doing your best to recover. It can be hard to be pregnant or a new parent while also trying to desperately understand what happened to you, and to do all of this without a guide. There is something that prompted you to pick up this book, perhaps in the hope there is support for what you're going through, that what you are feeling will change, and some validation that you are not alone. If no one else has said this to you yet, let me be the first: there is hope. Change is possible. This book will give you a road map, help you learn about what reproductive trauma is, what your trauma reactions are, and normalize and name what you may be feeling. You will learn how to build coping skills to manage these trauma responses so you can cope more effectively when you are triggered, anxious and overwhelmed. We will also talk about resources and treatment options, so if you decide to seek professional support at any point, you will know where to reach out for help in your area, no matter where you are in the world.

> **Healing from trauma is a process that takes time.**
>
> I admire you for being intentional in your healing, and for showing up for yourself.
>
> You still may be at the beginning or middle of your healing journey. You are right where you need to be.

DOI: 10.4324/9781003379973-2

What I wish every person knew about reproductive trauma

As a perinatal mental health therapist specializing in Perinatal Mood and Anxiety Disorders (PMADs, for short) and reproductive trauma for over 25+ years, I hold space for clients healing from all different types of struggles throughout their reproductive journeys. People can experience distress throughout the process of trying to conceive, their pregnancies, birth experiences (no matter how they actually gave birth), and into their postpartum recoveries. While birth trauma is probably the most talked about form of trauma in the perinatal journey, reproductive trauma encompasses more than birth trauma. It's important we name this so that people can identify what they're feeling and seek help no matter what they experienced. We will talk a lot about how trauma is independent of outcome, meaning you (or your baby) can now be healthy and OK, and at the same time you can still feel frightened or broken. You may even be feeling a mix of feelings, such as gratitude for your baby, but hating parts of the journey that led to becoming a parent. We will explore why people's reassurances and attempts to have you focus on the positive often don't work. What you went through is important. No matter how you have been impacted, you deserve support.

How to use this book

This entire book is devoted to helping you feel better, manage your symptoms related to your experience, and learn skills to help promote your healing. The first third of this book will help you identify what you're feeling, unpack what you experienced, and name and validate what you're going through. Because many people do not know a lot about trauma until they've experienced it, learning the language to describe your full experience can leave you feeling more empowered and allow you to become the expert on you. The second third of this book will help you build skills to manage what you're experiencing: trauma triggers, mood symptoms, the impact on your relationships, the connection and bond with your baby, and more. The final third will help you create a map for your future, by providing some hope of what ongoing healing can look like. We will discuss ways to manage fears and complex decisions about subsequent pregnancies and review professional treatment options.

> If any of the parts of this book feel like they're not a good fit for you for any reason, please skip them.
>
> You will notice I am purposefully repetitive with some concepts to help reinforce the information you will be learning, also recognizing how hard it can be to absorb new material as a sleep-deprived and traumatized new parent.

Please take your time going through this book

I get it. When you are suffering, you want to feel better, and relief can't come soon enough. That's why you picked up this book. With healing from a traumatic event, it can be helpful for your nervous system to pace yourself. Every little bit of growth helps. Don't push yourself to rush through or do all the activities. While the chapters build on each other, and this book can be read from cover to cover, you can also pop in and pop out, paying close attention to how activities and sections make you feel. Some topics or activities may also not be a good fit, which does NOT mean that you're a failure or you've done something wrong because you're not doing ALL the homework. In fact, this can be a helpful practice of learning how to tune back into yourself, and finding what feels okay, and what doesn't.

A note on language

We will talk about the disproportionate impact of perinatal mental health disorders and trauma on people of color and the LGBTQ+ community, yet the vast majority of the research has largely focused on cisgender women and race is not addressed in many studies. I also recognize that not all parents who experience reproductive trauma are women and moms. You will learn that dads and partners, too, are impacted by reproductive trauma. While the research is still limited and highlights the need for research with other populations, you will see me vacillate between using the term "woman" or "mother" when the research has been based on these folks, and the more general terms like "parent" when applicable.

A note on trauma triggers

I purposefully wanted to write a book that was accessible to people who have experienced trauma throughout the perinatal period, including the path of conception, pregnancy and the postpartum recovery period, and not limit the focus to birth traumas. While birth trauma is certainly the strongest focus of research and social media content, it's important that people who have experienced trauma with other aspects of their reproductive journey also have a resource for healing.

If you have difficulty with any of the topics or exercises in this book, it does not mean that you are doing anything wrong; you are still healing. It's important to remain curious and gentle with yourself. You will learn grounding and self-soothing skills to use when triggered. If this happens at any time when reading, please put the book down for a time and practice your skills. There may be parts of the book that just don't resonate with you, or that feel particularly difficult. I recognize that it could be triggering for some people to read some parts of this book at various parts of their journey. For example, those who are grieving a pregnancy loss, or currently going through infertility treatments may find the sections on promoting healthy secure attachment with a baby to not be a good fit right now. Please feel free to skip the parts that do not apply or do not feel supportive for your healing right now.

This book avoids real world stories on purpose

It can be triggering for people recovering from their own trauma to hear about all the various possible awful situations that can occur during the perinatal period. I hear this a lot from my clients who have felt more upset after they heard about another parent's birth trauma, or felt more activated after reading about someone's pregnancy complications. This is part of the reason I wrote this book by avoiding real-life examples. It can simply be too overwhelming or feel too raw for some people. However, being a survivor of reproductive trauma can also be isolating, and hearing about others' experiences can provide a sense of reassurance that you are not alone. I try to be mindful of this in this book and strike what I'm hoping is a helpful balance. Brief examples are provided that will help normalize what you're going through, while trying thoughtfully to avoid oversharing too many details that might be overwhelming to your system. If you are craving connection with others who have gone through similar experiences, there are additional resources for support at the end of the book.

I trust you to be the expert on you

Your story is unique, and it is important to get help for what you're going through. Chapter descriptions and section headers can help you decide what information may be helpful for you at this stage in your journey, and which information might not be a good fit for you right now. Trauma-sensitive modifications will be provided for many of the skills and activities that you will be introduced to so you will have choices and options. As you read, please notice how the skills you learn will also help you to pay attention to your body and emotions if topics feel particularly tender to you. You can skip certain sections and take breaks, if needed, putting down the book to practice self-soothing skills that you will be taught in the second part of this book. You will learn what you might need at various times in your process. Chapter 2 will help us lay some important groundwork together. We will talk about some foundational trauma concepts and help you discover more about why you might be responding and feeling the way that you are. We will start there to help you start your journey of healing and find your way back home to yourself.

You are not alone

A final note that you might find yourself working through this book on your own and notice you could use some additional support to manage challenging triggers or stages in your healing journey. Perhaps some sections are overwhelming or would feel better to do with the help or a mental health professional. This book can be a great companion resource when working with a trauma-informed mental health professional. If you find this is the case, the Resources and support chapter will give you some ideas of how to find providers who specialize in reproductive trauma. Time alone does not actually heal all wounds. Reproductive trauma healing is complex and nuanced, and as such, treatment from qualified and trained perinatal mental health experts is vital. This book can also be a good resource for professionals who work with and support people throughout the reproductive journey, such as psychiatrists, ObGyns, midwives, doulas, physical therapists, lactation consultants, and more.

A final note for professionals using this book with your clients/patients

I am so glad you have picked up this book to use with your clients! I wrote this book to use with my own clients who have survived reproductive trauma and who are working their way through the aftermath of their own experiences (and perhaps, still living with very real life impacts, such as physical pain, loss, and uncertainty about their futures). I'm honored you will use this workbook in a way that works for your practice, and apply it as needed in your work. I personally find that before introducing worksheets or take-home material, it is helpful to discuss the information in a way that makes sense and feels personally relevant. I encourage you not to use this workbook in a task-oriented *homework* way, but instead, use pertinent sections when those concepts come up with your clients.

Aiding our clients in finding their agency is part of trauma-informed care, and often part of their trauma experience was feeling forced to do something, being overpowered, not listened to, etc. As such, pacing and taking breaks will be crucial. Exploring present-day triggers together (including any distress brought up when working through this workbook) can be a good place to start. Fellow EMDR and somatic-oriented therapists will notice familiar language and concepts throughout. If you are looking for additional training opportunities to further your own professional learning, or if you are seeking consultation for your perinatal/reproductive trauma cases, you will find some options in the Resources and support chapter at the end of the book.

Chapter 2

What is reproductive trauma?
Why you might be feeling the way you do

As a Perinatal Mental Health therapist who specializes in trauma, I am used to talking about and treating trauma symptoms as a part of my everyday professional life. I love talking about trauma recovery and seeing trauma survivors heal. However, I realize that most people do not spend as many hours of their day focused on this concept. In fact, although the word *trauma* is becoming more widely used in popular culture and social media, not every survivor identifies that they've been through something traumatic. Sometimes, people think that trauma is only caused by *horrifically* massive things, like wars, natural disasters, significant violence, sexual assault, and violation from oppressive systems such as racism and ableism. As such, they might dismiss what they've been through as not fitting into this category. They may just know they're not feeling like themselves and are having a harder time than usual coping with everyday life. As new parents, they might be super worried about their baby or have a hard time thinking about their birth experience without feeling upset about how it all happened.

In this chapter, you will learn what trauma is, why your body might be responding in confusing ways, and why you might be easily reactive to certain situations and people. We will explore why you might be having a completely different healing journey than your partner, or even a friend who went through a similar experience. Before we begin, I want to recognize that you may not describe what you've been through as traumatic. So before we start labeling your experience, let's get curious together.

Here are some of the ways I frequently hear my clients describe how they are feeling or what they are thinking in the aftermath of their experience(s). Feel free to check which one(s) feel familiar to you:

☐ It's hard to "just get over" what happened and *how* it happened.

☐ Parts of my experience keep looping over and over in my mind or pop up when I'm not wanting to think about it.

☐ There are certain people, places, or situations that are more anxiety-provoking or emotional than I would expect them to be (i.e. triggering).

☐ I can't help but be hard on myself about what happened.

☐ I feel like what happened is my fault.

☐ I feel numb.

DOI: 10.4324/9781003379973-3

☐ Sometimes I'm acting in ways that are perplexing or embarrassing to me (like overreacting to situations, reacting in ways that don't logically make sense, or having really strong emotions at times).

☐ I have been avoiding certain situations or people; I've become easily frightened or timid.

How was that to read through? Were there any "aha" moments, or confirmation of what you were already felt with your experience(s)? Anything that was lacking that would better capture how you are feeling right now?

I find that survivors of reproductive trauma can struggle with needing, yet not receiving, *validation* from others to acknowledge that their experience was traumatic. There is already a lot of societal pressure for pregnancy and birth to be a joyful experience (and especially with some social media portrayals and what we see on TV and in movies). And sometimes people surrounding new parents may inadvertently invalidate you by focusing on all the *good things*, ignoring what actually *did* happen that wasn't okay. Perhaps this happened to you; maybe nobody reassured you that what you went through was real and not your fault. You also may be stuck in a paradox of wanting help but being reluctant to name what actually happened to you because that will make it real. Perhaps you are feeling some internal conflict of being grateful for your baby, yet are very angry and regretful about the experience that led to you becoming a parent. All of these feelings are valid, and I am again very thankful that you've picked up this book as a way of understanding yourself and your experience.

Let's talk about trauma

A trauma response is a symptom of your central nervous system responding to a distressing event. As Dr. Gabor Maté, physician and trauma researcher, so astutely says: "Trauma is not what happens to you, it's what happens inside you as a result of what happened to you."[1]

Sometimes you can experience something traumatic or distressing and your brain can work through it, processing and integrating all the various information. You eventually move through it, and eventually, the event truly feels like it is a distant memory that happened in the past. Even when you think about it, it does not cause distress, and it may even feel fuzzy and remote. On the other hand, some events that you experience can still cause distress even long after they're over. When your nervous system can't differentiate between what is in the past and what is in the present, it feels like you are still in *trauma time* (as if it's still happening). When your nervous system has difficulty discerning what is and isn't urgent, *everything* feels like it's an emergency. Your body may frequently feel like it's in a 10 out of 10 distress, when in reality, the danger may have passed and you are actually safe now. Your body is still living in *trauma time*, even if your logical brain may know that it's okay now. Because you are frequently feeling so activated as if everything is an emergency, it's no wonder you might be feeling so irritable.

When you're feeling pressured and constantly on edge, relief can't come fast enough, and your partner or loved one's response may feel woefully inadequate addressing what you need. If it feels like you're living in an intense situation and everyone else around you is feeling calm, you may feel rage at their responses, or lack thereof! Perhaps you're distressed that breastfeeding is not going well and are panicked your baby is not eating enough, for example. Why doesn't everyone around you seem to get it? Why aren't they responding with urgency like you are? It's not that it's not important to them; rather it's likely they're not triggered and activated in the same way you are.

Processed vs. unprocessed traumatic events

Processed Traumatic Event ↑

Processed Traumatic Event:

• Person initially feels scared about what happened, more emotional afterwards, and gradually over time, less on edge.

Eventually with time, the person may look back at their experience with relief and feel like it is truly "in the past" and behind them.

The person can make sense of what happened from a clear or organized perspective.

Unprocessed Traumatic Event:

• Person may feel initially scared about what happened, or have a delayed emotional response about their experience.

• Their reaction to their experience stays the same or worsens over time. It doesn't lessen.

• Memories may feel fragmented, and hard to remember in a logical order.

• It feels to them as if they're still living in their past experience sometimes, as if it's still happening to them.

Unprocessed Traumatic Event ↓

The subjective nature of trauma

Trauma is very subjective. For example, two separate people can both have an urgent, unexpected cesarean section and find it incredibly distressing at the time, yet one might continue to feel distress even months after it was over despite the reassurance there was a good outcome. This person might later internalize their experience as, "I failed, I did something wrong," whereas the other person might describe their birth experience as "intense but I'm proud of myself for how I got through it." This is why sometimes partners can have a very different lived experience of the birth of their baby. Did this happen to you? Perhaps your partner was present throughout your birth but you both have different responses to what you went through. You may be replaying it over and over in your mind and feel terrified, while your partner may be focusing on the present now and reassured that everything is okay. Why is this?

Our nervous systems are able to respond to perceived danger and distress automatically. When we are in *fight/flight/freeze* mode (or the lesser known *fawn*), our sympathetic nervous systems are activated, and we are no longer in logic brain mode. But here's the thing: emergency responses can sometimes get a bad rap, but this is exactly what is needed during a potentially dangerous event or crisis so that we can truly survive. Think about if you've ever had something suddenly come into your lane as you're driving. You need to be able to respond very quickly and not be delayed and distracted. Your heart rate becomes elevated, and you have your sympathetic nervous system to thank for your fast reflexes and focus, as you hopefully either quickly stop your car, or swerve into the next lane. We have mere seconds (or less) to make a decision, and can't think about anything else more complicated in our lives at the time.

Trauma exists when the nervous system struggles to recognize and trust the presence and conditions of actual safety.

You might feel like you are still living in *trauma time* even if the distress is over.

Yet, it can become problematic for both our physical and mental health when we stay stuck in that emergency response mode despite the crisis situation being resolved. When we are still responding as if we are in danger (even though we are safe now), we are living in *trauma time*. We might still feel like we did when we were in the crisis – with the same physical and body sensations (shortness of breath and nausea), same emotions (terror or shame), same negative thoughts ("I can't handle this," "I am broken"). Our brains might perceive danger or distress, even if logically we know that we are fine. Plus, a present-day situation might remind us of other times we felt overpowered, terrified, or powerless, such as difficult situations we experienced as children, and our nervous system again kicks into survival mode. Remember, a trauma response is a symptom of your central nervous system responding to a distressing event and NOT an indicator that you've done something wrong or that you've failed. If an event felt traumatic to you, then it was. It was real, it happened, and it has had a lasting impact. Trauma is often less about the details of the event than it is about the impact the event has on our body and emotions. As trauma specialist Dr. Pat Ogden poignantly says, "our experience that is stressful enough to leave us feeling helpless, frightened, overwhelmed, or profoundly unsafe is considered a trauma."[2]

You can feel traumatized even if:

- you or your baby had a good outcome

- logically you know that you're fine now (but don't feel like you are)

- you know you're out of danger now but you're still easily triggered and activated

- people around you are able to move on (and perhaps want you to do the same, or are asking you to focus on the positive)

This is why an experience can be traumatic regardless of the outcome. You may have had a healthy baby and recovered well, but continue to feel unsafe and scared when you think about your delivery. In other words, your body is still living in *trauma time* even if logically you know the distress and danger are over. Or, your excruciating infertility treatments and journey may have resulted in a successful pregnancy, but you may still feel hypervigilant and afraid, unable to enjoy your pregnancy or connect with your developing baby yet. It can still feel as if the other shoe is going to drop at any moment, even if the factual proof is in front of you that it's fine now. As a result, it's quite common to feel a jumbled mix of conflicting emotions and feelings right now. In the next two chapters, we'll help you sort through a bit more of what you're feeling, and address why you might be holding some of this internal conflict and ambivalence.

What is survival mode? How did it serve you at the time?

If you are finding yourself hypervigilant and on guard, easily activated and jumpy, irritable and more emotional than usual, you are likely experiencing a stress response, which means your sympathetic nervous system (SNS) is activated. Your SNS is trying to protect you by going into *survival mode*. SNS and endocrine reactions will attempt to increase energy, arousal, and hypervigilance to try to restore your body's homeostasis (or balance) following a traumatic event, and return things to normal. Yet, during a stress response, your body becomes flooded with stress hormones, like adrenaline and cortisol, and this stress response can become prolonged.[3] What this means is, you may feel like you are in a perpetual *fight/flight/freeze response*, or you become easily triggered and activated by situations that previously were not so stressful (such as loud noises, feeling like you cannot tolerate being touched, or feeling intensely afraid to leave your baby's side). It can then be hard to accurately read a situation and unhealthy for our minds and bodies in the long term.

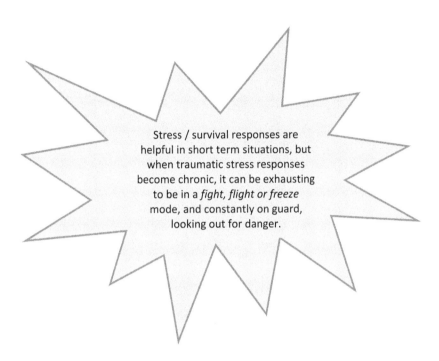

Stress / survival responses are helpful in short term situations, but when traumatic stress responses become chronic, it can be exhausting to be in a *fight, flight or freeze* mode, and constantly on guard, looking out for danger.

When you were in survival mode, you were doing a good job of protecting yourself. You did the best job you could at the time of surviving. In retrospect, you may look back and question why you did what you did, or why you said the things that you said. That's the nature of a trauma response. It isn't logical and well thought out. It's instinctive and a knee-jerk reaction. If you're in *fight or flight* mode, you're in super-protector mode, and cannot be still or calm, even if you tried. On the other hand, if you are in *freeze* or *fawn* mode, you probably had a difficult time speaking up or advocating for yourself, or maybe even had difficulty responding at all. All of these modes are self-protective and serve to protect you from danger. A *fawn* response additionally serves to appease and please others to facilitate the danger being over faster. There are also trauma responses of shut down and *dissociation*,[4] which we will talk about throughout the book, but these four basic concepts are an important place to start.

Examples of trauma responses

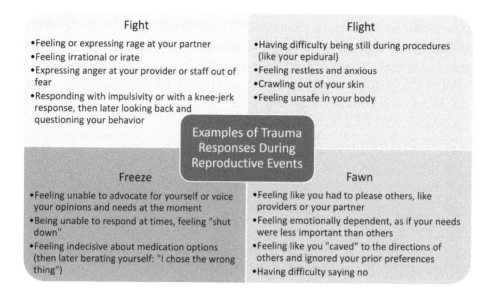

Fight

- Feeling or expressing rage at your partner
- Feeling irrational or irate
- Expressing anger at your provider or staff out of fear
- Responding with impulsivity or with a knee-jerk response, then later looking back and questioning your behavior

Flight

- Having difficulty being still during procedures (like your epidural)
- Feeling restless and anxious
- Crawling out of your skin
- Feeling unsafe in your body

Examples of Trauma Responses During Reproductive Events

Freeze

- Feeling unable to advocate for yourself or voice your opinions and needs at the moment
- Being unable to respond at times, feeling "shut down"
- Feeling indecisive about medication options (then later berating yourself: "I chose the wrong thing")

Fawn

- Feeling like you had to please others, like providers or your partner
- Feeling emotionally dependent, as if your needs were less important than others
- Feeling like you "caved" to the directions of others and ignored your prior preferences
- Having difficulty saying no

Fight responses can look like feeling activated in your body, or having bigger emotional responses that felt overwhelming or confusing to you at the time. Or perhaps, your emotions, such as anger, were quite justified given what was happening, but may have felt out of control and it took quite a while to come back down afterwards.

Flight responses can also look like being activated, with tension in your body, and a desire to actually flee. This might have been possible (such as leaving the NICU or doctor's office), or impossible if you were immobile (such as during a cesarean section or epidural), which can be that much more awful to tolerate.

Freeze responses can also look like feeling activated with tense muscles and a tense body while feeling incapable of responding or moving. Perhaps you could not speak up, or felt incapable of moving, as if you were paralyzed and your nervous system had both the gas and brake on at the exact same time.

Fawn responses can look like trying to please or appease others, and then later feeling confused or ashamed about your actions. Maybe you were going along with procedures or examinations that felt uncomfortable or awful, and then later questioned yourself why you didn't speak up. Perhaps you allowed visitors that you had previously set boundaries with, and then later beat yourself up for not saying something. This might look like being a nice complacent patient, so to speak, when in actuality you were not okay with what was happening to you.

Do you recognize any of these responses during everything that you went through? Is it possible you had more than one trauma response at various times of your experience(s)?

Please remember that these responses are part of our autonomic (or automatic) nervous system that activates instinctively when faced with a perceived threat. These are trauma responses that served to protect you at the time in your reproductive trauma, even if you look back now with confusion or frustration. Now let's think about trauma specifically in reproductive situations and learn more about what you went through.

What is reproductive trauma?

Reproductive trauma is a term to capture any event(s) that are distressing during the perinatal period, including fertility treatments, conception, pregnancy, delivery, and postpartum. Instead of just using the term *birth trauma*, which singularly focuses on a traumatic or distressing birth experience, *reproductive or perinatal trauma* addresses events during the entire reproductive experience.

Unfortunately, reproductive trauma is fairly common, as 34% of women report a traumatic birth experience,[5] and anywhere between 9–41% of women experience symptoms of Postpartum Posttraumatic Stress Disorder (PPPTSD) following childbirth.[6] As we talked about earlier, there are many events throughout the reproductive journey beyond childbirth that can be traumatic and distressing, for example when the baby has emergency interventions or spends time in the NICU. Mothers with a baby in the NICU are 40% more likely than moms of healthy infants to experience depression, anxiety, and trauma symptoms.[7] And reproductive trauma can begin prior to conception: people going through infertility experience significant psychological burdens, including higher rates of depression, anxiety, trauma, as well as financial and other stressors.[8] Those who experience miscarriages and later pregnancy losses can also experience such traumatic grief, with around 25% of people developing Posttraumatic Stress Disorder (PTSD) after a loss.[9] In other words, you are not alone and, unfortunately, unrelated life stressors can also add to the negative impact of reproductive trauma, a poignant example of which is that statistics rose during the early COVID-19 pandemic.

> ### The impact of the pandemic on reproductive trauma
>
> Postpartum PTSD rates rose to 30% early in the pandemic in 2020, with researchers citing social isolation, loss of control, lack of support, working from home, and lack of consistent and reliable childcare as contributors.[10]
>
> Higher rates of depression, anxiety, dissociation, and PTSD were seen during the pandemic in 2020, with people reporting less positive feelings during the pregnancy and postpartum period. Women in lower income areas, and with a previous psychiatric illness seemed to be at higher risk.[11]
>
> Eighty-six percent of participants in a study in 2020 whose infertility treatments were suspended, delayed, or canceled reported a negative impact on their mental health as a result.[12]

Let's talk about what situations reproductive or perinatal trauma might include. **Please checkmark any that you have experienced that were distressing:**

❑ Infertility treatments and procedures	❑ Learning infertility treatments were unsuccessful
❑ Doctor's appointments	❑ Pelvic exams
❑ Pregnancy complications (e.g. hyperemesis, bleeding, gestational diabetes, placenta previa)	❑ Pregnancy bedrest
❑ Miscarriages	❑ Ectopic pregnancy losses
❑ Pregnancy losses later in pregnancy	❑ Pregnancy after the loss of a child
❑ Difficult decisions during pregnancy	❑ Unmet expectations
❑ Terminations	❑ Terminations for medical reasons (TFMR)
❑ Negative interactions with providers	❑ Feeling overpowered, coerced, silenced, or harmed by providers
❑ Having your pain dismissed or not being adequately medicated	❑ Gender, sex, size, or other discrimination experienced from providers
❑ Racism, bias and/or microaggressions experienced from healthcare professionals	❑ Unwanted medical procedures or medical procedures done without your consent
❑ Feeling devastated by the way things went	❑ Distress or fear during birth
❑ Not having the birth you planned or wished for	❑ Postpartum complications and impacts on physical health / functioning
❑ Being injured during birth, or baby with medical issues or injuries	❑ Baby going to the NICU or requiring emergency interventions
❑ Delivering a premature baby	❑ Difficulty surrounding breastfeeding / chestfeeding
❑ Distress around mental health symptoms or a mental health diagnosis	❑ Difficulty finding adequate care or treatment
❑ Emergency interventions or procedures	❑ I experienced distress around: _____

What do you notice about some of the events listed? What was it like as you were reading through them?

_____

_____

_____

_____

Why might this have happened?

We've started to explore *what* you went through. Now let's talk about *why* this might have happened. You might have worked so hard towards becoming a parent. Maybe you've even dreamed about it since childhood, and perhaps have spent years (and countless financial resources and effort) on your fertility journey. Certainly, nobody dreams of a catastrophic loss or a traumatic event occurring during such a precious and important time. Or, perhaps you became pregnant unexpectedly, with themes of feeling out of control from the very beginning of your pregnancy, and at various touchpoints such as your delivery or postpartum recovery. Without understanding why this might have happened, it can be common to turn inward and blame yourself, or be stuck in a feeling of confusion about the *why*. When there are no easy answers, we can try to find some smidgen of control and order by turning blame inward. I find this to be the case particularly when it comes to reproduction, conceiving, carrying, and birthing a baby. These are such emotionally evocative minefields for many of us.

There are a number of reasons why a person might experience events during their reproductive journey as traumatic. First, this is such a vulnerable time of life, right? There are so many things to be fearful of and anxious about and many potential interventions to face. There are also many possible interactions with providers that might be positive and supportive, or the opposite, negative or even worse. You might have had to make hard decisions you never thought you would have to make, and sometimes with little or no warning or during a crisis. You have to become an expert on your body, learn a lot about fertility procedures, your baby, and your medical issues (and health issues you may not had known you had, or had never even heard about before!). You have had to learn how to practice advocating for yourself. It's a lot. And to add to this, if your reproductive experience has been impacted by any additional life stressors, such as the challenges of the pandemic, it makes it that much harder. For instance, perhaps you have been alone during appointments or ultrasounds, have had virtual appointments, or felt separated from your providers at times. Maybe you have been isolated from your support and the full range of treatment options has been unavailable to you. You might be fearful for your health, and frustrated by an inability to engage in social activities you would normally be doing, particularly to tend to your mental well-being. These challenges have all contributed to the risks of trauma responses and higher rates of depression, stress, and anxiety.[13]

> How you *feel* about what happened throughout your reproductive journey is just as important as *what* happened to you.

If what you have been reading in the previous paragraphs has been resonating with you, you are not alone. We see this reflected in the research, too, with studies showing a number of factors that are predictive of a person having a trauma response or Posttraumatic Stress Disorder (PTSD) during the reproductive period.[14] Sometimes it's the severity or level of intervention itself. For instance, mothers who deliver babies who require emergency intervention (such as resuscitation or going to the NICU) tend to be at higher risk of trauma symptoms. Those with high-risk pregnancies are also at higher risk for later trauma symptoms, as are those with pregnancy complications such as placenta previa or hyperemesis.[15] But equally impactful to what happened to you is how you *feel* about your experience. *That's what I mean when I say that trauma is subjective.* The majority of birth trauma survivors (66%) share that at the core of their trauma was the way they were treated by their provider.[16] Additional research shows us it is the level of intervention (i.e. an emergency cesarean section or crisis experience) along with the person's perception of their care that is the strongest predictor of birth trauma.[17] For instance, if someone has negative interactions with staff during their reproductive journey (felt demeaned, overpowered, coerced, or their pain was minimized by a provider), *and* they felt scared or experienced a crisis intervention such as an urgent or intense procedure, they have a higher likelihood of experiencing posttraumatic symptoms later on.

> We just covered a lot of important material. Here is a noteworthy risk factor to highlight:
>
> **Crisis event + negative perception of care = higher risk factor for posttraumatic symptoms**

Here is a list of the most common risk factors for reproductive trauma, or PTSD related to reproductive trauma. **Circle any of the risk factors that you identify with.** This can be a useful exercise to highlight the complexity of reproductive trauma, illuminate your specific circumstances, and lay the groundwork for your healing in the future.

Negative interactions with providers/staff	Having hyperemesis	Having a high-risk pregnancy
Emergency interventions (e.g. urgent cesarean section, baby with a health crisis)	Having untreated depression or PTSD	Being a person of color (experiencing racism/implicit bias)
Having a history of mental illness	Fear of the upcoming birth	Pregnancy complications (placenta previa, etc.)
Being from a low socioeconomic background	Being of younger age	Being in a relationship where there is violence
Having a history of sexual assault	Having little or no support	Baby went to the NICU

What was that experience like for you as you read through this list? What thoughts do you have about risk factors?

_____

_____

If you had any of the listed risk factors, it does not mean that you did something wrong, or that you were destined to have an experience that was traumatizing. Instead, this could help you figure out part of *why* you are feeling the way you are and remind you that you are not alone. As much as we would like this to be an incredibly rare event, as you saw from reading some of the statistics earlier in this chapter, you truly are not alone in this experience even though this can be an isolating time. These risk factors can also be very helpful information to have as you look at your future. In Chapter 11 we will explore risk factors in more depth when we talk about complicated decisions such as whether or not to have another baby. This helps shift the focus to an empowering lens on prevention, controlling the controllable, and creating a supportive treatment team and plan. Whether you choose to pursue another pregnancy or not, it can be empowering to learn more and take back some control.

> What happened to you during your reproductive journey *and* how you feel about it matters.
>
> If you had negative experiences with any of your providers *and* had an intense or frightening experience, this put you at higher risk of experiencing a traumatic response.
>
> Your subjective distress and any emergencies encountered are the most important risk factors predicting the development of PTSD after childbirth.[18]
>
> This all may have had an impact on how you processed your experience, and how stuck you might still feel.

Exploring risk factors in more depth

Here's the thing as we talk about risk factors. You may have been very prepared for your delivery, educated about what to expect, empowered to speak up for yourself, and still have had a traumatic experience. As we highlight what is within your control, and what is outside of your control, it's important to say that what you went through was not your fault. These words may be hard to hear if you are still healing and might be blaming yourself for some aspects of what happened. There can be numerous outside factors that contribute to reproductive and perinatal trauma, such as what you learned about negative interactions with providers. Even if you know this was not your fault, but are struggling with guilt and self-blame, perhaps learning more helps build curiosity about your and others' experiences. An important example is that there can also be systemic issues that contribute to reproductive trauma, such as implicit bias and racism in healthcare. A person's trauma history, as well as their cultural, identity, and socioeconomic factors can also contribute. Women of color are at higher risk for perinatal PTSD and also face higher rates of maltreatment from their providers.[19] As Serena Williams highlighted after her own birth experience: "In the U.S., Black women are nearly three times more likely to die during or after childbirth than their white counterparts. Many of these deaths are considered by experts to be preventable. Being heard and appropriately treated was the difference between life or death for me; I know those statistics would be different if the medical establishment listened to every Black woman's experience … Giving birth to my baby, it turned out, was a test for how loud and how often I would have to call out before I was finally heard."[20]

Since subjective distress and negative interactions with staff are important risk factors in predicting PTSD throughout the reproductive journey, and there are significant issues with implicit bias in healthcare settings, there is still so much work to be done on changing systems. While this book does not focus on this important work of changing systems, and instead focuses on your healing, there still has to be recognition that your experience likely occurred within a larger system. Please know that birth providers are also being called upon to provide the best quality, equitable, trauma-informed, unbiased, and culturally informed care. There are resources for those doing advocacy and reproductive justice work at the back of this book, and for those fighting for women's and trans people's treatment during pregnancy and childbirth.

> The social movement of reproductive justice was initiated in the 1990s by Black midwives and activists passionate about addressing systemic inequality and reproductive vulnerabilities among women of color and other marginalized communities.
>
> Reproductive justice affirms that *all* reproductive bodies deserve access to the care and resources to support their reproductive needs in safe and life-affirming environments with dignity and respect.[21]

As you've been reading about risk factors, perhaps certain ones have jumped out at you that feel similar to your experience. Or, maybe you don't see yourself or your experience adequately represented. If that's the case, it's okay – your experience still matters, and your reactions are still valid. After working in this field for more than two decades, I've learned that research is important, but it is still evolving and limited, and of course does not fully capture our human, lived experiences. *You are more than research*; in other words; there are many nuanced, complicated reasons why you may experience a situation as traumatic or why you may develop PTSD symptoms.

Reflection activity

As you have been reading through this chapter and learning more about reproductive trauma, your nervous system's responses, and the various risk factors that might have contributed to your experience, this may be a good time to pause and do a check-in. Part of trauma recovery is learning how to take breaks and soothe the nervous system, as you will learn in future chapters. I find this particularly important to do early on when learning vital information, so that it doesn't feel like a tsunami of facts coming at you. Let's take a break now for reflection.

What has stood out to you most significantly so far in your reading and learning?

_____

_____

What have you learned about your reproductive experience that you may not have thought about before?

_____

_____

How are you doing emotionally as you have been reading? Is there anything you need right now? Examples might include changing the pacing of reading and taking more breaks, reading at optimal times of day when you can better absorb the information without feeling overwhelmed, talking with your partner about key takeaways, etc.

_____

_____

Are there any particular parts that have been more challenging than others? Are there any parts that have brought validation or comfort?

_____

_____

You have learned a lot of important information in this chapter, and as you are learning how to check in with yourself, this might be a good place to pause. Take the time that you need to revisit information that resonated with you. Perhaps you need some time to reflect and let some of these concepts marinate. In the next chapter we will learn more about trauma and explore more of what specific symptoms you may be experiencing.

Chapter highlights

- A trauma response is a symptom of your central nervous system responding to a distressing event or series of events.

- _Reproductive trauma_ means a distressing event or events that occur during any part of the reproductive/perinatal journey, from conception through pregnancy, birth and postpartum recovery.

- Trauma is incredibly subjective. If you felt your experience was traumatic, then it was, regardless of the outcome or if others are minimizing your experience.

- There may be certain risk factors that could have contributed to the likelihood of you having a traumatic experience, and yet what happened to you was still not your fault. Your experience matters.

Notes

1 Caparotta, M. (2020, September 24). Dr. Gabor Maté on Childhood Trauma, The Real Cause of Anxiety, and Our "Insane" Culture. *Human Window*. https://humanwindow.com/dr-gabor-mate-interview-childhood-trauma-anxiety-culture/

2 Ogden, P., & Fisher, J. (2015). *Sensorimotor Psychotherapy: Interventions for Trauma and Attachment*. W.W. Norton.

3 Guy-Evans, O. (2021, May 11). Sympathetic nervous system functions. *Simply Psychology*. www.simplypsychology.org/sympathetic-nervous-system.html

4 Fisher, J. (2021). *Transforming the Living Legacy of Trauma: A Workbook For Survivors and Therapists*. PESI, Inc.

5 Beck, C.T., Driscoll, J.W., & Watson, S. (2013). *Traumatic Childbirth*. Routledge.

6 Anderson, C. (2010). Impact of traumatic birth experience on Latina adolescent mothers. *Issues in Mental Health Nursing*, 31, 700–707.

7 Fowler, C., Green, J., Elliott, D., Petty, J., & Whiting, L. (2019). The forgotten mothers of extremely preterm babies: A qualitative study. *J Clin Nurs*, 28(11–12): 2124–2134. doi:10.1111/jocn.14820; Tahirkheli, N.N., Cherry, A.S., Tackett, A.P., McCaffree, M.A., & Gillaspy, S.R. (2014). Postpartum depression on the neonatal intensive care unit: current perspectives. *International Journal of Women's Health*, 6, 975–987.

8 Aiyenigba, A.O., Weeks, A.D., & Rahman, A. (2019). Managing psychological trauma of infertility. *African Journal of Reproductive Health*, 23(2), 76–91. https://doi.org/10.29063/ajrh2019/v23i2.8; Rooney, K. L., & Domar, A.D. (2018). The relationship between stress and infertility. *Dialogues in Clinical Neuroscience*, 20(1), 41–47. https://doi.org/10.31887/DCNS.2018.20.1/klrooney; Schwerdtfeger, K.L., & Shreffler, K.M. (2009). Trauma of Pregnancy loss and infertility for mothers and involuntarily childless women in the contemporary United States. *Journal of Loss & Trauma*, 14(3), 211–227. https://doi.org/10.1080/15325020802537468

9 Fernández-Ordoñez, E., González-Cano-Caballero, M., Guerra-Marmolejo, C., Fernández-Fernández, E., & García-Gámez, M. (2021). Perinatal grief and post-traumatic stress disorder in pregnancy after perinatal loss: a longitudinal study protocol. *International Journal of Environmental Research and Public Health*, 18(6), 2874. https://doi.org/10.3390/ijerph18062874; Wesselmann, E.D., & Parris, L. (2022). Miscarriage, perceived ostracism, and trauma: a preliminary investigation. *Frontiers in Psychology*, 6576.

10 Ostacoli, L., Cosma, S., Bevilacqua, F., Berchialla, P., Bovetti, M., Carosso, A.R., Malandrone, F., Carletto, S., & Benedetto, C. (2020). Psychosocial factors associated with postpartum psychological distress during the Covid-19 pandemic: a cross-sectional study. *BMC Pregnancy and Childbirth*, 20(1), 703. https://doi.org/10.1186/s12884-020-03399-5

11 Berthelot, N., Lemieux, R., Garon-Bissonnette, J., Drouin-Maziade, C., Martel, É., & Maziade, M. (2020). Uptrend in distress and psychiatric symptomatology in pregnant women during the coronavirus disease 2019 pandemic. *Acta obstetricia et gynecologica Scandinavica*, 99(7), 848–855.

12 Gordon, J.L., Balsom, A.A. (2020). The psychological impact of fertility treatment suspensions during the COVID-19 pandemic. *PLoS ONE*, 15(9), e0239253. https://doi.org/10.1371/journal.pone.0239253

13 Ajayi, K.V., Harvey, I.S., Panjwani, S., Uwak, I., Garney, W., & Page, R.L. (2021). Narrative analysis of childbearing experiences during the COVID-19 pandemic. *MCN. The American Journal of Maternal Child Nursing*, 46(5), 284–292. https://doi.org/10.1097/NMC.0000000000000742; Racine, N., Eirich, R., Cookee, J., Zhu, J., Pador, P., Dunnewold, N., & Madigan, S. (2021, May 7). When the bough breaks: a systematic review and meta-analysis of mental health symptoms in mothers of young children during the COVID-19 pandemic. https://doi.org/10.31234/osf.io/u8pnh

14 Silverstein, R.G., Centore, M., Pollack, A., Barrieau, G., Gopalan, P., & Lim, G. (2019). Postpartum psychological distress after emergency team response during childbirth. *Journal of Psychosomatic Obstetrics and Gynaecology*, 40(4), 304–310. https://doi.org/10.1080/0167482X.2018.1512095; Grekin, R., & O'Hara, M.W. (2014). Prevalence and risk factors of postpartum posttraumatic stress disorder: a meta-analysis. *Clinical Psychology Review*, 34(5), 389–401. https://doi.org/10.1016/j.cpr.2014.05.003

15 Kjeldgaard, H.K., Vikanes, Å., Benth, J.Š., Junge, C., Garthus-Niegel, S., & Eberhard-Gran, M. (2019). The association between the degree of nausea in pregnancy and subsequent posttraumatic stress. *Archives of Women's Mental Health*, 22(4), 493–501. https://doi.org/10.1007/s00737-018-0909-z; Dekel, S., Stuebe, C., & Dishy, G. (2017). Childbirth induced posttraumatic stress syndrome: a systematic review of prevalence and risk factors. *Frontiers in Psychology*, 8, 560. https://doi.org/10.3389/fpsyg.2017.00560

16 Reed, R., Sharman, R., & Inglis, C. (2017). Women's descriptions of childbirth trauma relating to care provider actions and interactions. *BMC Pregnancy and Childbirth*, 17(1), 21. https://doi.org/10.1186/s12884-016-1197-0

17 Creedy, D.K., Shochet, I.M., & Horsfall, J. (2000). Childbirth and the development of acute trauma symptoms: incidence and contributing factors. *Birth (Berkeley, Calif.)*, 27(2), 104–111. https://doi.org/10.1046/j.1523-536x.2000.00104.x; Grekin, R., & O'Hara, M.W. (2014). Prevalence and risk factors of postpartum posttraumatic stress disorder: a meta-analysis. *Clinical Psychology Review*, 34(5), 389–401. https://doi.org/10.1016/j.cpr.2014.05.003; Dekel, S., Stuebe, C., & Dishy, G. (2017). Childbirth induced posttraumatic stress syndrome: a systematic review of prevalence and risk factors. *Frontiers in Psychology*, 8, 560. https://doi.org/10.3389/fpsyg.2017.00560

18 Lamont, R.F., & Joergensen, J.S. (2012). Risk factors for developing post-traumatic stress disorder following childbirth: a systematic review. *Acta obstetricia et gynecologica Scandinavica*, 91(11), 1261–1272. https://doi.org/10.1111/j.1600-0412.2012.01476.x

19 Vedam, S., Stoll, K., Taiwo, T.K., Rubashkin, N., Cheyney, M., Strauss, N., McLemore, M., Cadena, M., Nethery, E., Rushton, E., Schummers, L., Declercq, E., & GVtM-US Steering Council (2019). The Giving Voice to Mothers study: inequity and mistreatment during pregnancy and childbirth in the United States. *Reproductive Health*, 16(1), 77. https://doi.org/10.1186/s12978-019-0729-2

20 Williams, S. (2022, April 5). How Serena Williams saved her own life. *Elle.* https://www.elle.com/life-love/a39586444/how-serena-williams-saved-her-own-life/

21 Ross, L., & Solinger, R. (2017). *Reproductive Justice: An Introduction.* University of California Press.

Chapter 3

Reproductive trauma vs. Posttraumatic Stress Disorder: Your experience and distress matters no matter the label

You will hear me say a lot that your experience, and how you feel about it, was valid. By that I mean you do not need someone else's validation (even though it is incredibly helpful) to tell you what you already know: what you went through was distressing and it had an impact on you. This is important when it comes to your mental health as well. Did you know that you can be impacted by trauma and may or may not have a full Posttraumatic Stress Disorder (PTSD) diagnosis?

We talked a lot about reproductive trauma in the previous chapter, and we also talked about Posttraumatic Stress Disorder (PTSD) symptoms. These two things are not the same even though there is overlap. When distressing symptoms continue after the event, this is posttraumatic stress. When symptoms become pervasive and impactful to your functioning, this can eventually become significant enough to warrant a diagnosis of Posttraumatic Stress Disorder.

The current edition of the *Diagnostic and Statistical Manual of Mental Disorders* defines a traumatic event as exposure to actual or threatened death, serious injury or sexual violation.[1] This can result from either experiencing this event directly or witnessing the traumatic event. (This second part is important when we talk about your partner's experience in Chapter 9.) This can also result from repeated exposure to details of the trauma (such as the physical aftermath of reproductive trauma with body sensation triggers of cramping, difficulty with physical recovery reminders like scarring or pelvic floor injuries, etc.). Many of us who work with trauma will tell you that we find the diagnostic criteria lacking, however. Not everyone who experiences traumatic reactions or posttraumatic stress feels like their trauma involved "actual or threatened death, serious injury or sexual violation," and yet they were traumatized. This is part of why trauma is so subjective.

You might have only some of the symptoms of PTSD, yet you feel traumatized. Some people feel like their incident was not "bad enough" or not as significant as someone else's trauma to warrant how they're feeling, and yet they can't just talk themselves out of it. Your body is responding to distress and your experience is legitimate. Let's think about how people of color, people in larger bodies, people who are not able-bodied, and those in the LGBTQ+ community have experienced numerous microaggressions in their lives (such as not being believed or listened to, and being mistreated or bullied). Now consider the traumatic impact when this happens yet again, this time during their fertility, pregnancy, or birthing experiences. Examples include: experiencing medical maltreatment, being shamed, having intense fear during procedures or birth, begging for pain relief that isn't coming, or not being believed when saying something doesn't feel right. Examples during infertility include being discriminated against due to size or sexual orientation throughout their infertility treatments, or being demeaned or overpowered during procedures. Any of these examples are legitimately distressing and traumatic, even

DOI: 10.4324/9781003379973-4

if they may not fit a tidy diagnostic label. These are understandably awful and traumatic situations for a person to experience. Whether these examples represent you or your experience, your experience matters, and your story is for you, not a diagnostic manual.

As you reflect on the concepts introduced above, does this resonate with you? And, did you ever minimize your experience, feeling as if it were not as bad as someone else's, or not serious enough to warrant attention or reflect how you were feeling?

The symptoms listed next are part of the diagnostic criteria for PTSD; yet again, you do not have to have a full PTSD diagnosis in order for your experience to have had a negative, lasting impact on you. Whether you are experiencing some trauma symptoms and feeling *off* during your reproductive journey, or have actual diagnosable PTSD, what you are experiencing is real and valid. If you are suffering, you can benefit from and deserve support.

> Please remember:
>
> You may have some (or all) of the symptoms of PTSD to warrant a full diagnosis, and your reproductive experience still matters.
>
> Trauma is essentially *how* your body and nervous system responds to an event; PTSD is a diagnosis.
>
> Whether or not you have a PTSD diagnosis, you are likely suffering, deserve support, can benefit from treatment, and can heal.

Trauma reactions are symptoms of how your nervous system has responded to a distressing event. In Chapter 2 we talked about how unprocessed and *stuck* memories from our past can feel fragmented. On the other hand, when we fully process and integrate all the information from an event, we can put it behind us, and it feels like it is in the past. Posttraumatic stress causes this *fragmentation* and *disintegration*, meaning the images, thoughts, memories, body sensations, and other aspects of the traumatic event are fragmented and not fully processed and integrated by our brain. These can be very confusing to experience, particularly when you are also trying to focus on being as healthy as possible during your pregnancy, healing from your delivery, or bonding with your baby. These feelings can also be particularly difficult to tolerate if you are surrounded by messages from others encouraging you to "focus on the positive" or dismissing and minimizing your experience.

Trauma reactions can be indicative of posttraumatic stress. These trauma reactions, or fragmented aspects of the traumatic experience, show up as symptoms that can include **(please check any that you may have experienced or that resonate with you):**

☐ Triggers: people, places, or situations that now feel unsafe or anxiety provoking

☐ Sensitivity to sounds (reminding you of similar events like the IV machine beeping, or being reactive to loud noises)

☐ Flashbacks or replaying the event(s) over and over

☐ Unwanted intrusive thoughts, memories, or images from the event(s)

☐ Nightmares

☐ Negative self-referencing beliefs related to the event(s), such as "I'm permanently damaged," "I failed," "I'm still unsafe," "I can't trust myself"

☐ Intense emotions such as shame, anxiety, sadness, rage, guilt, or anger

☐ Numbness (feeling a lack of or dulled body sensations or emotions)

☐ Difficulty thinking or talking about the event(s)

☐ Difficulty looking at or touching your body, feeling disconnected from yourself

☐ Feeling overstimulated by or aversive to touch, even by your partner or baby

☐ Feeling hypervigilant or intensely overprotective of your baby, afraid for their safety

☐ Feeling disconnected from, or avoiding contact with, your baby

☐ I am experiencing _____

As you reflect on your symptoms, certainly these can be challenging, and have likely had a big impact on your life. How might your feelings change about yourself as a result of seeing some of your symptoms outlined on the page?

_____

_____

How did some of your symptoms help you survive or get through the situation at the time it was happening? Remember you might have been in survival mode during your traumatic event(s). An example might be, "being on guard helped me get through some scary situations with my baby" or "feeling disconnected from my body helped me get through some awful pain."

_____

_____

_____

_____

Delayed onset of symptoms

I've noticed an interesting phenomenon with reproductive trauma. Some people experience symptoms almost immediately after their event or as they're going through the distressing situation. For example, some people almost immediately start feeling hypervigilant and unsafe while in the hospital after having a traumatic birth experience. I've also noticed it's quite common for some parents' symptoms to start later on, and it seems to coincide with the timing of returning to safety once the danger has passed. It feels like the ultimate paradox, right? Once you (and maybe the baby) are safe and out of danger, you're unable to actually feel safe. You're in go mode while you're in the middle of the storm. But once it feels okay to rest, your system does not know how to downshift because it doesn't feel capable of doing so.

We see this reflected in research as well, with several studies showing that high numbers of NICU parents still have PTSD symptoms over a year after their NICU experience regardless of their baby's gestational age (meaning, even if their baby was not a young preemie).[2] This highlights that there are numerous contributing factors to trauma, and symptoms can show up later after the danger seems to be over. While these symptoms can be quite surprising to parents when they are just starting to notice their situation improving, this can actually be reflective of how hard chronic stress is. I often have parents come into my practice months (or more) after their challenging situation(s) has ended, expressing confusion about their symptoms. Once we explore what they have gone through, they can then find clarity about what they're experiencing and we can create a treatment plan together.

Does this sound like your experience at all?

_____

_____

This delay in symptoms can happen in situations such as:

- Delivering a healthy baby after years of infertility but feeling unable to settle into parenthood without the feeling of pending doom.

- Hormonal shifts, such as the start of your first postpartum period, restarting birth control, or weaning from breastfeeding.

- Feeling more hypervigilant and anxious months after your premature baby has come home (even though the baby is doing well now).

- Seeing your traumatic delivery playing out repeatedly as you think about conceiving again, feeling terrified and unsafe.

- Feeling unable to do any baby care by yourself, having intrusive images of horrible things happening and feeling ashamed, telling yourself, "But I should be able to do this, we worked so hard for this baby with IVF."

- Feeling triggered when going to early pregnancy appointments, remembering when you were there during your miscarriage last time.

- Hypervigilance and worry kick in after breastfeeding challenges finally start improving.

- Feeling relief now that your birth injury is being addressed in physical therapy, yet wondering why your flashbacks and other symptoms are worsening.

How soon after your experience(s) did you start noticing you were feeling off?

_____

_____

Were you able to understand your emotions, symptoms, or reactions as connected to your reproductive journey? Was there any confusion about what you were feeling at the time?

_____

_____

What were the responses of your loved ones when you started feeling off?

_____

_____

Activity

Remember, regardless of when your symptoms started, experiencing a traumatic event and having a PTSD diagnosis are two different things. You can be negatively impacted by your experience(s) and not have a diagnosis of PTSD. At the same time, it can be useful to identify what posttraumatic symptoms you do have. These symptoms are treatable and respond to trauma therapy.

This is the PTSD Checklist for the DSM-5 (PCL-5).[3] This self-administered scale can be useful to identify your trauma symptoms, and explore how your experience is impacting you today. Taking these results with you to a mental health provider can be a great place to start trauma treatment and begin a conversation around your healing journey. It can also be used over time while in treatment to track progress and improvement in symptoms.

Please answer, in the past month, with regards to your reproductive event(s) that you've been dealing with, how much you were bothered by:

1) Repeated, disturbing, and unwanted memories of the stressful experience?	(0) Not at all	(1) A little bit	(2) Moderately	(3) Quite a bit	(4) Extremely
2) Repeated, disturbing dreams of the stressful experience?	(0) Not at all	(1) A little bit	(2) Moderately	(3) Quite a bit	(4) Extremely
3) Suddenly feeling or acting as if the stressful experience were actually happening again (as if you were actually back there reliving it?)	(0) Not at all	(1) A little bit	(2) Moderately	(3) Quite a bit	(4) Extremely
4) Feeling very upset when something reminded you of the stressful experience?	(0) Not at all	(1) A little bit	(2) Moderately	(3) Quite a bit	(4) Extremely
5) Having strong physical reactions when something reminded you of the stressful experience (*for example, heart pounding, trouble breathing, sweating*)?	(0) Not at all	(1) A little bit	(2) Moderately	(3) Quite a bit	(4) Extremely
6) Avoiding memories, thoughts, or feelings related to the stressful experience?	(0) Not at all	(1) A little bit	(2) Moderately	(3) Quite a bit	(4) Extremely
7) Avoiding external reminders of the stressful experience (*for example, people, places, conversations, activities, objects, or situations*)?	(0) Not at all	(1) A little bit	(2) Moderately	(3) Quite a bit	(4) Extremely
8) Trouble remembering parts of the stressful experience?	(0) Not at all	(1) A little bit	(2) Moderately	(3) Quite a bit	(4) Extremely
9) Having strong negative beliefs about yourself, other people, or the world (*for example, having thoughts such as: I am*	(0) Not at all	(1) A little bit	(2) Moderately	(3) Quite a bit	(4) Extremely

(Continued)

bad, there is something seriously wrong with me, no one can be trusted, the world is completely dangerous)?					
10) Blaming yourself or someone else for the stressful experience or what happened after it?	(0) Not at all	(1) A little bit	(2) Moderately	(3) Quite a bit	(4) Extremely
11) Having strong negative feelings such as fear, horror, anger, guilt or shame?	(0) Not at all	(1) A little bit	(2) Moderately	(3) Quite a bit	(4) Extremely
12) Loss of interest in activities that you used to enjoy?	(0) Not at all	(1) A little bit	(2) Moderately	(3) Quite a bit	(4) Extremely
13) Feeling distance or cut off from other people?	(0) Not at all	(1) A little bit	(2) Moderately	(3) Quite a bit	(4) Extremely
14) Trouble experiencing positive feelings (*for example, being unable to feel happiness or having loving feelings for people close to you*)?	(0) Not at all	(1) A little bit	(2) Moderately	(3) Quite a bit	(4) Extremely
15) Irritable behavior, angry outbursts, or acting aggressively?	(0) Not at all	(1) A little bit	(2) Moderately	(3) Quite a bit	(4) Extremely
16) Taking too many risks, or doing things that could cause you harm?	(0) Not at all	(1) A little bit	(2) Moderately	(3) Quite a bit	(4) Extremely
17) Being "super alert" or watchful or on guard?	(0) Not at all	(1) A little bit	(2) Moderately	(3) Quite a bit	(4) Extremely
18) Feeling jumpy, or easily startled?	(0) Not at all	(1) A little bit	(2) Moderately	(3) Quite a bit	(4) Extremely
19) Having difficulty concentrating?	(0) Not at all	(1) A little bit	(2) Moderately	(3) Quite a bit	(4) Extremely
20) Trouble falling or staying asleep?	(0) Not at all	(1) A little bit	(2) Moderately	(3) Quite a bit	(4) Extremely

While a definitive diagnosis can only be given by a mental health clinician trained in diagnosing symptoms of trauma, it can be helpful to identify common symptoms of Posttraumatic Stress Disorder when healing from a traumatic event. There are different ways of interpreting these results with a clinician, but a general rule of thumb for this scale is that a score of 31 or higher indicates probable PTSD. That does not mean that if you scored 30 or less that what you went through is not impactful. Please remember this scale does not diagnose or identify whether or not your experience was traumatic (after all, only you are the expert on that). Instead, it helps further identify which symptoms you may have and their intensity.

How was that for you? Any surprises or insights with how you answered? Was there further confirmation of what you've already suspected about how you have been feeling, or how hard this has been?

_____

_____

Did you score higher or lower than you would have thought? Any additional reflections you had after taking this scale?

_____

_____

_____

Activity

How are you doing? While it's important to learn about reproductive trauma so you can feel validated about what you went through, it's also important to learn to take breaks. Thinking about what you went through can be exhausting and overwhelming. In future chapters you'll learn more self-soothing skills, and more ways to help you shift attention away from *trauma time* and back into the present in safer ways. Let's introduce a brief exercise here now to help you practice this attention-shifting, or *oscillation*.

Looking around you now, can you notice something that brings you a small bit of happiness? Is there an item, an animal, or a person that brings even a bit of relief or pleasure as you look at it/them? Notice as you look at this object/animal/person that even for a brief moment you can shift away from the thoughts or task at hand. Spend as long as you'd like looking at this point of focus.

What did you notice?

_____

_____

In Chapters 5 and 6, you'll learn more about what is happening to your brain when you are triggered, or feel overwhelmed or numbed out. You will learn important self-regulation skills to help come back home to yourself. In the next chapter, we'll talk more about your emotions, and help you sort through some of the complexity of everything you might be feeling right now (and why it's so hard to stay within your *window of tolerance*). You learned a lot of important information in this chapter; keep working through this book at the pace you need.

Chapter highlights

- Please remember – a trauma response is a symptom of your central nervous system responding to a distressing event or series of events while PTSD is a diagnosis.

- The PCL-5 (The PTSD Checklist for the DSM-5) can be a helpful tool to assess for symptoms of PTSD.

- Whether you have a full PTSD diagnosis or are only experiencing some of the symptoms, you can still be suffering and deserve support and treatment.

- Symptoms of trauma can start immediately after you experienced your distressing event(s) or can be delayed even months later.

Notes

1 American Psychiatric Association. (2022). *Diagnostic and Statistical Manual of Mental Disorders* (5th ed., text rev.). https://doi.org/10.1176/appi.books.9780890425787
2 Kim, W.J., Lee, E., Kim, K.R., Namkoong, K., Park, E.S., & Rha, D.W. (2015). Progress of PTSD symptoms following birth: a prospective study in mothers of high-risk infants. *Journal of Perinatology: Official Journal of the California Perinatal Association*, 35(8), 575–579. https://doi.org/10.1038/jp.2015.9; Schecter, R., Pham, T., Hua, A., Spinazzola, R., Sonnenklar, J., Li, D., Papaioannou, H., & Milanaik, R. (2020). Prevalence and longevity of PTSD symptoms among parents of NICU infants analyzed across gestational age categories. *Clinical Pediatrics*, 59(2), 163–169. doi:10.1177/0009922819892046
3 Weathers, F.W., Litz, B.T., Keane, T.M., Palmieri, P.A., Marx, B.P., & Schnurr, P.P. (2013). The PTSD Checklist for *DSM-5* (PCL-5). Scale available from the National Center for PTSD at www.ptsd.va.gov

Chapter 4

Trauma, grief, and mood changes: Sorting through your conflicting emotions and feelings

Emotions can feel so convoluted and jumbled after experiencing reproductive trauma. You might be feeling jealous or envious when hearing about a friend's positive birth experience while also feeling relieved for them at the same time. Maybe you're noticing some internal conflict like loving your baby fiercely while also being resentful of your journey getting to this point or feeling overstimulated or triggered by their cry sometimes. Perhaps you have deep-seated anger around some aspects of your experiences, while at the same time being so proud of and grateful for other parts of it. You can feel both broken and capable, both a failure and amazing all at the same time. You can grieve your pregnancy losses and be happy for a loved one as they become a parent. Our hearts are quite remarkable for being able to hold many emotions at the same time.

It's common for people to feel guilty (or even confused) about these many conflicting feelings. The shame can lead to keeping these feelings and thoughts internalized. But here's the thing: you're not alone in feeling this way, and having mixed emotions is a common part of a traumatic experience. It makes sense that each event has a mix of both joy and suffering, because reproductive journeys are so complex. Learning you were pregnant after such an arduous fertility process may have brought both relief and a new onset of terror. Difficult pregnancy symptoms like all-day nausea and vomiting might be both reassuring to you that you're still pregnant while also awful to experience and maddening to not know when you're going to feel better. The traumatic birth that you're resentful of is also what brought you your precious baby. Again, you are capable of holding multiple emotions at the same time. Here and in later chapters, we will be talking about additional ways to identify and unpack some of these jumbled thoughts and feelings. As you learn more about what you're experiencing, and learn ways to build resiliency and heal through this time, you can work towards feeling safe in your body again.

What are your initial thoughts about holding conflicting and multiple emotions? Does this resonate with you?

_____

_____

What conflicting emotions might you be experiencing currently?

_____

_____

DOI: 10.4324/9781003379973-5

How might this information help you see some of your reactions in a new way?

_____

_____

Why it might be difficult to feel safe emotionally or physically right now

Are you finding yourself shutting down, going numb, or spacing out sometimes? Or are you on guard and hypervigilant, such as being hyper-focused on your baby's safety? Are you confused and surprised by your emotional reactions at times, for instance, embarrassed by how irritable and tense you are with your partner? If any of this rings true for you, you are not alone.

Let's talk a bit more here about why it might be difficult for you to tolerate some of your emotions at times, or why you might sometimes find yourself shutting down. The *window of tolerance* is a term coined by psychiatrist Dr. Dan Siegel to describe our *internal zone of regulation.*[1] When we are within our window of tolerance, we feel stable, present in the here and now, and our nervous systems and emotions are regulated. When we're outside of our window of tolerance, we're more likely to feel triggered, out of control, and our nervous systems and emotions are dysregulated. After experiencing a trauma, our nervous systems can have difficulty staying inside our window of tolerance.

The window of tolerance and common responses after a trauma[2]

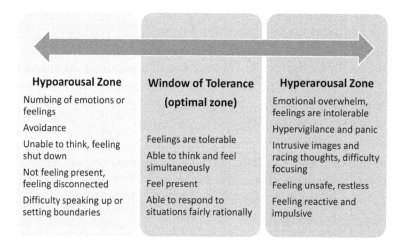

Hypoarousal Zone	Window of Tolerance (optimal zone)	Hyperarousal Zone
Numbing of emotions or feelings		Emotional overwhelm, feelings are intolerable
Avoidance		Hypervigilance and panic
Unable to think, feeling shut down	Feelings are tolerable	Intrusive images and racing thoughts, difficulty focusing
Not feeling present, feeling disconnected	Able to think and feel simultaneously	Feeling unsafe, restless
Difficulty speaking up or setting boundaries	Feel present	Feeling reactive and impulsive
	Able to respond to situations fairly rationally	

What is this like for you as you learn about the *window of tolerance*, and some of the common responses of hypoarousal and hyperarousal? Are any of these responses familiar to you, and if so, can you understand some of your responses in a new way? For example, can you see your reactions in a new light, such as having a tendency towards shutting down, or the opposite, spinning with frantic energy?

_____

_____

_____

_____

How often do you think you swing outside of your window of tolerance since your trauma? (It's okay if it's frequent; that's a common trauma response. You will learn skills to stay within your window of tolerance and find yourself able to do this more often.)

_____

_____

Does any of this information help you understand why some of your emotions and body sensations are so confusing to you at times, and why your emotions might change drastically?

_____

_____

Let's keep exploring the complexity of your emotions and learn more about what you went through. This next part is specifically for those who went through fertility struggles or infertility treatments. If fertility issues didn't impact your experience and this doesn't feel relevant to you, you can catch up with us in the next section about perinatal mental health.

Complex feelings during and after infertility treatments

I don't think the trauma of infertility gets talked about enough. This is a complicated time when you might be feeling a myriad of emotions all at once. There can be such a rollercoaster of emotions with each uncertain month, holding both hope and fear, hitching your dreams to procedures while perhaps also remaining guarded and afraid. The vulnerability during each treatment, the pain and discomfort with procedures, the mood changes and pain experienced with injections; all can have cumulative impacts of trauma. The financial aspect of infertility treatments can be incredibly traumatic as well; there is uncertainty in investing so much in a procedure that is often not covered by insurance and has unpredictable success rates. Then there is the potential trauma of facing financial debt and still not having a pregnancy/baby. You probably also had numerous interactions with different providers with varying bedside manners and skill levels, some with kind and gentle approaches, and some who may have caused harm. In other words, there could have been numerous traumatic touchpoints throughout your fertility journey.

The trauma of getting your period and realizing it did not work also cannot be minimized. It can be truly devastating. These big feelings can be confusing and also isolating, particularly if you're surrounded by well-meaning people who are cheering you on, keep asking if you're pregnant yet, and encouraging you to "just think positive and keep trying." There can be a challenging balance of needing support and at the same time sometimes finding that support to be draining.

For people who eventually conceive, there can still be a lot of complicated feelings. For example, I've held space for countless clients who voice anxiety and fear about their successful pregnancies, while also feeling guarded and protective for themselves, not wanting to bond or connect with this baby yet out of concern they may lose this pregnancy. They live with such a heightened level of fear and guardedness that can roll into parenthood. Even if everything is going relatively smoothly, it doesn't feel like it internally. They may also have anxiety about the "what if this hadn't worked" thoughts even though things were successful. There can sometimes be limited support from others in recognizing or being able to tolerate all of these feelings. Loved ones can sometimes have difficulty understanding these very real but complex feelings and may inadvertently invalidate you by attempting to refocus on the positive (e.g. "but that's not what happened," or "just be grateful for what you have" type of messages). Perhaps others have tried to use humor that landed flat and caused harm, or have put pressure on you that just adds to you feeling more overwhelmed and isolated.

> Complex feelings both during and after infertility are common, and your support might have limited capacity to help you tolerate those feelings.
>
> There can be a lot of internal and external pressure to be happy and grateful right now when that is not realistic.

Similarly, it's common for parents who've gone through infertility to feel guilty about expressing any negative feelings about their parenting journey once the baby is here. (By the way, literally everyone has negative thoughts about being a parent sometimes; that's normal and realistic.) After going through infertility, some parents feel they don't deserve to complain or that they have to appreciate most everything about being a parent since they worked that much harder to get there. This guilt and pressure can be that much more amplified if the parent(s) are reminded by others about how much they wanted this.

We talked about some of the distressing and traumatic event(s) that can happen throughout fertility challenges (such as financial stressors, getting your period, etc.) as *trauma touchpoints*. If you went through fertility challenges in conceiving, or infertility procedures, what *trauma touchpoints*, or distressing experience(s) on your journey, stand out for you?

_____

_____

_____

Can you relate to the idea of conflicting emotions along your journey? If so, which conflicting or confusing emotions did you experience at times?

_____

_____

_____

Which messages about your fertility journey did you receive from others that were unhelpful? Which were helpful and validating?

_____

_____

_____

_____

Trauma and perinatal mental health

Let's talk about another common factor that might be contributing to how you are feeling right now: it's possible you are experiencing other Perinatal Mood and Anxiety Disorder symptoms (PMADs for short) in addition to your trauma symptoms. For some people, having a Perinatal Mood and Anxiety Disorder *is* the primary source of the reproductive trauma. For example, it can be quite traumatic for parents to experience intrusive awful thoughts, go through postpartum psychosis, or struggle with their mental health for prolonged periods. For other people, PMADs symptoms happen in conjunction with their other reproductive trauma symptoms. I know that it may seem like the ultimate cruelty with everything else you're dealing with to also be struggling with other mental health symptoms such as depression. At the same time, it's important that you're educated about what to look out for so you can, again, be the expert on you. These symptoms are temporary and respond well to treatment.

Depression and trauma

In addition to some of the trauma symptoms you might be experiencing, have you been noticing any feelings of sadness, irritability, lack of motivation, loss of energy, or tearfulness? We have talked previously about a prior history of depression (particularly when it's untreated) being a potential risk factor for experiencing a reproductive trauma. While there are numerous other reasons why a woman may develop depression after having a baby, a traumatic birth experience is a significant reason. Women who have traumatic birth experiences are more likely to develop both Postpartum PTSD and Postpartum Depression, and in general, women who develop Postpartum PTSD are at higher risk for developing Postpartum Depression.[3] We also see this with women going through infertility treatments as well, as they can have increased rates of depression.[4]

To add to this, many of the symptoms between depression and trauma overlap (such as irritability and sadness), so it can sometimes be confusing for people to figure out what they're experiencing. If this is resonating with you, please know you're not alone, and what you are experiencing is temporary and treatable. Many of the skills you are learning in this book to help you address your trauma symptoms can also help manage and reduce any mood symptoms. If you would like to seek professional help or explore more about your mood, there are resources at the end of the book that can help you find your way.

Common symptoms of Perinatal Depression can include (check any that resonate with you):

☐ Depressed or sad mood most of the day (or more frequently than usual)

☐ Hopelessness

☐ Tearfulness (more than normal)

☐ Feelings of irritability, rage, or anger

☐ A loss of interest in pleasurable activities

☐ A change in appetite (either an increase or decrease) and not just because you are busy and preoccupied now with your baby

☐ Sleeping more or less than normal (Again, not because of the baby. Not being able to fall back asleep after the baby does is an indicator that something may be going on with you.)

☐ Feelings of worthlessness or guilt

☐ Loss of energy and fatigue (Again, I know this one may sound funny given that you have pregnant or postpartum changes in sleep but does your loss of energy seem abnormal for this stage?)

☐ Recurrent thoughts of death or suicidal thoughts*

☐ Urges to harm yourself or your baby**

*While this is not always a part of depression, it's important to talk about. People who don't have depression can also have suicidal thoughts and urges. If you are experiencing suicidal thoughts or urges to harm yourself, you need and deserve professional support right away. Emergency resources are located at the end of this book in the Resources and support chapter.

** While this is not a common aspect of perinatal depression, it's important to name this and notice I say "urges" and not thoughts as we will talk about later with anxiety and OCD. Again, emergency resources are at the back of the book in the Resources and support chapter.

What did you notice as you were identifying common depressive symptoms? Did any stand out to you?

_____

_____

Increased anxiety and vulnerability

After a traumatic and distressing event, it feels like you have just had the rug pulled out from under you because something awful just happened. How you experienced it has had ripple effects. You may have new fears about bad things happening to the people you love, or even hearing about people around you getting pregnant might be overwhelming. Following reproductive trauma, the idea having or delivering another baby may feel incomprehensible right now. We will talk in future chapters about how to manage these thoughts and triggers as they come up, but for now, please know that these are common responses to such difficult events. You don't have to have a full diagnosis of anxiety to recognize that anxiety symptoms still might be affecting you. You can benefit from support and building skills to manage the impact of anxiety and worry.

Many people still have anxiety about what happened to them during their perinatal journey starting from when they were trying to conceive. As we have talked about, people who have experienced fertility struggles and infertility have higher rates of anxiety and depression.[5] This is also true for those who had pregnancy complications, traumatic or stressful births, and postpartum complications. It's a complex causal relationship just like with trauma. Some studies have shown, for example, that while stressful birth experiences certainly have an impact on whether or not someone will develop postpartum anxiety, a lack of support from hospital staff and a lack of perceived control during birth tend to contribute to the risk of developing an anxiety disorder more than the birth experience itself.[6] This means that there are numerous contributing factors that are all potentially impacting your emotions and why you may be struggling now.

Common symptoms of Perinatal Anxiety can include (check any that might resonate with you):

☐ Frequent or constant worrying

☐ Racing thoughts

☐ Intrusive thoughts or images that are unwanted and possibly disturbing and distressing

☐ A bad feeling like something awful might happen

☐ Restlessness, difficulty sitting still for long periods of time

☐ Hypochondriasis (worrying about you, your loved ones', or your baby's health)

☐ Changes in sleep (again, not because you're up with the baby, but if you have difficulty falling back asleep or difficulty shutting your brain off)

☐ Physical symptoms such as a racing heart, nausea, shakiness, dizziness, clamminess, etc.

What did you notice? How often are you experiencing anxiety symptoms?

_____

_____

Perinatal Obsessive Compulsive Disorder (OCD)

There are also other Perinatal Mood and Anxiety Disorders that can start or worsen during this reproductive journey, such Bipolar Disorder and Psychosis. The last one we will touch on here is Obsessive Compulsive Disorder, as it, too, is highly connected with trauma and PTSD.[7] Upwards of 90% of all new moms report having scary and intrusive thoughts at some point.[8] It's common, in other words, to have awful images and thoughts pop up sometimes about harm coming to you, your baby, or someone you love. This is different from OCD, which is marked by persistent, repetitive worries and unwanted thoughts that cause significant distress and are difficult to talk yourself out of or turn away from. Around 3–9% of new moms have a diagnosis of Perinatal OCD.[9]

Common symptoms of Perinatal OCD can include (check any that might resonate with you):

☐ Intrusive and unwanted thoughts or images are persistent, unwanted, and possibly disturbing and distressing.

☐ Thoughts and images cause distress and uncomfortable feelings. Actions are done to try to get rid of these feelings.

☐ Compulsive behaviors are actions done to try to reduce the distress related to the thoughts and fears. These can be frequent checking, cleaning, counting, seeking reassurance, mental rituals, or avoidance.

We've talked a lot about the common overlapping symptoms of trauma and some other mood symptoms so you can see how confusing this time can be and why you might be feeling such complicated emotions right now. Notice how many of the symptoms of depression, anxiety, and OCD can be shared with trauma. This is why it can be beneficial to work with a mental health provider with specific training in perinatal mental health and reproductive trauma.

The overlap between trauma and other mood symptoms

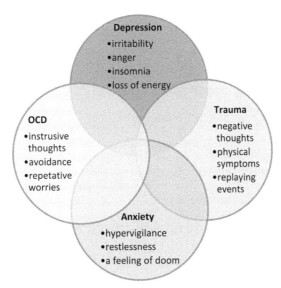

Given what you went through, it's no wonder why you might be experiencing heightened fears and anxieties, reacting with hypervigilance, and being easily startled and agitated. You have likely experienced a lot of loss: the loss of control, the loss of trust in others (or maybe even your own body), the loss of feeling safe, etc. This may now have an impact on how you see your world and interact in it. We will continue to help you build tools to manage these fears and body sensations over the next few chapters. Let's explore more of the impact and meaning of these losses.

Trauma and grief

Why trauma and grief are so intertwined

Let's honor that there are many different losses you might have experienced throughout your reproductive journey. You may be grieving the actual loss of your pregnancy. Perhaps you've had to make heartbreaking decisions. I'm writing this chapter as the United States is going through a tumultuous time impacting reproductive rights and this has had a tremendous impact on parents as they experience pregnancy losses, those needing medical interventions and support, and those terminating for medical or a myriad of other personal reasons.

Whether or not you experienced the loss of your precious baby, you also likely experienced loss in other forms. Many people who have endured reproductive trauma have had secondary losses as well. **Common feelings or sources of loss include (check any that might resonate with you):**

☐ A loss of trust that your body will be able to do whatever you ask it to do

☐ A loss of feeling safe or calm

☐ A loss of taking your mental health for granted

☐ A loss of belief that "everything works out okay"

☐ A loss of faith or anger and confusion at God or a higher power for what happened

☐ Grieving the changing relationship with your partner

☐ Grieving the changing relationships with loved ones

☐ A loss in income, and/or work identity

☐ A loss of belief in the goodness of others

☐ A loss of belief that "good things happen to good people"

☐ A loss of feeling of safety or trust with medical providers

☐ An unexpected loss or change in your body (e.g. a hysterectomy or pelvic floor injury during your birth)

☐ A loss of physical capability during your healing

☐ Grief around changes in family dynamics

☐ Grief and change around who you go to for support and who you thought was a good listener

☐ A loss of your friend group

☐ A loss of dreams and expectations

☐ Grieving the "old you"

☐ A loss of belonging

☐   Another source of grief and loss you are experiencing right now is: _____

_____

Do any of these resonate with you? Have you ever thought about these as secondary losses before?

_____

_____

How does this help you understand your complex emotions and feelings right now? Does this help you revisit some of your emotions with a new perspective?

_____

_____

_____

_____

Understanding grief

Dr. Elisabeth Kübler-Ross was a psychiatrist who identified 5 stages of grief.[10] You may have heard of these commonly discussed stages that she most often saw in those who are dying and grieving: denial, anger, bargaining, depression, and acceptance. While Dr. Kübler-Ross's research was groundbreaking and has been profoundly helpful for countless people, this model can often be misused with people who are grieving. There are sometimes misunderstandings about this model that these stages are linear, and that everyone's experiences will be neatly captured in these stages. It is most certainly not a to-do list that must be accomplished. Some people feel like this model passively tells them what they may be in store for with their feelings, and not what they can do about these feelings instead. While it can be helpful to know what common feelings may come when experiencing grief and loss, these stages are not an exhaustive list. This model does not name more nuanced feelings such as the hypervigilance of anxiety that commonly occurs after a traumatic loss.

Some clinicians, when working with grief, prefer instead to take a more active view, empowering the impacted person through therapeutic grief work. For example, drawing upon psychologist J. William Worden's research on grief, he posits that there are four tasks of grief:[11]

1. acceptance of the reality of the loss

2. process through the pain of loss

3. adjust to an environment without the lost person/object

4. establish a changed but continuing connection with the deceased while embarking on a new life.

Whether your loss is more literal or figurative (or a combination of both), what do you think of grieving involving actively moving through various tasks? How might these four tasks listed be applied to your healing journey?

_____

_____

_____

How might you explore acceptance of your reality? What could this look like? (Examples might include making a physical therapist appointment to address your pelvic floor pain that you have been avoiding, or requesting your medical records with your ObGyn to review your birth process.)

What might it look like to process through the pain of your grief and loss? (Examples might include using this workbook, going to therapy, or sharing your story with a safe person.)

What steps could you take that would help you adjust to your environment as it is now? We can't rush or skip to this phase, so you might not be here yet. You can return to this at another stage of your healing, or jot down some ideas of what you would like this to look like. Examples could include wanting to be more socially active with other parents eventually, or learning how to manage your trauma triggers.

How might you want to have a changed relationship with what happened to you? Put another way, how do you want to think about your reproductive experience in the future? Again, this might be more difficult to imagine earlier on in your healing journey, and in Chapter 12 we will talk a lot more about instilling hope and looking towards your future. (Ideas can be wanting to eventually talk about your experience comfortably or one day feel more compassionate towards yourself about what you went through.)

Disenfranchised grief

Have you been feeling as if you're the only person who has felt the way you do? Do you ever feel isolated and alone, like you can't speak up about your experience without people becoming uncomfortable around you? *Disenfranchised grief* and trauma occur when a person's experience is restricted in some way. This often happens when there is societal pressure for fast-tracked healing, or stigma around the person's mourning or healing process. I see this frequently happen around pregnancy loss, pregnancy complications, infertility, and birth trauma. There is so much of a desire for the perinatal period to be a happy time that often people who have experienced pain are left suffering alone. Some loved ones surrounding you may not even acknowledge what you went through due to their own discomfort. For example, there may be pressure from others to focus on the baby, or to move on, particularly if they perceive that the danger is now over.

Disenfranchised grief means that while ultimately many of us will experience the same type of losses through our lifetimes (grandparents, parents, jobs, etc.), there are many losses only experienced by some.

As a result, these losses tend to be more socially stigmatized, depending on the culture in which we experience them, and how well versed our community is at handling grief and loss.

Please know that however you are grieving and adjusting to your life now, your feelings are important and legitimate, and there is no one way to heal. In the next few chapters, we will explore more about what you are specifically feeling by identifying symptoms that influence your life, and start talking about ways you can help manage and move through these. We also will help you identify who your key support people are, and how to better engage with those who are important to you, and who may not exactly know how to help you (due to their own discomfort or lack of information).

Cultural, family, and community impacts on grief and trauma

How was grief, mourning, and/or coping displayed in your family or community growing up? What you are experiencing may be overwhelming to you, not just because what happened to you was so hard, but also because you might be learning new ways to cope with it now. Or maybe you feel like you're forging new paths as you might be the first person in your family to be talking about or experiencing these feelings or symptoms. Perhaps you grew up in a family where emotions were not overtly shown, mourning was not done publicly, or mental health was not openly discussed. Some families and communities can have stigmas about mental health, which may mean that speaking up about grief or trauma is unwelcome. Perhaps there are some other barriers to mental health resources or accessible, safe care. Alternatively, you might have culturally based models for healing that are helpful and that you can draw on now and integrate into your journey. You may have rich traditions around grieving and loss that might be bringing you great comfort. Or you might be noticing a mix of all of the above. In other words, how you cope will inevitably be impacted by your culture and society in which you were raised.[12] As a result, there cannot be a one-size-fits-all approach to your healing journey.

As you are thinking about your experience, can you think about how your culture, faith, family, and community may influence how you are experiencing your emotions or trauma?

_____

_____

_____

What messages did you learn about grieving and/or expressing emotions as you were growing up? Did you see any positive examples of people receiving help? Any examples that you do not wish to emulate?

_____

_____

_____

What are the messages you have learned around support or mental health treatment in your community, faith, or family? Are there any you might want to draw from as you are healing from your experience?

_____

_____

_____

What is the availability of mental health treatment and support in your community? Is this a barrier? (If you need some additional ideas, resources can be found at the back of this book.)

_____

_____

_____

Do you have any friends or family who have modeled that it is okay to get help for their mental health? What did this look like? How might you draw from their experiences?

_____

_____

_____

_____

_____

As you are journaling, notice what themes stand out for you, what inspiration you are drawing from, and what supports you already have around you. This is particularly important as you are on your healing journey.

Trauma and isolation

Have you been able to talk to anyone about what you've been feeling? You might feel isolated right now, particularly if you've received any of those unhelpful messages we have been talking about. In Chapter 8 we'll talk more about ways to build and expand your support system and find ways to safely express your needs. For now, at this stage in your journey, it might help to identify even 1–2 safe people to share some of what you have been feeling. Some ideas can be **(put a check next to any that might appeal to you right now):**

☐ A friend that you have previously been able to easily talk to

☐ Your partner

☐ A trusted family member who is typically non-judgmental and supportive

☐ A person whom you know had a similar experience with trauma or loss

☐ A confidant from your religious organization or community

☐ A mental health professional (resources are at the end of the book if you have not made connections with one yet)

☐ A birth trauma, infertility, NICU, or other specialty support group

Messages from others

We've explored a lot of what complex feelings and thoughts you might be experiencing. Lastly, let's talk about the messages you might be surrounded by right now. Experiencing a reproductive trauma is hard enough – period. What can make it exponentially more difficult in the healing journey afterwards is if the people around you, even inadvertently, invalidate your experience.

Perhaps you are being encouraged to focus on the baby, the future, or all the good things. Maybe when you try to talk about your birth, or your pregnancy complications, people seem to get uncomfortable, and try to change the subject. Or maybe when you have shared your story, you are met with responses that make you feel ashamed or guilty, like you are being pessimistic and should just be grateful for what you do have. I have found that these messages are often coming from a well-intended space, meant to bring peace or a little nugget of wisdom. Sometimes these words are said in order to mask a person's own discomfort, and platitudes end up causing great harm, instead of the help that was intended. People who give unwanted advice and try to find meaning (such as trying to superimpose one's own beliefs onto someone else) can be so hurtful when what you actually needed was a listening ear.

I am especially not a fan of "at least" statements as they are invalidating, even if unintentionally so. These messages can diminish and minimize what you actually went through. Perhaps you may now feel like you are unable to voice how you are actually feeling to someone who is trying to find the meaning or positive perspective for you. We'll talk more about this in Chapter 8 as we explore how to connect with your support system following a reproductive trauma or loss. You will learn how to voice your needs to others in a way that feels safe and within your bandwidth right now. There are activities and prompts you can use with your loved ones, and you can even copy sections of that chapter to hand out. For now, as we are exploring your emotions, let's look at how the messages you've received may be contributing to how you feel.

What kinds of messages have you received from others that have not been helpful, or have felt invalidating, or unsupportive? Examples I often hear are (check which ones are familiar):

☐   At least you are healthy now

☐   At least the baby is fine

☐   Thankfully you can try again

☐   You can always adopt

☐   At least you know you can actually conceive

☐   Everything happens for a reason

☐   You just need to have faith

☐   You're all home now, it's all behind you

☐   It probably wasn't that bad

☐   At least your period comes regularly

☐   Some people have it so much worse

☐   You'll be fine

☐   At least you don't have to go back to work yet

☐ It's probably just stress, just relax and …

☐ Let's not focus on the bad stuff

☐ Other messages I have received that have not felt good: _____

_____

On the other hand, what kinds of responses to your experience(s) have you found helpful, validating, or supportive?

_____
_____
_____

As you wrap up this chapter on emotions, consider whether you have previously been able to voice any of the complexity of the emotions and thoughts that you have about your journey. Very often, just getting started with naming those complex and jumbled emotions in a private place such as this can be helpful before you start sharing them with others.

What contradictions or jumbled emotions are you noticing? An example might be: "I feel both hopeless and hopeful about my physical recovery from my pelvic floor injuries," or "I'm angry about what happened to me and I'm also so glad to be a Mom."

_____
_____
_____
_____
_____
_____

You have done some important work in this chapter exploring the complexity of what you have been feeling emotionally. In the next chapter, you will start building skills to cope with these challenging feelings.

Chapter highlights

- It is common to experience numerous complex and conflicting emotions all at once following a reproductive trauma.

- Our *window of tolerance* describes our internal zone of regulation. After experiencing trauma, our nervous systems can have difficulty not becoming either *hyperaroused* or *hypoaroused*.

- Trauma symptoms and other Perinatal Mood and Anxiety Disorder symptoms often overlap, such as Depression, Anxiety, and Obsessive Compulsive symptoms.

- There is a strong link between trauma and grief, particularly with *disenfranchised grief*, in which your grieving may be restricted, stigmatized, or isolating.

- How you were raised, and the family, faith, culture, and community you were raised in, may inform how you are grieving and coping today.

- Grief and trauma can be incredibly isolating, particularly if loved ones do not know how to properly communicate their support, and if they inadvertently share harmful messages. Support can be very powerful.

Notes

1 Siegel, D.J. (1999). *The Developing Mind* (Vol. 296). Guilford Press.

2 Ogden, P., Minton, K., & Pain, C. (2006). *Trauma and the Body: A Sensorimotor Approach to Psychotherapy*. Norton.

3 Grekin, R., & O'Hara, M.W. (2014). Prevalence and risk factors of postpartum posttraumatic stress disorder: a meta-analysis. *Clinical Psychology Review*, 34(5), 389–401. https://doi.org/10.1016/j.cpr.2014.05.003; Kountanis, J.A., Muzik, M., Chang, T., Langen, E., Cassidy, R., Mashour, G.A., & Bauer, M.E. (2020). Relationship between postpartum mood disorder and birth experience: a prospective observational study. *International Journal of Obstetric Anesthesia*, 44, 90–99. https://doi.org/10.1016/j.ijoa.2020.07.008

4 Williams, K.E., Marsh, W.K., & Rasgon, N.L. (2007). Mood disorders and fertility in women: a critical review of the literature and implications for future research. *Human Reproduction Update*, 13(6), 607–616. https://doi.org/10.1093/humupd/dmm019

5 Clayton, E., & Nonacs, R. (2020). Infertility – the intertwining effect of mood disorders and infertility. *Psychiatric Times*, 37(12).

6 Ford, E., & Ayers, S. (2009). Stressful events and support during birth: the effect on anxiety, mood and perceived control. *Journal of Anxiety Disorders*, 23(2), 260–268. https://doi.org/10.1016/j.janxdis.2008.07.009

7 Franklin, C.L., & Raines, A.M. (2019). The overlap between OCD and PTSD: Examining self-reported symptom differentiation. *Psychiatry Research*, 280, 112508. https://doi.org/10.1016/j.psychres.2019.112508

8 Kleiman, K. (2019). *Good Moms Have Scary Thoughts: A Healing Guide to the Secret Thoughts of New Mothers*. Familius LLC.

9 Fairbrother, N., Collardeau, F., Albert, A.Y.K., Challacombe, F.L., Thordarson, D.S., Woody, S.R., & Janssen, P.A. (2021). High prevalence and incidence of obsessive-compulsive disorder among women across pregnancy and the postpartum. *The Journal of Clinical Psychiatry*, 82(2), 20m13398. https://doi.org/10.4088/JCP.20m13398; Zambaldi, C.F., Cantilino, A., Montenegro, A.C., Paes, J.A., de Albuquerque, T.L., Sougey, E.B. (2009). Postpartum obsessive-compulsive disorder: prevalence and clinical characteristics. *Compr Psychiatry*, 50(6), 503–509. doi: 10.1016/j.comppsych.2008.11.014

10 Kubler-Ross, D., & Kessler, E. (2014). *On Grief and Grieving*. Simon & Schuster.

11 Worden, J.W. (2018). *Grief Counseling and Grief Therapy: A Handbook for the Mental Health Practitioner* (5th ed.). Springer Publishing Company.

12 Fernández-Basanta, S., Coronado, C., & Movilla-Fernández, M.J. (2020). Multicultural coping experiences of parents following perinatal loss: a meta-ethnographic synthesis. *Journal of Advanced Nursing*, 76(1), 9–21. https://doi.org/10.1111/jan.14211

Part II

From surviving to thriving: How can you start feeling better?

Chapter 5

Rescue when you're drowning: Essential coping skills following a traumatic reproductive event

Following a traumatic event, it can feel like the rest of the world continues on while yours has just come to a screeching halt. I've had many clients describe their experience of leaving the hospital after a traumatic birth feeling disoriented, as if their entire world changed while they were inside. Similarly, people experiencing the devastation of unsuccessful infertility procedures and losses can feel like they are living in a bizarre parallel universe, watching people going about their regular lives. It can feel weird when you are going through something so life-changing while everyone else is not. Even being in traffic, in public, or seeing the sun shining might make you feel discombobulated. While some people might notice an immediate change in how they feel after the traumatic event, others might notice feeling *off* days or even months later, which can add to the disorientation. Whether you fall in the latter category or are currently in shock and feeling like your world just suddenly shifted, this chapter is for you. You can think of this chapter as providing first-aid skills. If you're a bit further along in your healing journey and still noticing bouts of heightened emotion and trauma responses that are difficult to manage, the skills in this chapter will be useful for you, too. This chapter will help you learn to identify what aspects of your situation are within your power, so you can eventually control the controllable, so to speak.

Addressing your basic needs

While addressing your basic needs may sound, well, basic, it's actually an important place to start following a traumatic event or crisis. Some people may find it relatively easy to return to their normal rhythms of life after experiencing a distressing event, while others might struggle with returning to anything that even closely resembles their previous state of normalcy. To add to this, as we talked about before, your reproductive trauma might not be the first traumatic event that you've experienced in your life. Trauma tends to be cumulative, and our bodies certainly remember what it was like to feel unsafe, overpowered, or paralyzed even if the present scenario is quite different. As such, finding safety or returning to a sense of normalcy may not be a fully realistic ask right now. If that's the case for you, there are still things you can learn that will help.

DOI: 10.4324/9781003379973-7

You may be struggling with some of the basics right now, and that is okay.

It can be helpful to begin your journey of healing with finding more and more moments of relief and reprieve.

Let's start simple with some concepts of what is within your control: your basic needs.

Once the wheels come off the bus, it can be incredibly difficult to gain back control. It's amazing how quickly our mental health can spiral if we let our sleep, hygiene, diet, and routines lapse, and yet that can often be what unintentionally happens following an upsetting life event. But the opposite is also true. Returning to our normal routines, as much as possible, can often help us feel a degree of safety and predictability when the rest of our perception of safety and predictability has just been shattered. I certainly don't mean that you have to hyper-perform right now, fake it, or push yourself through your discomfort. Instead, this can look like finding a gentle balance of the nurturing self-maintenance measures that you need in order to build your resilience and start your path of healing.

What might some of your basic needs be? Notice this is subjective, as we're not putting limits on what may be considered a basic need to you. You are the expert on you and will know what areas you are lacking support in or where you're needing more stability. **Check any that you are already addressing to some degree, and circle any that might need attention.**

☐ Sleep and rest

☐ Regular hygiene maintenance like showering

☐ Regular intake of nutritious food

☐ Safety in the present moment (e.g. is the distress or danger over? Do you currently have what you need regarding your physical health?)

☐ Pain control

☐ Emotional support (therapist, friend, partner, neighbor, family member, etc.)

☐ Tangible support like help with household chores or care for other children

☐ Help with your baby

☐ Body/physical recovery needs (e.g. pelvic floor rehab team, lactation specialist support, wound care, etc.)

☐ Predictability and some semblance of a routine

☐ Other needs _____

_____

What was it like for you to review this list? Any insights or surprises?

_____

_____

Which of your basic needs have you been able to attend to regularly?

_____

_____

Which needs of yours could use some attention?

_____

_____

Now that you see which of your basic needs have not been adequately addressed, what do you think the impact has been on how you've been feeling (e.g. how might your energy have been impacted if you are not eating regularly)?

_____

_____

Are there any barriers to you being able to address your basic needs (e.g. lack of support, your overwhelming emotions such as anxiety, etc.)? These barriers can sometimes feed the cycle of posttraumatic stress.

_____

_____

Where can you begin to focus your energy on some basic self-care (e.g. "even though it's hard, I will ask my partner for more support with nighttime feeds so I can get more sleep" or "we need to problem solve how to ensure we are eating more regularly such as getting food delivered or asking friends for help")?

_____

_____

Sleep

While so much may feel out of your control right now, your sleep may be one of the areas most significantly impacted. Whether you are going through infertility cycles and dealing with hormones and unpredictable stressors, are currently pregnant dealing with a changing body (and bladder!), or postpartum and adjusting to life with a newborn, you see how challenging it is when sleep is disrupted. Sleep is so precious; I swear, it's worth a million dollars to get a good night's rest. The tough thing, though, is a lack of quality sleep can worsen mood symptoms, including trauma reactions. The opposite is true as well, that insomnia is a common symptom of PTSD, depression, and anxiety. It can be a big feeding cycle. As you might be noticing, when you're tired, it's more difficult to cope, and you might find that you're more irritable (and less rational!). Everything can feel intensified, and it's easier to be triggered and anxious.

You may not have control of the _amount_ of sleep you are getting in this stage of life, so instead let's focus on different ways to address the _quality_ of sleep you are able to get right now. If getting more quality sleep is possible, it can help you manage your symptoms by allowing you to think more clearly. Then, as your trauma symptoms improve, you may notice your sleep also improves. A bonus of some of the skills you will learn in this book, such as meditation and breathing skills, is that they may naturally improve your sleep. Let's help you learn some basic ways to address your sleep.

> Addressing your sleep can be one helpful way to address your mental health and one of your foundational basic needs.

Here are some ideas for maximizing some quality sleep during conception, pregnancy, or postpartum recovery **(check which one(s) you already are doing or want to try interweaving into your sleep routine):**

☐ **Maintain a sleep schedule and routine as much as possible.** While a rigid schedule might be completely unrealistic given the season of life you are in, aiming for some consistency with bedtime can reinforce your sleep–wake cycle and help you fall asleep easier.

☐ **Practice soothing bedtime rituals.** Calming routines can help your brain start to slow down and prepare for sleep, just like how nighttime routines help babies wind down and become sleepy. This might include listening to calming music, doing relaxing yoga or stretches, using a meditation app, reading a book, or taking warm showers around the same time every evening.

☐ **Ensure you have a comfortable and ideal space for sleeping.** A dark space with cooler temperatures is the most optimal for sleeping. Adding darkening curtains, wearing comfy pajamas, and getting rid of distractions or clutter in your space, as much as possible, can be helpful.

☐ **Manage stimulation as much as you can before going to bed.** The two hours before bedtime helps your brain prepare for sleeping, a crucial time for repair and rest. Avoiding bright screen time (phones, TVs, computers) and stressful activities (tense conversations, paying bills, etc.) if possible during this time can help the quality of your sleep. This can be hard for many parents as this might be the one time they have to connect and catch up on social media and emails while the kids are sleeping, although it often comes at the cost of quality sleep. There's no all-or-nothing here, but as a new or pregnant parent trying to be protective of your mental health and sleep, this can be a helpful tip to focus on right now.

☐ **Move your body, get outside, and get sunlight daily, if possible.** Moving your body (even a gentle brief walk) earlier in the day is preferable so you aren't trying to go to bed right after being active. An added bonus of being outdoors earlier is that sunlight exposure helps regulate neurotransmitters responsible for the regulation of mood, sleep, and cognitive functioning.[1] Even 5–15 minutes of sunlight can help, or if it's not the season to go outside currently, sitting near a window or indoor bright light works too.

☐ **If you are postpartum, aim for protecting 3–4-hour blocks of sleep, if possible.** You might be able to split the night into two or more blocks, depending on factors such as the age of your baby, the feeding method you're using, and if you have support at night. One example to try: one person does the last feed of the night and one does the first feed of the morning so that each can be *off duty* for a block of time. Other people will trade off entire nights so that only one parent is *on duty* a few nights a week. Single parents can benefit from family or friends staying overnight early on during the challenging first weeks, and postpartum doulas can be additional resources. Find what works for you depending on your available support, your trauma symptoms, and what feels tolerable.

Of the sleep ideas we just talked about, what 1–2 things can you incorporate into your sleep routine?

_____

_____

_____

_____

Basic grounding skills

Part of tending to your basic needs can be learning how to soothe yourself when things feel overwhelming. Think of grounding skills as helpful *rescue skills* when your system is flooded and overwhelmed. Reorienting yourself to the present brings a reminder that you are out of the danger (as much as possible, even if you are still physically healing, or still impacted by what happened to you). Think of using these skills like you are getting your bearings by standing still after you've been spinning around in circles. Grounding is a way to reorient yourself to the calm and safety that exists in the present.

Grounding skills can also be very helpful when you are in perpetual *survival mode* (frequent *fight/flight/freeze* responses), or you become easily triggered and activated by situations (such as loud noises, feeling like you cannot tolerate being touched, or feeling intensely afraid to leave your baby's side). Let's look at other signs you may be triggered.

> A gentle reminder that if you feel on guard, easily activated, jumpy, irritable, and more emotional than usual, you are likely experiencing a stress response, which means your sympathetic nervous system (SNS) is probably activated.
>
> Your SNS is trying to protect you by going into *survival mode* even if the danger has passed.
>
> Grounding skills can be helpful to bring your body back into the present.

How might you know that you are being triggered?

Realizing that you're being triggered can be helpful in figuring out your more perplexing reactions, emotions, and sometimes even behaviors. Following a trauma, it's common to have more intense emotional and behavioral reactions to situations sometimes, which does not mean that your reaction is not important. It means your body is responding as if you are still in danger, and there is more below the surface.

Some common signs of being triggered (check any that you might recognize recently)[2]

❏ Doing something out of character	❏ Feeling terrified or panicked
❏ Having overwhelming emotions	❏ Feeling out of control
❏ Having difficulty breathing	❏ Having sudden intense physical reactions
❏ Feeling unexplained rage	❏ Body wanting to collapse
❏ Going numb	❏ Shaking, quivering
❏ Having sudden intense emotional reactions	❏ Wanting to run away
❏ Churning or pit in stomach	❏ Dissociating (more on this later)
❏ Hating yourself	❏ Hating others
❏ Avoiding usual activities or relationships	❏ Feeling shut down

How was this for you to review?

_____

_____

When you recognize signs of being triggered, it can be helpful to remind yourself that this is a trigger, it's a trauma response, and it will pass. Even after the fact, it can be empowering to learn more about yourself and why you responded the way you did. In the following chapters, you will learn more about your specific triggers, and ways to soothe yourself.

What is dissociation?

Like so many other psychiatric concepts, the term *dissociation* gets misused in pop culture so often that people may not have a good grasp of what it actually is. Dissociation symptoms during and after a reproductive trauma can be difficult to navigate but are actually quite common. Sometimes people don't even know that they've been dissociating, they just know they feel *off*. As you are discovering more about your central nervous system's response and why you are feeling and reacting certain ways, learning about dissociation can be empowering in case you are experiencing this.

You can think of dissociation as your brain's way of trying to protect you by shutting it all down. It's a really sophisticated way your brain has of buffering you from feeling the intensity of everything happening at the time.

Dissociation with reproductive trauma can look like[3] (check any that resonate with you, if it feels comfortable to do so):

☐ Feeling numb, like you're disconnected from reality, or floating away in your mind

☐ Feeling like your world is unreal, like you're in a fog, or your surroundings feel strange or off

☐ Losing time: you don't remember parts of the event(s), you are more forgetful than you would expect as a pregnant or new parent

☐ Feeling disconnected from your body, or not recognizing parts of it (note: this is different than looking in the mirror while pregnant or post baby and feeling emotions at your changing body)

☐ Zoning out, going somewhere else during difficult situations such as when baby cries, or *coming to* mid conversation

☐ Feeling shut down emotionally, like everything is blunted

☐ Swinging from having strong intense emotions to shutting down

Do you connect with any of these indicators of dissociation?

_____

_____

Perhaps you remember that you responded during your traumatic event(s) with dissociation, and that you still do so when overwhelmed or triggered sometimes. Your nervous system is doing its very best to protect you. While numbing out or floating away during something awful can be useful to buffer against the distress and trauma, it's not helpful if your system keeps responding in that same way even though the danger is over, right? It's like being stuck in a trauma loop if your system still shuts down at loud noises or when being touched, even though logically you may know you're actually safe. This is why you can't talk yourself out of a trauma response. Your brain and central nervous system (CNS) are responding in *survival mode* and you can't reason your way out of that. Now let's talk more about stress responses, some ways you can learn to ground yourself, and help reorient yourself to the present.

The good and the bad about stress responses

Like we talked about in Chapter 2, while stress gets a bad rap, we actually need stress responses in our lives sometimes because this shuts off our rational thinking part of our brain, and prepares our body for immediate reaction. Let's use a driving example again. Consider if you're driving and the car in front of you slams on their brakes – you immediately do as well, without even thinking about the steps to take. You're not thinking about what you need to buy at the store later, that you forgot to call your friend back, or how hungry you are. Your brain hones in on the immediate need: stop the car! Stress responses are helpful in short-term situations but after traumatic stress responses become a pattern; our nervous systems have difficulty accurately reading situations to determine whether or not they are truly dangerous. This is why you might be feeling constantly on alert and on edge even if everyone around you reassures you nothing is wrong.

Relaxation techniques help suppress a continued stress response and slowly help your brain recalibrate. We'll go over several more calming techniques in the next chapter. Professional trauma treatment can also help people gain mastery over these triggers that incite and perpetuate a trauma response.[4]

Whether this is the first major traumatic event you have experienced, or you have had a history of trauma, it is profoundly helpful to learn how to self-soothe with grounding skills.

Your body may not be used to quiet or calm, so if this is uncomfortable or difficult, that is okay! This is part of learning and trauma recovery.

Take your healing at your own pace.

Grounding skills can help activate your parasympathetic nervous system (PNS), which then calms you, slowing down your nervous system and helping you return to present. One of the easiest and quickest things to do to activate your PNS and cool your system down is to slow your breath down. Think of it this way: if you were being chased by a bear (I don't know why we always use this metaphor … Go with it …), you would be terrified, your heart rate would be sky-high, and you would be solely focused on getting away. In other words, your sympathetic nervous system would be activated and you would be in *survival mode*. And once the bear went on its way (in our pretend scenario, we always get away from the bear, thankfully) and we knew we were safe, what's the very first thing that our body would do (other than pee with relief, probably)? We would instinctively take a huge breath of relief, in and out. A big deep breath often activates the parasympathetic nervous system, because it reminds us we're safe now. The breath is calming.[5]

When in doubt, breathe it out

When helping clients healing from trauma, I like to start with some simple breath work so they can learn how to soothe themselves. In the next chapter, we will review several additional types of breathing skills, and you can choose which one you prefer to practice regularly. For this chapter, though, as we're focusing on grounding skills and rescue tips that tend to work quickly, we will start with the simplest breathing practice to learn. Slowed breathing out is a quick way to return to neutral and to yourself when you're feeling activated and triggered. If you played tag as a kid, you know how you found safety by going to *home base*? You can think of slowed breathing like returning to your home base. By slowing your breath, you can activate your parasympathetic nervous system, and calm yourself.

Slow breathing not only helps you feel calmer, it can also:[6]

• shut off the overactive, stressed, and flooded brain

• help you reconnect to your body

• release endorphins, which help you perceive and feel pain differently

A note on choices – slowed breathing is helpful when you are feeling anxious and activated. It is not helpful for a different trauma response, that of feeling *numbed out* or *dissociated* (disconnected), as this may make you feel further zoned out. As you are learning more about yourself and your reactions, it can be helpful to think about the right tool for the right job. As we have talked about before, working with a trauma therapist can be invaluable for learning these different nuances and skills.

Breath meditation for calming your nervous system

1. Start by breathing in with a regular breath (whatever your regular breath is at the moment) through your nose, and then breathe slowly out through your mouth as long as you can tolerate it. Think of it as if you have a birthday candle in front of you that you are actively trying NOT to blow out. It may flicker with your breath, but you are not exhaling so quickly that it will go out. Do this for several rounds.

2. Next, try inhaling through your nose, and exhaling slowly through your mouth and see if you can make them both the same length. Do this for several rounds.

3. Next, keep inhaling and exhaling just as you were but now try to see if you can lengthen the exhale slightly. If it helps you to count, see if you can extend the count out by 2–3 this time. Do this for several rounds.

4. Do this for 5 rounds. Again, if it helps you to anchor yourself by counting, aim for counting in by 5 on the inhale, and out by 8 on the exhale. These numbers are just a guide.

5. After several minutes, or whenever you need to take a break, you can let go of watching and directing the breath and allow it to return to your version of normal.

How did that feel? Do you notice any changes in your body or heart rate? Can you see a shift in anything else like your attention or focus?

_____

_____

You may want to do another round, or may have found that one round was sufficient for now and you can try again later. Remember that if any of these grounding skills are difficult for you, you are not failing. This is part of trauma recovery, and by practicing regularly, your body's stress response will change. It can be helpful to start out practicing when you are not in the most stressful of situations so you can gain a feeling of mastery and capability.

Other good times to try breath practices are when you are (check one or more of these scenarios that resonates with you and you want to try this week):

☐ *Triggered* (e.g. in the middle of a fertility procedure, driving by the hospital, or thinking of your delivery)

☐ *Anxious* (e.g. feeling hypervigilant and afraid, or worried about your baby)

☐ *Angry* (e.g. rage is building at your spouse, you are irritable when stuck in traffic)

☐ *Overwhelmed* (e.g. your baby's cry is making you feel paralyzed, you're on the brink of melting down)

☐ *Sleepless* (e.g. racing thoughts are keeping you awake)

☐ *Needing grounding* (e.g. when feeding your baby and wanting to feel more present)

☐ *Out of Your Window of Tolerance* (the more you practice tuning into whether you are hypo-aroused, or hyper-aroused, and you need help coming back to neutral)

It can be helpful to practice for 2–5 minutes twice a day, even at times when you might be feeling more neutral or happy.

Physical/body grounding skills

These next skills can be particularly useful for rescuing when you are flooded, overwhelmed, or if it feels difficult to calm and soothe yourself (such as if you are in your *hyperarousal* zone). Grounding is also useful when triggered or if you are *numbed out* or *dissociating* (i.e. your *hypoarousal* zone), and need a physical anchor to help you come back to the present. These skills remind your body and mind that you are *here* and *now*, when you may have just felt like you were catapulting into the past. As with any grounding skills, these listed here are not a one-size-fits-all situation; instead it's important to find something that is easy for you to do in the moment of feeling activated, so that you will have something that is easily accessible.

Check any that appeal to you:

☐ Bite a lemon (or suck on a sour candy)

☐ Smell nearby aromatherapy/perfume/scented candles/essential oils/coffee

☐ Use a weighted blanket

☐ Snuggle with your animal or pet (my personal fave), noticing the feel and smell of their fur, the sound of their breath

☐ Hold on to a grounding object such as a smooth stone or seashell

☐ Hold on to ice or run your hands under cool water

☐ Put a cool or warm washcloth on your face or neck

☐ Try standing on one leg, if possible, or balancing on an exercise or birthing ball

☐ Get into the shower, noticing if either cooler or warmer temperatures help you feel more stable

☐ With your feet firmly on the ground, flex and dig your toes into the floor or rug beneath you

☐ Pick a color, such as green, and count how many objects you can see around you that are that color

☐ Stretch and move your body

☐ Notice the sounds both inside and outside of the room you are in

☐ If you are outside, notice what natural and human-made noises you are hearing. See if you can count how many you hear

☐ Other ideas you like for grounding/rooting yourself _____

_____

Notice how these skills are focused on the senses, such as taste, touch, balance, and smell. Paying attention to what you feel, smell, hear, see, and touch can help you come back into the present and tune back into your body if your system has gone offline or if you are dissociating. This ability to shift attention back to one or more of your senses is helpful when feeling triggered.

Mental/mind grounding skills

It can also be helpful to have some tools in your toolbox that call upon your mental focus. This helps you learn to refocus your attention back to the present, and away from the past (or from wherever it was currently spinning). Ideas for mental grounding skills include:

☐ Try saying the alphabet backwards

☐ Sing your favorite childhood song to yourself and try to remember all the words

☐ Do a mental puzzle such as counting backwards from 100 by 7's, or forwards with odd numbers

☐ Try spelling your full name backwards

☐ As you practice slow breathing, remind yourself of today's date, and repeat your address, your phone number, and your birthdate. Try to remember your childhood phone number or quiz yourself on other similar memory challenges

☐ Say various words that rhyme with the objects you see around you

☐ Other ideas you like for mentally grounding yourself: _____

_____

Activity

It can be helpful to have a plan for when you need immediate support. **With all of these ideas you have learned, and perhaps some ideas you created on your own, which 2–3 physical grounding skills were the most appealing to you?**

_____

_____

Which 2–3 mental grounding skills stood out the most to you?

_____

_____

When would these physical or mental grounding skills be most useful to practice (e.g. when are you usually triggered, overwhelmed, on edge, or more emotional)?

_____

_____

Write these ideas down, either in your phone, or somewhere visible in your house, like on a note on your bathroom mirror or on the refrigerator. These will serve as a reminder for some simple soothing grounding skills the next time you are activated.

Taking mental breaks/shifting your attention

There will be times, in the immediate aftermath of your distressing reproductive experience, and all throughout your healing journey, that you desperately need to take breaks from your trauma. It's actually healthy and understandable to not want to or be able to sit in a *trauma bath* at all times, to need to attend to real-life demands, and to want to focus on other things. Especially as a new parent, you have so many demands vying for your attention! Learning to breastfeed, pump, or bottle-feed your little one while also staying on top of taking care of yourself, dealing with changes in your sleep, and trying to stay afloat while also managing an emotional roller coaster: it's a lot.

Learning to *oscillate*, or shift focus back and forth between your trauma and back to regular life tasks, is part of a healing journey for grief and trauma.[7] You may need to focus on what happened and attend to your emotions at times, and at other times, it may feel like too much. You might need a little dose of your grief and trauma, in other words, and then take a breather, returning to your life. Of course, complete avoidance of your feelings and ignoring what you went through all together does not serve you, and only leads to further numbing out, shoving down, and dissociating from your experience. Oscillation is a helpful practice to support you returning to your *window of tolerance*.

> Suppressing our emotions can actually make the emotions feel stronger, while also leading to memory and health problems.[8]
>
> Learning how to focus back and forth between the distress and taking breaks, shifting your attention in a safe way, can be helpful for your immediate distress as well as your long-term healing.

The skills in both this chapter and the next will help you do this *oscillation* practice. For example, if you're feeling activated and triggered at your doctor's appointment, it would be useful to practice some self-soothing skills such as a grounding technique you learned in this chapter, or some breath skills you'll learn in the next chapter.

What activities bring you a little pleasure or relief, or help take your mind off your negative thoughts and distress even for a brief moment?

_____

_____

What are some ways you can thoughtfully incorporate these activities into your daily routine?

_____

_____

_____

_____

Activity

This can be a good place to keep track of when you have practiced this oscillation and used your skills to shift your attention back to your body, and then back to the present. Notice if, with practice, you find it easier to soothe yourself and refocus on your present surroundings. **Which grounding or soothing skills are you finding that you're returning to more frequently?** (You may want to continue returning to this activity as you learn more skills in the upcoming chapters.)

Day/time   Stress level before (0–10)   Grounding skill used   Stress level after (0–10)

_____

_____

_____

_____

_____

_____

_____

_____

_____

_____

Dealing with indecisiveness

It can often be quite difficult to make decisions in the aftermath following a traumatic event, particularly when there are complex decisions such as choices around your or your baby's healthcare, financial or insurance decisions, work and medical leave choices, and other life decisions that rudely won't stop just because you had a life-altering experience. Often, I either see people shutting down entirely, feeling paralyzed with indecisiveness, or spinning their wheels, such as pouring themselves into organizing something they've been neglecting (cleaning out closets, anyone?). This is often due to the internal feeling of restlessness and anxiety, and needing somewhere to divert that energy. Sometimes this can be an important part of coping and grieving (to feel a sense of mastery and controlling something when everything feels out of control). Yet, when the task undertaken feels too large, this often leads to burnout and worsening trauma symptoms.

> If you're feeling restlessly indecisive or paralyzed, this can be a helpful time to ask yourself some questions to find clarity in what you actually need.
>
> • Is this going to help me or hinder me?
>
> • Is this going to aid in my ultimate healing, or drain me of my precious energy?
>
> • What choices do I have right now?

Let's think about what situations make you feel better, and which situations make you feel worse. Once we've done that, you will have a better idea of some control and choices you actually have right now. That's a big deal if it feels like everything else has been stripped out of your control.

What makes you feel better right now (e.g. sleep, cozy soft clothes, walking by yourself, being with certain people, following specific social media accounts, quiet, snuggling with your baby, having some time away from your baby, having small tasks or projects you can complete and feel good about)?

☐ _____

☐ _____

☐ _____

☐ _____

☐ _____

☐ _____

What makes you feel worse right now (e.g. loud noises, specific social media accounts, feeling like you have to fake it around certain people, going to places where you're around parents who look like they have it all together, seeing pregnant people, hearing other people's delivery stories, other people taking care of your baby, or feeling like you have to do it all yourself)?

☐ _____

☐ _____

☐ _____

☐ _____

☐ _____

☐ _____

As you reflect on the lists you made, what choices DO you have right now (e.g. is there anything you can cut out of or reduce from your life, such as unfollowing some social media accounts or pausing certain responsibilities for now)? Is there anything you can focus on more?

_____

_____

Remember, trauma and grief reactions are automatic and beyond your control right now.

Making small choices about your life, on the other hand, can feel like you are controlling the controllable.

Let's help you bring back in some small bits of control when it may feel like you've lost all control. This can be as simple as making little micro-decisions about what you can do to help yourself feel even a tiny bit better, or noticing what makes you feel worse. Especially when you're feeling indecisive, overwhelmed by choices, or when everything feels urgent, it can be helpful to break your choices down into short- and long-term goals.

What are some short-term decisions you can or need to make right now? Examples might be: when to schedule the next IUI cycle, whether to hire a lactation consultation or doula, deciding which loved ones you can ask for immediate help, how to arrange for care for your other children, figuring out your medical leave from work, ensuring your next doctor's appointment is scheduled, booking pelvic floor physical therapy, etc.

☐ _____

☐ _____

☐ _____

☐ _____

☐ _____

☐ _____

What are any long-term decisions you can put off making right now? The answer might actually be "none." Or, you may have some decisions you thought urgently needed your attention but can be paused for later on when you are feeling better, such as infertility procedure choices, big financial decisions, thoughts about career changes, deciding whether or not to write your doctor a letter about your birth experience, finalizing your child's childcare options, etc.

☐ _____

☐ _____

☐ _____

☐ _____

☐ _____

What did you notice? Even if many things feel beyond your control right now, such as your triggers and trauma reactions, what small choices might be within your control?

_____

_____

Chapter highlights

- Learning basic grounding and soothing skills can be incredibly useful when feeling panicked, distressed, triggered, or having flashbacks. This is all further practice learning to stay within your *window of tolerance*.

- When you have been traumatized, your sympathetic nervous system has been more activated, which means you are more likely to go into a *fight/flight/freeze* response.

- Slow breathing activates your parasympathetic nervous system, which helps you feel calmer.

- Addressing your sleep is one helpful way you can address your mental health and one of your foundational basic needs.

- Learning how to *oscillate*, or take small breaks from your trauma reactions, can be a helpful way of feeling some control.

- Keeping a routine and schedule can help you maintain a semblance of normalcy when your safety and stability have just been impacted.

- When feeling indecisive and overwhelmed, it can be helpful to identify what choices are serving you right now, and which are hindering you.

- Breaking decisions into short- and long-term goals can be helpful when feeling like everything is urgent and overwhelming.

Notes

1 Mead, M.N. (2008). Benefits of sunlight: a bright spot for human health. *Environmental Health Perspectives*, 116(4), A160–A167. https://doi.org/10.1289/ehp.116-a160
2 Adapted from: Fisher, J. (2021). *Transforming the Living Legacy of Trauma*. PESI Publishing & Media.
3 Adapted from: American Psychiatric Association. (2022). *Diagnostic and Statistical Manual of Mental Disorders* (5th ed., text rev.). https://doi.org/10.1176/appi.books.9780890425787
4 Scotland-Coogan, D., & Davis, E. (2016). Relaxation techniques for trauma. *Journal of Evidence-informed Social Work*, 13(5), 434–441. https://doi.org/10.1080/23761407.2016.1166845
5 Russo, M.A., Santarelli, D.M., & O'Rourke, D. (2017). The physiological effects of slow breathing in the healthy human. *Breathe* (Sheffield, England), 13(4), 298–309. https://doi.org/10.1183/20734735.009817
6 Busch, V., Magerl, W., Kern, U., Haas, J., Hajak, G., & Eichhammer, P. (2012). The effect of deep and slow breathing on pain perception, autonomic activity, and mood processing – an experimental study. *Pain Medicine*, 13(2), 215–228. https://doi.org/10.1111/j.1526-4637.2011.01243.x; Larsen, K.L., Brilla, L.R., McLaughlin, W.L., & Li, Y. (2019). Effect of deep slow breathing on pain-related variables in osteoarthritis. *Pain Research & Management*, 2019, 5487050. https://doi.org/10.1155/2019/5487050; Ma, X., Yue, Z.Q., Gong, Z.Q., Zhang, H., Duan, N.Y., Shi, Y.T., Wei, G.X., & Li, Y.F. (2017). The effect of diaphragmatic breathing on attention, negative affect and stress in healthy adults. *Frontiers in Psychology*, 8, 874. https://doi.org/10.3389/fpsyg.2017.00874
7 Stroebe, M., & Schut, H. (1999). The dual process model of coping with bereavement: rationale and description. *Death Studies*, 23(3), 197–224. https://doi.org/10.1080/074811899201046
8 Chapman, B.P., Fiscella, K., Kawachi, I., Duberstein, P., & Muennig, P. (2013). Emotion suppression and mortality risk over a 12-year follow-up. *Journal of Psychosomatic Research*, 75(4), 381–385. https://doi.org/10.1016/j.jpsychores.2013.07.014

Chapter 6

From surviving to thriving: Learning ways to calm yourself and reconnect with your body

Your body and mind have just been to hell and back. It makes sense if you are having a difficult time concentrating, feel unsafe at times, or feel uncomfortable in your own skin. In this chapter we will explore more about what's going on in your body and why it can feel like it's still living in *trauma time* sometimes. You will also develop skills to further calm and soothe yourself, building on the grounding and breath skills you learned in the last chapter.

People often share how disconnected they feel from their own bodies following a perinatal or reproductive trauma. So many previously routine and neutral activities are now distressing or triggering. For instance, some people have difficulties looking at themselves in mirrors, feeling like they don't even recognize themselves, or perhaps even feeling dissociated or disgusted by looking at themselves. Some have become uncomfortable with physical contact, and have a tough time touching their own bodies after their experience, not to mention being touched by others. Going to the bathroom, getting dressed, bathing (and certainly sexual intimacy!) can all be incredibly distressing activities. If this is your experience, you are not alone.

Perhaps you've heard the idea that trauma is stored in the body.[1] This is the concept of the disconnect that can happen sometimes between our minds and bodies. While logically we know that the event is over and we are (hopefully) safe now, our bodies are still living in *trauma time,* and we are easily triggered and physiologically activated. You may still feel as if you're reliving those awful moments. Coupled with this perception might be the reality that your body has changed and even been significantly impacted physically.

Perhaps you are **(check any that resonate with you):**

☐ Being triggered when being touched

☐ Having pregnancy complications that are scary and difficult (excessive vomiting, bleeding, bedrest, sciatic pain, requiring self-injected medication, etc.)

☐ Recovering from injuries sustained during your birth requiring follow-up surgeries and/or physical therapy

☐ Recovering from c-section pain

☐ Having breastfeeding or chestfeeding difficulties that have been traumatic in and of themselves

☐ Unable to touch your body and/or scar without being distressed

DOI: 10.4324/9781003379973-8

☐   Activated by hearing certain noises

☐   Overwhelmed by your menstrual cramping

☐   Triggered or dissociating with aspects of your physical healing

☐   Not recognizing your body, being upset by its changes, etc.

Suffice it to say, you've likely been through a lot and your body is still not only physically recovering, but still reactive as well. It may be challenging living in your body sometimes.

Let's explore some of the ways that you can slowly learn to safely reconnect with your body in a way that works for you. We will review some body skills that can help you find your way back home to yourself, so to speak, while simultaneously learning how to cool and soothe your nervous system. In the last few chapters, we talked a lot about *survival mode* and how it helped protect you at the time. As you begin the process of moving from surviving to thriving, let's go over some additional skills to help you continue to heal. Whether you are working through this workbook yourself, or with a therapist, this is an important chapter to help you build new tools to navigate through the reactivity your body is likely feeling. This chapter can also essentially serve to prepare you for psychotherapy, as these will be skills that will help you tolerate the work you will potentially be doing in any type of trauma therapy. Take these exercises at your own pace, and as always, there is no one way to do this.

First, some more nerdy bits about the brain:
Let's start with a review of all amazing things your brain is doing during this period of your life. Then we'll help you learn to refocus your mind when it wanders, and quiet your body when it's on overdrive.

Have you noticed you are an emotional mush now? Maybe you cry more now at certain commercials or you might not be able to tolerate stressful stories that you could before, like movies, news, or shows about harm coming to animals or children. During your pregnancy and postpartum period, your brain is undergoing one of the most dramatic changes it will ever experience. You are experiencing different hormonal fluctuations throughout each trimester of pregnancy. New circuits in your brain are continually created that enable you to better bond and respond to your baby's cues. The birth of your baby, interacting with them, and even feeding them are examples of actions that create these changes in your brain that help it develop a greater capacity for empathy.[2] I continually marvel at this remarkable process. It's the coolest superpower.

There are not only positive and adaptive changes in the brain during this perinatal timeframe, but after experiencing reproductive trauma, there can also be potential changes to the brain that can have negative impacts. For example, when a person has experienced a traumatic event or chronic stress, there are structural changes that can happen in the brain that can impact functioning.[3] These changes can account for why it is so difficult to focus, remember, and act rationally and calmly at times.

Changes to the brain with trauma/stress:

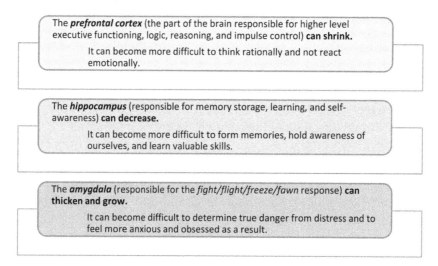

The *prefrontal cortex* (the part of the brain responsible for higher level executive functioning, logic, reasoning, and impulse control) **can shrink.**

It can become more difficult to think rationally and not react emotionally.

The *hippocampus* (responsible for memory storage, learning, and self-awareness) **can decrease.**

It can become more difficult to form memories, hold awareness of ourselves, and learn valuable skills.

The *amygdala* (responsible for the *fight/flight/freeze/fawn* response) **can thicken and grow.**

It can become difficult to determine true danger from distress and to feel more anxious and obsessed as a result.

As you read about the changes to the brain that can happen, and their potential negative impact of stress and trauma, did any of this help explain what you're experiencing right now? For instance, is it harder for you to concentrate or make any decisions? Are you having problems scheduling appointments, or completing tasks that previously felt easy, like paying bills or staying on top of your hygiene?

_____

_____

_____

The changing brain impacts how well we function. This can make an already hard situation even more challenging, which is why self-care skills for your mind and body are so important to your healing. They help your brain recover so that you can start to feel better.

Here's the good part:
Even though you've just learned that your brain can be impacted by trauma and stress, the great news is that you can do something about it, even as a busy, pregnant, or new parent focusing on recovering and healing. Our brains are capable of healing and growth!

Studies have shown us that reparative changes to the brain can occur when we practice regular meditation or other calming practices such as yoga and breath work.[4] This is part of what is called *post-traumatic growth* (we will explore this more in Chapter 12) and can be a remarkable process. While having hope that things can change is important, I also know it might feel completely overwhelming to think about how to learn and practice new skills when your whole world has been turned upside down. We'll talk about how to feasibly interweave healing practices into your busy life in a moment. For now, let's talk about the benefits that can come from these calming practices.

Positive benefits to the brain by practicing calming and self-soothing skills like yoga, slow breathing, meditation, or mindfulness:[5]

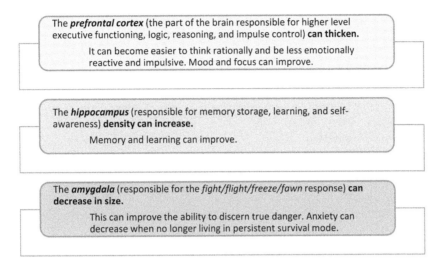

The *prefrontal cortex* (the part of the brain responsible for higher level executive functioning, logic, reasoning, and impulse control) **can thicken.**

It can become easier to think rationally and be less emotionally reactive and impulsive. Mood and focus can improve.

The *hippocampus* (responsible for memory storage, learning, and self-awareness) **density can increase.**

Memory and learning can improve.

The *amygdala* (responsible for the *fight/flight/freeze/fawn* response) **can decrease in size.**

This can improve the ability to discern true danger. Anxiety can decrease when no longer living in persistent survival mode.

Notice how these practices can have a reversing impact to the negative structural changes to the brain we mentioned previously! Regularly interweaving even *small moments* of calming, soothing practices like meditation and breathing into your busy life will help you quiet your racing mind, build an improved attention span and memory, and feel an internal sense of calm.

I see this in my clinical practice, when clients practice self-soothing skills, such as regular slowed breathing, or just brief five-minute meditations using a meditation app at night before going to bed. Even taking a short walk outside or sitting in the sun can make a big difference in clearing the mental cobwebs. Clients find themselves becoming calmer with an improved ability to focus and feel less reactive with regular practice. Noticeable impacts can be seen with small changes. Little steps can create big shifts!

Breathing skills

How often have you found yourself feeling panicky, short of breath, anxious, or overwhelmed since your trauma? Do you ever feel an abundance of restless energy, even though you're actually exhausted?

Like we talked about in the previous chapter, learning how to calm and soothe yourself through breathing can be a helpful skill for regulating emotion, particularly when you have experienced something traumatic, are being triggered, and/or are experiencing heightened anxiety. And here's why: some people who experience pain and anxiety tend to have subtle hyperventilation and inefficient breathing patterns.[6] These inefficient breathing patterns can make you even more susceptible to panic and anxiety, which means that you might be breathing a little faster than is optimal and *flight, fight* or *freeze* responses can be more easily triggered.[7] Also, rapid and shallow breathing is not only the consequence of anxiety (you breathe so much faster and superficially when you're scared and anxious) but your breath can also become the focus of your anxiety; meaning, if you're feeling panicked, you might feel shortness of breath or chest tightness, which then increases anxiety because you might become afraid of the physical symptoms you are now experiencing. It's a feeding cycle of worry and fear that can rapidly deteriorate if you haven't yet learned breathing techniques. To add to this can be catastrophic thinking such as "I can't handle this," "there's something wrong with me," or "I could die."

A cycle can look similar to this:

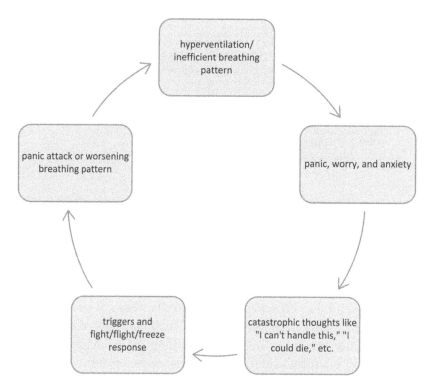

On the flip side, learning how to slow your breath can help to reduce panic and anxiety[8] as well as:

- decrease stress, anger, and sadness[9]

- improve sleep[10]

- decrease perception of and improve coping with pain[11]

- improve the immune system response and healing[12]

- slow heart rate and decrease blood pressure[13]

- improve concentration and attention[14]

In other words, all the benefits you crucially need when healing from trauma!

Disrupting the cycle can look like this:

Just like I do with my clients, we will review several different types of breathing skills, and you can choose which one you prefer to practice regularly. The point is not to feel like you have to choose the perfect one but to have several to choose from when you need help. Let's load up your toolbelt, in other words. You've already learned a good, basic slow breathing technique in the previous chapter to try if you're feeling activated, overwhelmed, or anxious.

> Remember that breathing skills are quick ways to return to a neutral state and to yourself.
>
> By slowing your breath, you can activate your parasympathetic nervous system, and calm yourself.

Modifications and options: part of learning breathing skills as a trauma survivor is to figure out what works for you and not force it. The general rule of thumb is if you're feeling activated (remember that bit about being in the *hyperarousal* zone?), learning to slow your breath down is helpful. On the other hand, if you're feeling numbed out or disconnected from your body (being in your *hypoarousal* zone), doing more of an activating breath skill can be helpful.

Breathing options to try:
Square or box breathing involves essentially making a "square" with the pattern of your breath. This can be a great one to practice if experiencing racing thoughts, panic attacks, or trauma triggers, because it involves both counting and a focus on the breath, which is helpful.

1. Breathe in by a count of 4, hold for a count of 4, breathe out for a count of 4, then pause for a count of 4 before restarting the pattern. Because each count is by 4, do you see that you are essentially forming a square with your breathing?

2. It is important that you're breathing by YOUR count of 4 and not by someone else's timing. Some people, after going through a traumatic experience, find it hard to tolerate breathing exercises if the pacing is too slow.

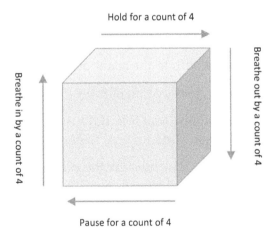

Remember that part of your trauma healing journey is finding what works for you, and taking back control, even in small ways. People who like this breathing exercise and find that the counting is helpful for focusing their active mind may want to start with a smaller square, so to speak, by counting by a few seconds at a time initially and then slowly building up to a larger count. You can also hold a square pillow on your chest and trace the edges with your hands as you count up, around, down, and back around. It can be comforting for some people to hug something close and another way of incorporating some *grounding skills* into your calming practice. For others, it may feel like too much to have close physical contact, even with an inanimate object.

Diaphragmatic breathing

Learning how to breathe diaphragmatically can also help you tune into your breath and help you move from superficial breathing patterns into more rich, deep breaths. What that means is, instead of breathing superficially from the top of your chest, you can learn how to breathe from the deeper part of your belly. Breathing diaphragmatically on a regular basis can reduce your susceptibility to panic attacks and provide the benefits of slowed breath.

1. Place one hand on your chest and the other on your belly, if tolerable. For some people who have experienced reproductive or other traumas involving the body, it might not yet feel comfortable to touch their own bodies. So if this is not yet available to you, it's absolutely okay to skip this part and place your hands in a comfortable, grounding place (e.g. at your side, palms face up, petting your dog, anchored to the floor, etc.).

2. As you breathe in slowly through your nose and slowly out through your mouth, notice the rhythm of your breath. Be mindful of allowing your belly to fill up with air like a balloon when you inhale, and deflate with exhalation.

Sip breathing involves taking 2–3 slow small "sips" of breath in through your mouth and then slowly exhaling out in one long breath. This can often be more tolerable for those who are feeling panicky or still learning to be more comfortable in their bodies following a trauma. Remember that there is not one way to heal or soothe yourself. Find what you like and then practice it regularly.

4–7–8 breathing is similar to the *square* or *box* breath in that you are incorporating slowed breathing with counting, but this time we're using counts of 4, 7, and 8. I like to imagine that with this breath skill, instead of making a square, we're making a lopsided triangle with our breath.

1. Count to 4 as you slowly breathe in through your nose (remember your count might be different from someone else's).

2. Breathe out slowly through your mouth to the count of 7.

3. Now pause, with your lungs empty, to the count of 8, before beginning the next cycle of breath in.

4. Try to do 3–4 cycles of this and see how you feel. If the 4–7–8 count is challenging initially, you can try a counting modification that works for you, such as 3–5–7.

5. If you feel any sense of panic when you pause after the exhale, you can move immediately to the inhale. Gradually, try to work up to a longer pause/breath suspension at your speed.

4–7–8 breath

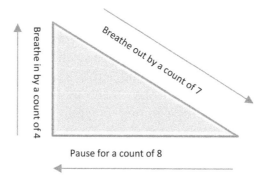

Modification tip: if sitting up and trying any of these breathing practices causes you to feel tense or you're unable to relax, you can try this lying down, or leaning up against a wall or the back of a chair. Sometimes, lying down can be triggering, or trying to stay upright can cause people to tense their muscles, which makes their breath feel even more constricted.

Before using these skills in stressful situations as a rescue, it can be helpful to practice any of these breath options for a few minutes twice a day, particularly at times of feeling more neutral or happy, if possible. Like anything, it can be hard to practice new things when you're in crisis. It can be much easier to practice regularly when you feel relatively calm or neutral. Imagine trying to learn a new language ONLY when you're stressed out! It would be virtually impossible (and not at all fun). It's much easier to learn something new when the situation is more optimal. Then, it's easier to draw upon your new skills you have learned when you are in times of stress.

Activity

1. Choose one of the breath practices you have learned. Set a reminder in your phone two times per day to practice one of the breath skills for about two minutes (remembering to practice times when you are feeling a bit more calm). Record your practices to track progress.

Date	Benefits noted	Difficulty practicing (0–10)	# minutes practiced

Notice with time if it becomes easier to practice. Pay attention to which modifications you prefer, such as if you've found that you prefer to lie down while practicing, or if you prefer to sit or stand. Which modifications feel safer and more comfortable to you?

2. When you are feeling triggered, stressed, anxious, flooded, or overwhelmed, write down when you have used your breath skills to manage those moments:

Date	Benefits noted	Difficulty practicing (0–10)	# minutes practiced

Is there a difference between #1 and #2? Do you notice a difference between which breath skills you tend to prefer when you are stressed and activated, versus which breath skills you lean towards when regularly practicing them?

Meditation

How you can practice meditation as a new or expecting parent

I know, I know. You're probably thinking that it's a joke to imagine how you could possibly interweave meditation into your life right now. Whether you're trying to conceive, are pregnant, postpartum, or recovering and sinking into new parenthood life (or maybe literally feeling like you're sinking), you are BUSY. To add to that, you've also experienced distressing events that have impacted your mental well-being. It's quite possible that it's difficult for you to sit still right now, and silence is uncomfortable. It is for many people who have been through trauma.

The great news is that even if you can incorporate only small moments of breathing practices or meditation into your day, these small moments can help with these positive brain changes we talked about before. Even five-minute meditation practices a few times a week can be particularly beneficial if you are experiencing any of the issues we've discussed. When you are *hyper-aroused*, meditation can be a quick way to cool your nervous system response, and slowly expand your capacity for quiet, stillness, and an internal sense of calm again. You also don't have to figure this out yourself. You can learn to do this with a therapist's help. I am also a big fan of free meditation apps and have shared some options in the Resources and support chapter.

Meditation is another incredibly useful tool in your trauma recovery toolbox, and the benefits are numerous. Research shows us that meditation can provide:[15]

- less of a "wandering mind"

- improved focus and memory

- relaxation and calming effects

- less emotional reactivity

- a greater sense of one's self

- greater self-control and decision making

- similar improvement in health and immune responses as with breath retraining

Meditation and breathing techniques can be helpful tools to help manage the symptoms that frequently occur with stress and trauma, particularly in conjunction with psychotherapy or other treatments. And let's face it, you deserve some time to recover and repair! I think of brief meditation and breath work as vital microbreaks that every new parent needs in their healing and parenting journey, but particularly something you need when you have gone through traumatic experiences.

Activity

Maybe you're thinking, "But I'm drowning right now. I am barely getting showers in if I'm lucky. How am I possibly supposed to add in time for meditating?" You're not alone if the thought of adding an extra activity seems overwhelming. Just like with breathing practices, I encourage you to use these microbreaks of meditating to help you when you're feeling overwhelmed. You don't have to schedule extra time to practice (because you probably don't have any extra time to give right now). Meditation can be particularly useful during times of transition that otherwise may be stressful.

Some ideas are (check some that feel reasonable for you, and that you want to try this week):

- ☐ While waiting for an ultrasound or medical exam

- ☐ When you are about to do your hormone injections or other infertility procedures

- ☐ When your nervous system feels overloaded

- ☐ When putting your baby down for a nap, before transitioning to your next task

- ☐ While lying down for a nap yourself, or when you try to rest

- ☐ Before starting the next item on your to-do list

- ☐ Before falling asleep to help quiet your mind

- ☐ When feeling indecisive

- ☐ As you are learning to take a few moments to yourself

- ☐ Before coming back inside the house from the car, while your baby is still asleep in the car seat

- ☐ After feeding your baby at night, to help you fall back asleep

If you already have one, choose one of your favorite meditation apps and write it here. If you don't, now would be a good time to check the Resources and support chapter for ideas.

_____

_____

Download a meditation app on to your device now so that when you need it in the middle of the night to help you quiet your mind/body and fall back to sleep, you have it ready to go.

Body scan meditation:
Most people, when learning how to meditate, find they prefer to have someone guide them through it, which is why I recommend you try an app or guided video first. I've been meditating for years and I still prefer to follow someone else's voice rather than do it on my own.

However, if you would like to practice a brief meditation exercise on your own, a body scan can be one place to start. If you find you have difficulty tolerating this (with a racing mind, feeling numb, uncomfortable body sensations, etc.), this is not uncommon. In fact, many people who have experienced trauma have difficulty tuning into their bodies at times.[16] So if this is your experience, you are not alone and I would recommend specifically searching for trauma-informed body scans or trying trauma-sensitive modifications that work for you, like keeping your eyes open, sitting upright rather than lying down, or skipping any parts that feel uncomfortable.

Remember that you can stop at any point. It does not mean that you have failed if you don't like doing this on your own. You might find that you prefer a guided trauma-sensitive meditation or to work with a professional like a trauma-informed therapist.

After reading the instructions, find a quiet space in your house (for example, I recommend choosing a time when you know you will not be interrupted for a few moments, such as when the baby is napping or while you are not the primary caregiver for your child(ren)). Calming music can be helpful in the background, if you prefer not to have silence. You might want to record these instructions for yourself on your phone and then play them back to yourself so you have a guide, or read them in advance so you know what to expect. Many meditation apps also have guided body scan practices.

Modifications and choices: You may prefer to have music on, keep your eyes open, and sit or stand up during this activity to help keep you oriented to the present. You can also have a grounding object with you, such as a stone or seashell, to help you shift attention if things become too overwhelming by focusing on your body.

1. Sit in a comfortable position or lie down with your body comfortably supported.

2. If it feels okay to do so, you can keep your eyes closed. Other options are to softly gaze downward or at a point across from you.

3. First, notice and tune into your breath. No need to force your breathing to be anything other than what it is. Just notice the rhythm of your chest and belly rising and falling.

4. With time, shift your attention to the top of your head, and notice any sensations you have there. The purpose of today's body scan is truly just to check in, as if you had a magnifying glass scanning your body from top to bottom. We are scanning and noticing, not trying to change or force anything.

5. Now, shift your attention to your face, jaw, and neck. Notice what you're feeling, and if you're holding any tension here.

6. Now bring awareness to your shoulders and chest, paying attention to any tightness, tensions, or other sensations. Pause here, again noticing your breathing.

7. Now notice your arms from your shoulders down to your hands, maybe even wiggling your fingers.

8. Bring your attention to your torso, stomach and back. This may be difficult, or not, given that this is a place where you may be holding, or have held, your baby and you may still be physically recovering. Just notice, as we shift our attention back to your breath.

9. Notice now your legs, paying attention to the sensations all the way down to your feet, perhaps wiggling your toes.

10. As we close out today's practice, let's return your focus back to your breath, perhaps taking one deep cleansing breath. Please thank yourself for the practice you did today, no matter how successful you felt or how challenging this was.

How do you feel in your body? Do you feel more or less physically relaxed? How do you feel emotionally after that practice?

_____

_____

When setting a goal for meditation, how often would you like to try to practice bringing in some brief meditation microbreaks into your week?

_____

_____

Yoga

I love yoga, not only for myself, but also for my clients, because it's like a "buy one, get one free" sale. It combines mindfulness and deep breathing, and like everything we've discussed in this chapter, has been proven to reduce stress and activates the calming parasympathetic nervous system response.

Yoga also:[17]

• reduces hyperarousal symptoms

• improves daytime functioning and sleep, and decreases PTSD symptoms

• decreases cortisol (stress hormone) levels

• increases psychological flexibility

And the great thing to know (at least this is a bonus for me) is that you don't have to be super strong or flexible. Restorative and gentle yoga practices are a great way to slowly tune back into your body after a traumatic experience and practice your breath work. It can be helpful to seek out pre- and postnatal yoga classes online and in your area. Again, working with trauma-informed providers is crucial at this stage in your journey so you can be offered modifications and choices.

Like everything else we've talked about in this chapter, find what works for you in this busy stage of your life. If you're in the postpartum recovery phase simultaneously caring for a newborn and healing from an injury from your birth, it might not feel feasible to attend a yoga class yet. It might also feel triggering to be around others while you're in a different stage of healing. Or if you're currently pregnant and dealing with complications, you might need to find gentle practices to do at home with your provider's approval. There are numerous free yoga videos online as short as five minutes, so chances are good you can find something that will fit into your lifestyle. Even holding a pose or two for a brief moment can be helpful. Studies have shown short prayer practices and yoga mantras bring the same benefits we've talked about with other skills, such as slowed respiration, improved concentration, and feelings of internal calmness.[18]

This would be a good time to practice a brief gentle stretch or yoga pose, if you are familiar with one. (See the Resources and support chapter for ideas.) How did that feel?

_____

_____

Muscle relaxation

The skills we've talked about in this chapter are mostly for self-soothing and quietening the nervous system. As we wrap up the chapter, let's explore one more skill specifically for the body, and that's Progressive Muscle Relaxation. As we talked about at the beginning of the chapter, you have been through something tremendously traumatic and distressing. It's likely your body is still responding as if it were still happening. From being easily startled at noises, to being tense and having physical pain (and everything in between), your body has been impacted by what you've gone through. You're also likely still on your healing journey. Suffice it to say, your body is likely carrying a lot of stress.

By learning how to calm your body, your parasympathetic nervous system is activated, which is calming and enables faster healing, more rational and logical thoughts, and recovery from your symptoms. When your body feels calmer, your mind can learn to be calmed. Everything can eventually slow down, and you can think more clearly.

Progressive Muscle Relaxation (PMR) is one type of relaxation exercise that is helpful for some trauma survivors. It can be incredibly beneficial to help your body remember how to get into a physiological state of relaxation again.[19] Please notice how tolerable this is for you, because PMR is another skill that involves tuning into your body as you practice tensing and relaxing your muscles. For some survivors of reproductive trauma, PMR may not be a tolerable exercise, and that is okay if it's not a good fit for you. This is not an exercise to rush through, particularly as you might be learning how to tune into your body in new ways.

You might want to record these instructions for yourself on your phone and then play it back to yourself so you have a guide, or read it in advance so you know what to expect. Many meditation apps also have PMR practices.

Modifications and choices: you can choose to either sit or lie down, and have your eyes open or closed (or you can also change this up throughout the practice) in order to help you stay grounded and connected to the present. It's okay to stop at any point if you feel uncomfortable physically or emotionally, or if you feel disconnected from your body or like you are floating away. You can also try this out with parts of the body to see how comfortable it is (such as with your hands and feet only).

1. Let's start either with eyes open or a softened gaze again, either sitting or lying down, whichever is most comfortable. Take a few deep breaths, practicing *diaphragmatic deep breathing* in and out. Notice how it feels as the air fills your lungs, and allow whatever tension can leave your body with each exhalation.

2. Take in another deep breath and see if you can do so slower this time, again noticing whatever tension leaves your body as you exhale.

3. Now, move your attention to your feet. Tense your feet by curling your toes and the arch of your foot. Holding the tension for a few seconds, notice what that feels like, and then release the tension.

4. Notice what this new feeling in your feet is like, and then focus on your lower legs. Tense the muscles in your calves, holding it tightly for a few seconds, noticing the tension here. Then release the tension, ensuring you are still breathing slowly.

5. Notice what you are feeling in your legs now, and then focus on your upper legs (notice that activating the pelvic area may be triggering or difficult given what you've just experienced throughout your reproductive journey, and you can skip this section if so). Tighten the muscles by squeezing your thighs together, if this feels okay, and then release.

6. Notice what that felt like, and then shift your attention to your stomach and chest, again skipping this area if it feels better to do so. Tense this area and hold the tension, and then release it, allowing your body to relax. Notice the feeling afterwards. Continue to take slow, deep breaths throughout.

7. Tense the muscles in your back by bringing your shoulders together, if tolerable, and hold for a few moments, and then release. Notice how this feels, and allow yourself to continue to breathe.

8. Tense your arm muscles, making a fist, squeezing all the way up your arm, and then release.

9. Now tense your face and neck by pursing your lips or tensing your jaw and forehead, and then release. Notice what this relaxation feels like.

10. Finally, tense your entire body for several moments, holding the tension. Now release, allowing your whole body to be a relaxed, cooked noodle. Pay attention to the difference, and how relaxation in your body feels different than tension. Try this whole-body tension and relaxation again.

11. As a final thank-you to yourself for your practice, you can wiggle your fingers and toes, stretch your body wherever it feels good, and take a few cleansing, deep breaths before opening your eyes and returning to the present.

How did that feel? Was any part of it more intolerable or difficult than others?

_____

_____

These are not signs of pass/fail but areas for practice, or indicators that it might be helpful to work with a therapist or meditation support. Of course, any areas of tension can also be areas of your body that are still healing and need gentle attention.

Notice how PMR is similar to the body scan exercise you learned earlier in the chapter, with the added element of tightening and relaxing the muscles. Which one do you prefer?

_____

_____

Of all of the skills outlined in this chapter to promote relaxation and help you slowly return home to yourself, which feels best, or is the most attainable to you at this stage in your healing?

_____

_____

As you practice these skills, I hope you can give yourself compassion and encouragement, as this takes time and patience. Remember that you do not have to do this alone. In fact, these relaxation techniques are quite beneficial in conjunction with trauma psychotherapy, as I have found that people who are in therapy and regularly practicing these skills often find faster healing.

Chapter highlights

*   There are structural changes to the brain that can occur with trauma and chronic stress that can cause us to become more emotionally reactive, and have less ability to be rational and calm.

*   However, breathing practices, mindfulness, relaxation, and meditation can reverse the changes to the brain caused by trauma and stress, and improve overall brain functioning.

*   Breathing practices help to rewire the brain, decrease stress, and calm the body and mind.

*   Relaxation practices help activate the parasympathetic nervous system, which enables a more calm, logical, and rational response.

*   All of these activities can be done in just brief moments and can be easily interwoven into your busy life!

Notes

1   Van der Kolk, B. (2015). *The Body Keeps the Score: Brain, Mind, and Body in the Healing of Trauma*. Penguin Books.
2   Barba-Müller, E., Craddock, S., Carmona, S., Hoekzema, E. (2019). Brain plasticity in pregnancy and the postpartum period: links to maternal caregiving and mental health. *Arch Women's Ment Health*, 22, 289–299. https://doi.org/10.1007/s00737-018-0889-z
3   Van der Kolk, B. (2015). *The Body Keeps the Score: Brain, Mind, and Body in the Healing of Trauma*. Penguin Books.
4   Hölzel, B.K., Carmody, J., Vangel, M., Congleton, C., Yerramsetti, S.M., Gard, T., & Lazar, S.W. (2011). Mindfulness practice leads to increases in regional brain gray matter density. *Psychiatry Research*, 191(1), 36–43; Lazar, S.W., Kerr, C.E., Wasserman, R.H., Gray, J.R., Greve, D.N., Treadway, M.T., McGarvey, M., Quinn, B.T., Dusek, J.A., Benson, H., Rauch, S.L., Moore, C.I., & Fischl, B. (2005). Meditation experience is associated with increased cortical thickness. *Neuroreport*, 16(17), 1893–1897.
5   Pagnoni, G. (2012). Dynamical properties of BOLD activity from the ventral posteromedial cortex associated with meditation and attentional skills. *Journal of Neuroscience*, 32(15), 5242–5249. https://doi.org/10.1523/JNEUROSCI.4135-11.2012; Yang, C.C., Barrós-Loscertales, A., Li, M., Pinazo, D., Borchardt, V., Avila, C., & Walter, M. (2019). Alterations in brain structure and amplitude of low-frequency after 8 weeks of mindfulness meditation training in meditation-naïve subjects. *Scientific Reports*, 9(10977). https://www.nature.com/articles/s41598-019-47470-4
6   Hegel, M.T., & Ferguson, J. (1997). Psychophysiological assessment of respiratory function in panic disorder. *Psychosomatic Medicine*, 59(3), 224–230.
7   Paulus, M.P. (2013). The breathing conundrum-interoceptive sensitivity and anxiety. *Depression and Anxiety*, 30(4), 315–320. https://doi.org/10.1002/da.22076
8   Meuret, A.E., Rosenfield, D., Hofmann, S.G., Suvak, M.K., & Roth, W.T. (2009). Changes in respiration mediate changes in fear of bodily sensations in panic disorder. *Journal of Psychiatric Research*, 43(6), 634–641. https://doi.org/10.1016/j.jpsychires.2008.08.003
9   Zaccaro, A., Piarulli, A., Laurino, M., Garbella, E., Menicucci, D., Neri, B., & Gemignani, A. (2018). How breath-control can change your life: a systematic review on psycho-physiological correlates of slow breathing. *Frontiers in Human Neuroscience*, 12, 353. https://doi.org/10.3389/fnhum.2018.00353
10 Jerath, R., Beveridge, C., & Barnes, V.A. (2019). Self-regulation of breathing as an adjunctive treatment of insomnia. *Frontiers in Psychiatry*, 9, 780. https://doi.org/10.3389/fpsyt.2018.00780
11 Busch, V., Magerl, W., Kern, U., Haas, J., Hajak, G., & Eichhammer, P. (2012). The effect of deep and slow breathing on pain perception, autonomic activity, and mood processing – an experimental study. *Pain Medicine*, 13(2), 215–228. https://doi.org/10.1111/j.1526-4637.2011.01243.x; Larsen, K.L., Brilla, L.R., McLaughlin, W.L., & Li, Y. (2019). Effect of deep slow breathing on pain-related variables in osteoarthritis. *Pain Research & Management*, 2019, 5487050. https://doi.org/10.1155/2019/5487050
12 Kox, M., van Eijk, L.T., Zwaag, J., van den Wildenberg, J., Sweep, F., van der Hoeven, J.G., & Pickkers, P. (2014). Voluntary activation of the sympathetic nervous system and attenuation of the innate immune response in humans. *Intensive Care Medicine Experimental*, 2(Suppl 1), O2. https://doi.org/10.1186/2197-425X-2-S1-O2
13 Pramanik, T., Pudasaini, B., & Prajapati, R. (2010). Immediate effect of a slow pace breathing exercise Bhramari pranayama on blood pressure and heart rate. *Nepal Medical College Journal*, 12(3), 154–157.
14 Ma, X., Yue, Z.Q., Gong, Z.Q., Zhang, H., Duan, N.Y., Shi, Y.T., Wei, G.X., & Li, Y.F. (2017). The effect of diaphragmatic breathing on attention, negative affect and stress in healthy adults. *Frontiers in Psychology*, 8, 874. https://doi.org/10.3389/fpsyg.2017.00874
15 Brewer, J.A., Worhunsky, P.D., Gray, J.R., Tang, Y.Y., Weber, J., & Kober, H. (2011). Meditation experience is associated with differences in default mode network activity and connectivity. Proceedings of the National Academy of Sciences of the United States of America, 108(50), 20254–20259. https://doi.org/10.1073/pnas.1112029108; Kox, M., van Eijk, L.T., Zwaag, J., van den Wildenberg, J., Sweep, F., van der Hoeven, J.G., & Pickkers, P. (2014). Voluntary activation of the sympathetic nervous system and attenuation of the innate immune response in humans. *Intensive Care Medicine Experimental*, 2(Suppl 1), O2. https://doi.org/10.1186/2197-425X-2-S1-O2; Mrazek, M.D., Franklin, M.S., Phillips, D.T., Baird, B., & Schooler, J.W. (2013). Mindfulness training improves working memory capacity and GRE performance while reducing mind wandering. *Psychological Science*, 24(5), 776–781. https://doi.org/10.1177/0956797612459659
16 Treleaven, D. (2018). *Trauma-Sensitive Mindfulness: Practices for Safe and Transformative Healing*. W.W. Norton & Company.
17 Eda, N., Ito, H., & Akama, T. (2020). Beneficial effects of yoga stretching on salivary stress hormones and parasympathetic nerve activity. *Journal of Sports Science & Medicine*, 19(4), 695–702.; Dick, A.M., Niles, B.L., Street, A.E., DiMartino, D.M., & Mitchell, K.S. (2014). Examining mechanisms of change in a yoga intervention for women: the influence of mindfulness, psychological flexibility, and emotion regulation on PTSD symptoms. *Journal of Clinical Psychology*, 70(12), 1170–1182. doi:10.1002/jclp.22104; Staples, J.K., Hamilton, M.F., & Uddo, M. (2013). A yoga program for the symptoms of posttraumatic stress disorder in veterans. *Military Medicine*, 178(8), 854–860.
18 Bernardi, L., Sleight, P., Bandinelli, G., Cencetti, S., Fattorini, L., Wdowczyc-Szulc, J., & Lagi, A. (2001). Effect of rosary prayer and yoga mantras on autonomic cardiovascular rhythms: comparative study. *BMJ (Clinical research ed.)*, 323(7327), 1446–1449. https://doi.org/10.1136/bmj.323.7327.1446
19 Toussaint, L., Nguyen, Q.A., Roettger, C., Dixon, K., Offenbächer, M., Kohls, N., Hirsch, J., & Sirois, F. (2021). Effectiveness of progressive muscle relaxation, deep breathing, and guided imagery in promoting psychological and physiological states of relaxation. *Evidence-based Complementary and Alternative Medicine*, 2021, 5924040. https://doi.org/10.1155/2021/5924040

Chapter 7

When your brain feels stuck: Gentle skills to help your mind through trauma time

Do you find yourself avoiding certain places, people, or certain situations since your traumatic experience(s)? It's common with trauma, particularly when dealing with PTSD symptoms, to instinctively avoid distressing situations, even unconsciously. While that may be self-protective, such as driving out of your way to avoid seeing the hospital where you gave birth, or not looking at your postpartum body whenever you undress, it can also be a common trauma reaction meant to avoid distress. What about zoning or numbing out? Do you often find yourself feeling "spacey," like it's hard to focus on even the simplest of tasks? How about worrying about the past or future; does your brain seem to be on overdrive about all the bad things that could (or did) happen? All of these can be indicative of trauma responses as well.

Let's be honest. Being pregnant or a new parent is hard. Sleep deprivation, feeling like you are juggling a dozen breakable plates in the air at the same time, never getting to sit down without jumping right back up again, and feeling isolated can compound this challenging life stage. How many times have you come across your abandoned tea or coffee, now completely cold? How often are you completely forgetting to eat? When was the last time you had a proper shower? If you went through infertility on your journey, you may have experienced similar overwhelm as that can be all consuming sometimes. In addition to feeling preoccupied with tasks of parenthood, it's also very common for parents to be easily distracted by thoughts of the past and future, experience frequent worry, and feel scattered. To top it all off, you also may be experiencing physical and emotional symptoms as well during your trauma recovery. All of this is a whole lot on your nervous system, and where mindfulness can be a useful practice to help you during this difficult time, to help you slow things down and move out of *trauma time* and into the present moment.

> This is an incredibly busy phase of life and it can be hard enough to simply keep your head above water sometimes, much less cope with all the symptoms you are currently experiencing.

What is mindfulness?

To be mindful means simply learning to bring your awareness to the present without judgment. Yet, it's not always so simple as it seems, especially if we're distressed, overwhelmed, and anxious. It's common following a trauma (and living in the aftermath of it, such as still being in pain, feeling constantly hypervigilant about your baby, etc.) to have system overload and numb out at times. Or

DOI: 10.4324/9781003379973-9

in order to avoid feeling your feels, so to speak, you might notice yourself staying busy and bustling around, but not truly tuning into your mind or body sensations, and thereby feel disconnected from yourself.

When the present situation is uncomfortable, learning to be mindful can help us focus on our surroundings, our thoughts, feelings, and eventually learn how to do this without judging ourselves or being self-critical. When struggling with PTSD symptoms or healing from trauma, it is especially helpful to learn how to shift our awareness to the present, because part of trauma means feeling like you might be stuck in the past (i.e. *trauma time)* or avoiding certain situations, and not actively present and engaged. Remember how we talked about *oscillating* between overwhelm and coming back into the present? Mindfulness practice brings a set of skills to help you shift back into the now.

> ### What's the difference between mindfulness and meditation?
>
> Practicing being mindful is truly learning how to be present. As John Kabat-Zinn (the founder of Mindfulness Based Stress Reduction) says, mindfulness is "the awareness that arises through paying attention, on purpose, in the present moment, non-judgmentally."[1]
>
> Meditation is a *practice* of learning to focus the mind or breath, etc.
>
> While there are Mindfulness Meditation practices (carving out time to practice being mindful), you can also practice mindfulness on the fly. We'll learn both options in this chapter.

Please know I'm not suggesting mindfulness is a magic cure-all or something that can replace trauma treatment, such as working with a trauma therapist. Instead, trauma-sensitive mindfulness, that is, mindfulness skills taught from a trauma-informed perspective, can be a tremendous resource for survivors of traumatic events.[2] This is particularly the case for reproductive trauma survivors, where much of the distress lingers and is stored in the body.

WHY mindfulness?

The benefits of mindfulness are numerous and include:[3]

- improvement in PTSD and OCD symptoms
- decreased depressive and anxiety symptoms
- less rumination (worrying over and over)
- improvement in cognitive functioning
- improved emotional regulation
- decreased emotional reactivity
- increased empathy

HOW can you feasibly practice mindfulness right now?

You might be wondering how you can realistically practice mindfulness when it feels downright impossible to be present in a life that may feel like a dumpster fire. I feel you; that's part of trauma. The bonus of mindfulness is that it doesn't take any extra time. It's simply a practice, an act of awareness. The example I like to give involves food, because, yay food! We've all had the experience of not eating mindfully – perhaps quickly scarfing something down while we're multitasking and reading emails, or watching TV and tuning out. We are barely paying attention to what we've eaten, much less the taste and texture, and we're likely plowing through our meal pretty quickly. And vice versa; we've also all likely had the experience of savoring a special meal. We tend to slow down, especially if we're around company that we're enjoying, and we pay attention to each and every bite. Maybe we even talk about it with our friends. We make happy *nom-nom* noises, and we savor the smells and texture of the entire meal. That's mindfulness.

When you catch yourself not being present (which is likely happening a lot right now because of how you're feeling), you can learn to practice bringing yourself into the here and now for even brief moments. Here's an example:

1. The first step of mindful awareness is actually catching yourself when you are not present. This can be so hard because you might not be aware it's even happening! What are some tells that this might be happening? **Check which ones feel familiar to you:**

☐   If you are triggered

☐   If you are worrying about something terrible that could happen in the future

☐   If you are ruminating about something that happened in the past

☐   If you are overwhelmed and feeling like you're spinning on a hamster wheel

☐   If you are feeling numb or "out of your body"

☐   If you feel frantic, doing a dozen things at once

☐   What else is an indicator or a tell that you are not present, or that you are disengaged?

2. Once you notice moments you have not been present for, you can begin to pay attention to yourself and your surroundings to help reorient to the here and now. What is happening right now? Talk yourself through it as you pay attention to the various aspects of your environment. Notice what you hear both in your immediate surroundings and further away from you. Pay attention to the feel of your surroundings: the texture of the floor as you shuffle your feet and curl your toes, and the arms of the chair you are sitting on. Does it feel tolerable to briefly notice what emotional state you are in? How about what body sensations you might be feeling? This dual attention to your emotions and your senses can be a helpful mindfulness practice taken in little doses as a trauma survivor. Or if you are with your baby, practicing tuning into the present: notice what they are wearing, look into their eyes, pay attention to what is actually happening (not what your mind was just focused on previously). Attend to the smells around you: the smell of their hair, lotion, and clothes. Listen to the noises: the ticking of a clock, a white noise machine, your baby's gurgle, a cry, a burp. Notice the feel of the softness of your baby's skin, or the texture of the blanket.

3. You can start small by doing this for a few seconds or a few minutes. Like we talked about in the last chapter, it will of course be easier to do this when you're not flooded and overwhelmed. Try first when you are feeling a bit closer to neutral, or at least a mid-range distress, if that's possible right now. Some trauma survivors often don't have a feeling of neutrality, and feel quite activated and charged, like everything is a ten out of ten. So, if that's the case, it's OK to start where you are. Learning how to take things at your pace, and/or working with a trauma therapist can be helpful to practice any of these skills so you're not alone.

What was that like for you to practice a small mindfulness exercise? Were any particular aspects easier to do or more challenging? If it was difficult, that does not mean that you have failed, or an indicator that it didn't work or that you should quit trying. Learning how to tune into yourself and what you are feeling can be an important part of trauma healing.

_____

_____

The act of paying attention to your senses can help bring you back into the moment, and avoid the avoidance. This can be hard because it may be new to you. This can also be challenging, because asking you to tune into your internal world might be uncomfortable. Your body sensations, thoughts, memories, etc. are likely distressing. This is why I've introduced mindfulness to you *after* I've introduced trauma concepts to you. It's important to first learn about *why* your body and mind might be responding the way they are before you start to safely learn ways to tend to yourself. As you continue to practice this, in a way that feels challenging but not overwhelming, it will allow you to be more present, and help you when you are struggling with catastrophic thoughts of an awful future or depressive thoughts of the traumatic past. It's okay to not be okay right now, and learning how to be present will eventually allow you to feel *all* of your feelings, whatever they are.

> ### Avoidance
>
> Avoidance may be unconscious and instinctive, and initially self-protective. You may be avoiding situations that are distressing, or even your own emotions or body sensations when it all feels like too much to bear.
>
> Avoidance, unfortunately, tends to prolong PTSD symptoms.
>
> The good news is that trauma-sensitive mindfulness can help us address avoidance, and learn how to attend to that which was previously distressing.[4]

Mindful self-compassion

Part of mindfulness is practicing allowing yourself to feel your feels, and eventually learning how to do so without judging yourself for having those feelings. That's hard to do when you might feel broken, or scared you might feel this way forever, or feel like everyone else has it all together. And let's face it, as humans we're not always so good about speaking gently to ourselves. We often are so much kinder to our loved ones than we are to ourselves, and yet expect that we can just snap out of it. How often have you slipped into self-talk where you berate yourself, such as: "I'm being so stupid," "I'm so weak for feeling this way," or "I can't stand myself."

Self-compassion is a concept heavily researched and studied by psychologists, like Dr. Kristin Neff, who defines this practice as learning how to be kinder to oneself, and being less critical and judgmental.[5] Practicing self-compassion is also the reminder that we are not alone (the shared human experience, and that we're all imperfect), and helps us honor mindful awareness of personal suffering. Isn't all of this (feeling isolated, blaming oneself, suffering, etc.) such a challenging aspect of surviving trauma? Mindful awareness of our personal suffering while also practicing self-compassion is just that, a *practice*. With time, you can learn to respond to yourself with less judgment, more kindness, and a greater awareness that you are not alone. This will help you build more and more tolerance to tune into your pain and discomfort.

The key components of self-compassion

Mindful awareness	• Paying attention to your suffering • Practice doing so without judgment/criticism
Shared human experience	• We are not alone • (Also, we're all imperfect and we all suffer)
Fierce self-kindness	• Practicing self-protection and boundaries • Noticing what you need

Learning to practice self-compassion can help you build more emotional resilience to manage all the challenges you're experiencing right now.[6] It's not just a matter of giving yourself a big hug and telling yourself you're amazing (even though you are, and you totally deserve that hug); it's a matter of learning how to talk to yourself in new ways. Think of it this way: you're going through a LOT right now, and if you had someone at your side constantly saying the negative things to you that you say to yourself, how would that make you feel? How would it impact your motivation if someone was constantly criticizing you or putting you down? Would it make you feel more or less alone, supported and validated if someone was pointing out all of the negative things?

On the other hand, what would it feel like if you were supported by someone speaking to you with loving kindness? What if they were regularly validating what you were feeling and going through? How would that impact you if they were providing encouragement that you are not alone and that your situation would eventually change? What would that do for you? As Dr. Neff summarizes so nicely: "This is a moment of suffering. Suffering is a part of life. May I be kind to myself in this moment. May I give myself the compassion I need."[7]

I recognize that it can be tricky for some people to receive compassion and loving warmth from others sometimes, depending on a number of factors, such as how they were raised, their cultural background, and their attachment style, to name a few. To learn to practice self-compassion can therefore be even more challenging, but it is not insurmountable. Remember the *oscillation* idea we've talked about? Even brief practices can be incredibly beneficial. Just even noticing how you're talking to yourself (more on this later in the chapter) can be profoundly useful.

Mindful self-compassion activity

Let's introduce some brief prompts to help you learn how to practice mindful self-compassion. If you like this and want to learn more, additional resources are located at the end of the book. These are adapted from Dr. Neff's self-compassion prompts to help you validate your truth, inspire courage, feel less alone, and to connect to your internal wisdom.[8]

1. Be mindful of your suffering:

Consider a prompt that validates the pain, hurt, injustice, or trauma you experienced (or are experiencing) (some ideas are: "I know what happened to me was real and was not okay," "I trust myself despite what others might be saying to minimize my birth experience," "I am so angry about what happened in the delivery room and it's understandable I would feel the way I do right now," or "My infertility journey was incredibly hard and has impacted me even today.")

_____

_____

_____

_____

_____

2. There is common humanity:

Create a prompt that empowers you to know you are not alone or inspires you to reach out to others who are in a similar situation (we will discuss ideas on how you can find more support in Chapter 8 and the Resources and support chapter). Some ideas are: "I am craving connection with at least one other mom who had a traumatic birth, so I will check out a birth trauma support group," "It helps me to read statistics and know I'm not alone in this even though I feel so isolated right now," or "This is such a lonely time but I take solace in knowing there are other parents like me who are healing from their traumatic pregnancies."

_____

_____

_____

_____

_____

3. Practice fierce self-kindness:

What might you need right now to protect your boundaries, stand up for yourself, or practice using your _no_? (We will work on some scripts for this in Chapter 8.) **What might be the wisest thing for you to do right now?** (Ideas might be: "I am learning how to speak up when others minimize my birth experience and tell me I should just be grateful for the healthy baby," "I want to use my voice to share parts of my story that feel comfortable when I decide it's helpful for me to do so," "I want to minimize the time I spend with _____ because I don't want to compare myself to them right now," or "I'm learning how to take care of myself in new ways after breastfeeding hasn't gone well.")

_____

_____

_____

_____

_____

How was that activity of creating self-compassion prompts for you?

You can take the three statements you created and put them into your phone, or somewhere visible in your house (like your bathroom mirror), or in a private place like a journal, so that you can come back to these prompts again and again. Remember that it is easier to practice a new skill like self-compassion when you practice repeatedly, and at times when you are not super activated. Let's learn another mindful practice now so you can load up your toolbox with options.

5 Senses

One of my favorite mindfulness practices to teach a client is the *5 Senses*. This can be particularly useful when feeling anxious, flooded, or having intrusive thoughts or memories, as it's a very effective skill to bring you back to the present.

1. Look around you and name five things you can see around you. Describe them in detail to yourself or out loud, paying attention to the various aspects of the item, such as color, texture, shape, and memory the item elicits, etc. Now take a deep, cleansing breath in and a slow breath out (or whatever breath is available and tolerable to you).

2. Next, name and feel four things you can directly touch nearby (for example, your pajamas, your baby's blanket, the arms of the chair you are sitting on), taking time to explore and describe the feel of each item. Take another deep, cleansing breath.

3. Slowing down, listen and name three things you can currently hear (maybe both inside and out of the room that you are in). Take another slow breath.

4. Notice and name two things you can smell. (You might have to "cheat" on this one and find something near you to smell such as your shirt or your baby's clothes.) Take another deep breath.

5. Finally, name one thing you can taste (maybe taking a sip or bite of something nearby to help you) and finish this practice with a breath.

The 5 senses

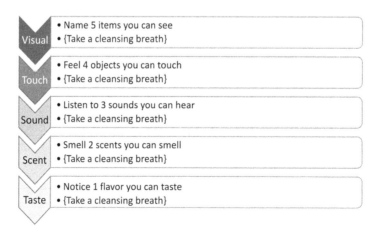

How are you feeling now? This practice can help to slow you down, and can be a brief *microbreak* as we've discussed, which you can learn to bring into your daily life when needed.

Mini mindfulness sense activity

An alternative to the 5 Senses is to briefly use a few of your senses to tune in to your environment around you. Close your eyes (or if it's more comfortable, keep your eyes open and soften your gaze looking at an object in front of you) for 20 seconds. Do this at a time that feels relatively okay to not be on guard (you're in a private space, you're not the primary caregiver on duty right now, etc.). Tune into the sounds around you. What do you hear? Pay attention to any smells around you. What do you get? Touch the area around you. What do you feel?

Try to practice this or the 5 Senses activity 2–3 times a day and mark how you feel when practicing either activity. How does it help you?

Day of practice	Time of day	Stress level before (0–10)	Stress level after (0–10)

Mindful movement

Yoga, meditation from the prior chapters, or some of these mindfulness practices might be challenging to you for a myriad of reasons, but particularly if you find quiet or stillness uncomfortable. Tuning into your body might be difficult right now as you are healing, and unfortunately that is a common experience. This will change and get better, but for right now if it's hard, it can be helpful to have options. Mindful movement is a great option when silence and stillness feel like too much to ask of your nervous system. Perhaps you just need to get your wiggles out if you feel too restless to sit still. Maybe paying attention to your body is too much right now at this stage in your healing journey, particularly if you're not yet working with a trauma therapist or are still physically in pain. That's okay, and quite common for trauma survivors to feel overwhelmed tuning in to themselves and their bodies. Instead, learning to move mindfully (instead of distractedly and tuning out from your emotions and yourself) can be another skill you can learn.

Some ideas to incorporate here into your movement are briefly *tuning into yourself* and practicing *dual awareness*. (Remember that oscillation concept we talked about before?) For example, as you're walking with your baby, pay attention to the sound of the stroller wheels. Notice your feet as they strike the ground, and the sound they make. Depending on the weather, and what's on the ground, what do you hear? Are there leaves? Puddles? Dry dirt? Allow your attention to briefly shift to how your body feels, if possible, and then connect back to what you're seeing around you in your neighborhood. What do you hear? What do you see? What do you smell?

See if you can tolerate a few minutes at a time of moving mindfully at various times throughout the day. Examples are **(check which options feel feasible for you to try this week)**:

☐   Stretching your whole body when you've been in the same position for a while

☐   Slowly stretching your head, neck, legs, and feet while feeding your baby

☐   Taking a walk or getting up to move your body when you feel restless or anxious

☐   Getting outside and briefly walking around and practicing breathing when feeling trapped inside your house

☐   Playing music and having a mini dance party. Even if you feel like an idiot, your baby (and your body) might love it.

☐   Another idea for mindful movement is: _____

_____

These mindfulness skills can be useful to help you manage some of the distress both in your body and in your mind following a traumatic event. Now that you've learned some helpful tools to practice, let's explore more about what might be going on in your mind, possibly contributing to the mental distress.

Negative beliefs

It is common for people to have negative self-referencing beliefs about themselves following traumatic or distressing events. You might certainly have thoughts and emotions externally towards a situation or provider, such as feeling rage about what happened to you, disappointment about how they spoke to you, or feeling let down, etc. In addition to your emotions and thoughts about the situation, there can often be intense internal, negative beliefs held about yourself as well. I often hear themes from clients after their reproductive traumas, such as "I failed," "I'm permanently broken," "I'm a defective mother," "I can't trust anyone," "I'm not safe anymore," or "I did something wrong." That's not to imply that you have only negative thoughts about your experience; you might be holding both negative thoughts AND positive ones about various parts of your journey, like recognizing that you did the best you could, that you are a survivor, and that you also feel broken and unsafe at times. As we talked about in Chapter 4, it's normal to have a lot of conflicting emotions and thoughts right now.

> It's common to have negative beliefs about yourself connected to what you went through. You might feel broken, unsafe, powerless, or voiceless, for example.
>
> This does not mean that universally you believe this about yourself, but there can be tender parts of your experience(s) that feel *stuck* and are difficult to move past.
>
> Notice how you might have both negative and positive beliefs about yourself during various aspects of your reproductive experience(s). For example, you might feel victorious and strong remembering one part of your birth whereas another part might bring feelings of shame or powerlessness.

You will have a chance to explore your thoughts in more depth later in this chapter, but for now, let's do a brief check-in. Does the idea of having both negative and positive beliefs about yourself throughout your experience ring true for you? What have you been saying to yourself about what you went through?

_____

_____

You're probably also finding that you can't talk yourself out of having these negative thoughts. You may wish you felt differently, maybe there is shame about what comes up for you as you think about your experience(s). It might even feel like you shouldn't feel this way, especially if you worked so hard to be a parent, like you should be grateful now. Yet because negative thoughts are part of a trauma response, you may be finding you can't reason your way out of how your trauma experience is being *felt*. In trauma therapy, you won't be asked to talk yourself out of how you're feeling. Instead, I like to think of trauma approaches such as EMDR therapy (which stands for Eye Movement Desensitization and Reprocessing Therapy, which we'll talk about more in Chapter 12) as the *nudge* to your brain to help you reprocess any of these *stuck* beliefs and find healthier, more adaptive beliefs about yourself.[9]

As we are talking about negative beliefs connected to your journey, notice how this is resonating with you. You will have a chance to explore some of your specific thoughts and beliefs in a moment. Once you learn to identify what negative beliefs you are having about what you went through in the past, you may also discover that you're having negative thoughts about yourself when you are triggered in the present day as well. This can happen when healing from trauma and distress. Remember how we talked about triggers as being situations, places, and things that activate your trauma response? Present-day triggers can also activate this negative held belief that was connected to your traumatic experience; meaning, both traumatic experiences themselves AND present-day triggers often have negative self-referencing beliefs tied to them.[10] For example, a woman who experienced trauma with both her pregnancy complications and delivery might feel like "I'm broken, I can't trust my body, I've failed" when thinking about her placenta previa and early delivery due to an abruption. Several months postpartum she is still being triggered when hearing about other people's happy and positive delivery experiences or when she sees other pregnant people. She feels jealous, and has similar feelings of "I wasn't able to have that, and I can't trust my body to do that," or even "I've failed as a woman." Distressing events in both her present and her past are being internalized in similar ways.

Negatively held beliefs: "I'm broken, I can't trust my body, I've failed"

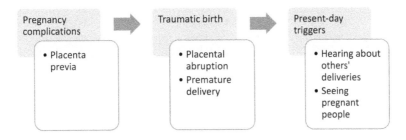

Notice the thread of the same negative core belief theme connects the past and present. This is typical with traumatic events. Present-day situations are often that much more distressing because of unresolved issues from the past. These unresolved issues may be experiences throughout your reproductive journey such as distressing infertility experiences, awful exams and procedures during your pregnancy, etc. This also might not be the first time you felt this way in your life, meaning there can be previous lived experiences linking all the way back to childhood. For example, during your infertility journey, you may have felt shameful and like a failure for not conceiving on your own (a commonly held negative belief I hear a lot). This may be a familiar feeling for you, that you have felt like a failure during other distressing moments throughout your life, making these stressful present experiences that much more tender. Traumatic experiences can get exacerbated, in other words, when other lived experiences of feeling unsafe, defective, or shameful get triggered. Aspects of your experience(s) might be particularly *sticky* and difficult because your body responds like "oh, there's that awful feeling again" and the intensity of the feeling is cranked up. Grief and distress are cumulative and tend to pile on previous lived experiences. The positive news is that you can continue to heal, no matter how many times you have experienced these feelings in your life, and one supportive place to do so is with trauma therapy.

> Your present-day stressors and triggers are distressing enough on their own.
>
> *And* present-day situations are often that much more distressing because of unresolved issues from the past.

Let's consider what this could look like with this example of the woman with negative beliefs of "I'm broken, I can't trust my body, I've failed," and see how her present-day triggers might be linked back to her past. Perhaps all the way back to childhood, she has lived experiences that were interpreted internally in similar ways. Perhaps when she was trying to conceive, it took longer than she expected and she felt a lot of shame and self-blame. Maybe she truly felt as if her body were broken and she failed at the task she thought was supposed to come easily: have a baby. Perhaps earlier in her life, she had numerous difficult memories as a teenager around feeling like her body was disgusting and broken, with self-image challenges. If we trace it all the way back to childhood, we see roots of when she learned how to talk to herself the way she did: early memories of times she relentlessness blamed herself when getting into trouble.

Negatively held beliefs: "I'm broken, I can't trust my body, I've failed"

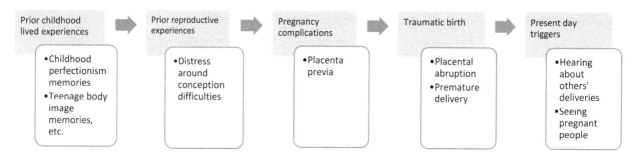

Reflection activity

You may or may not already have an idea of how you've been talking to yourself about your experience(s), and what negative beliefs you may have been holding. Let's help you explore a bit more about how you internalized what happened to you. Here is a list of common negative beliefs parents will often share about their reproductive experience(s).[11] These are based on common themes that Dr. Francine Shapiro, the founder of EMDR therapy, noticed about how trauma survivors would talk about their experiences.[12] You will notice these are broken into three separate themes of *responsibility/defectiveness, safety/vulnerability, and power/control/choice*.

Circle which ones resonate with you, or which ones you may have thought at various times throughout your journey.

Responsibility / Defectiveness	Safety / Vulnerability	Power / Control / Choice
I am a failure	I cannot protect myself	I'm powerless / helpless
I'm worthless / inadequate	I can't trust anyone	I can't handle (my emotions, my healing, etc.)
I am permanently damaged	I am still not safe	I can't trust my judgement
I am a disappointment	I am going to die	I can't let it out
I should have done something differently	I have to _ in order to be safe	I have no control (over my body, my emotions)
I did something wrong	I am still in danger	I can't get the birth (etc.) that I want
I should have known better	I cannot trust myself	I have to be perfect (as a mom, etc.)
I do not deserve _____	It's not safe for me to___	I can't succeed
My body is ___ (negative)	People will always let me down	I have no voice
Others:		

What did you notice as you were circling any beliefs you have? Did you notice certain themes (such as you had a strong safety theme that ran throughout your entire experience(s), or felt a mixture of feeling defective and having a lack of control at times)?

_____

_____

What positive beliefs do you have about yourself with regard to your experience? Now that you have identified some negative beliefs you may hold about your perinatal experience(s), what positive beliefs do you have, if any? For example, if you identified a strong theme of failure, were there any aspects of feeling capable, or deserving? (It's understandable if it's difficult to identify any positive thoughts right now. You can look ahead in this chapter for some ideas, or leave this section blank and return to it at various times in your healing.)

_____

_____

_____

Are there things that you would like to say to yourself now that you couldn't say then? What do you wish you thought about yourself with this experience instead? For example, "I feel like a failure but I know my pelvic floor injury wasn't my fault. Eventually I hope I'll feel like a survivor that endured something really hard."

_____

_____

_____

Were there any surprises for you, such as not realizing how frequently or intensely you have been feeling or thinking this way?

_____

_____

_____

Are there other times in your life that you can remember feeling similarly? We have talked about the cumulative impact of trauma and how sometimes the triggers and experiences during reproductive trauma may spark earlier held experiences. If this is the case, make a note here and you can certainly use this awareness journey throughout this book or with a trauma therapist at any point down the road.

_____

_____

_____

Grounding activity

We've just done some heavy work, and this may be the first time that you have ever thought about what you went through (or are currently going through) with this particular perspective. Now would be a great time to practice a self-soothing or grounding activity from either Chapter 5 or 6. If you don't yet have a go-to one yet, take the time to flip through those chapters again and choose one to practice now for a few minutes, or until you are feeling grounded and back in the present.

If you are having a difficult time choosing one, remember that simple slowed breathing practices are always a great place to start. Or, quite simply, what helps remind you that you are right here and now (e.g. looking at your baby, touching the arms of the chair you are sitting on, moving your body to not feel stuck or paralyzed)?

How are you doing right now?

_____

_____

_____

Triggers and beliefs

We've talked a lot throughout the book about the impact of trauma triggers on your nervous system and how you might identify that you are being triggered. As we're exploring the idea of negative beliefs, let's help you understand triggers in more depth so we can bring this all together. Trauma triggers are our nervous system's response to stimuli that reminds us of our traumatic event. These stimuli can set off body sensations, memories, or flashbacks. These can be people, situations, places, or even other sensory material like sounds, images, or smells. Your own body can be a source of triggers, too. After reproductive traumatic events, there can be a multitude of physical triggers, from menstrual cramps and bleeding, to feeling over-touched during breastfeeding/chestfeeding or intimacy.

I like to think of triggers as saboteurs, or reactions that ambush us. You might be feeling neutral in your body or even having a happy moment, and then WHAM! Suddenly, you might be feeling panicky, afraid, and anxious, with shortness of breath. Or you might dissociate and numb out, feeling disconnected from your body. You feel irritable or sad out of nowhere. Sometimes it might be obvious to you why you're feeling that way, such as feeling anxious when you're returning to the hospital for a check-up, or feeling on high alert hearing a noise that reminds you of the monitor in the NICU where you spent so much time with your baby. These triggers can also seemingly come out of nowhere and can be maddeningly perplexing. It can be common, for example, for the feeling of tight clothes or shirt sleeves to be inexplicably panic-inducing, until you might connect the dots that this feels similar to the feeling of the blood pressure cuff turning on during labor, or being unable to move during a cesarean section.

While we often can't prevent or avoid many sources of triggers, with treatment they can decrease and even resolve. As part of your healing journey, it can be empowering to further explore the source of your triggers to create a treatment plan, particularly with a trauma therapist's help. It can be helpful, first, to identify some common causes of triggers. While you did some initial exploration of this in Chapter 2, let's go more in depth now that you know more about trauma and yourself.

As you review the list, mark any that resonate with you:

☐   Being touched (by baby, your partner, or others)

☐   Certain sounds

☐   Quiet or stillness

☐   Certain smells

☐   Certain places

☐   Particular times of the day

☐   Feeling frustrated or out of control

☐   Not being heard/believed or understood by others

☐   Doing some aspects of caring for your baby

☐   Breastfeeding/chestfeeding your baby

☐   Certain people or medical providers (even the thought or memory of them)

☐   Seeing pregnant people

☐   Seeing others' babies

☐   Hearing other peoples' pregnancy or birthing stories

☐   Seeing certain parts of your body

☐   Going to the bathroom or doing certain hygiene rituals

☐   Additional triggers you've noticed:

_____

_____

_____

What did you learn about yourself as you looked through this list? Does this lead you to think about what you might need right now? For example, you may have identified some types of touch as a trigger. That is common for people following a reproductive trauma. With everything you've been through, it is understandable that you might have discomfort with being touched, or with certain activities. You might not want to be touched in certain places, or by certain people. You probably feel very protective of your body right now. When we talked about what you might need right now in Chapter 4, identifying the source of your triggers is incredibly helpful, because this can help guide what you might need more or less of. For example, if touch is triggering, it's important for everyone to seek permission before approaching you, or touching your body, including medical providers, lactation consultants, your loved ones, etc. Let's be real, that was *always* the case and is even more vital now. You also may notice that certain things that were not previously triggering are becoming more so now. That's okay, too, and you will keep learning how to address your specific triggers.

I'm learning this about myself when it comes to my triggers:

_____

_____

_____

I'm realizing I need more of (using headphones around the house because I'm easily triggered by noise, or talking to my partner about touch because I'm easily overstimulated and jumpy, etc.):

_____

_____

_____

I'm realizing I need less of (unstructured time, seeing that particular provider who doesn't listen to me, doing bath time alone because I'm overwhelmed with that task right now, etc.):

_____

_____

_____

Activity

You just identified some of the sources of your current day triggers and perhaps it inspired you to make small immediate changes. Let's help you unpack your triggers a bit more, including what negative beliefs and emotions are getting sparked. This might be challenging, because very few of us (myself included, even as a trauma therapist) are going through our lives looking out for trauma triggers and identifying our underlying negative core beliefs. Learning how to demystify your triggers is another big step towards figuring out why you're responding the way you are.

In other words, it's not likely that when distressing things happen that we will often have the ability to immediately say, "oh there that annoying trigger is, I'm saying to myself that I'm a failure again." Yet, when we are able to understand our triggers a bit better, it can be incredibly empowering to help demystify why we're feeling the way we are. It can feel less scary when we understand what is happening.

In the next worksheet, practice tracking some of your triggers over the next week or two. The first line is filled in with an example. A few notes before you start: the *Symptom* (third) column can sometimes be the most confusing one for people, but what this is asking you is, "How did you know it was a trigger?" In other words, what was the *symptom* that indicated you were triggered? Did you have a strong emotional reaction? A behavior that confused you? An urge to do something (like drink alcohol to numb out, or throw something)? The other column that can be a challenge sometimes for people after being triggered is the *Negative belief* column. Spend time with this one if it feels tricky, and go back to page 91 to look at the list of some common negative beliefs to see if any capture how you might have been talking to yourself, or what you believed about yourself at the time.

Trigger tracking worksheet:[13]

Date	Trigger	Symptom (Emotion, behavior, urge)	Emotions at the time of trigger	Intensity of trigger (0–10)	Body sensations during trigger	Negative belief about yourself	Time it took to recover
Wednesday	I snapped at my partner for trying to help me when I was having difficulty nursing	Got irritable, lashed out, wanted to scream at him and give up and stop breastfeeding	Rage Irritability Impatience Frustration	9	Felt flushed throughout my body and short of breath. Headache after I snapped at my partner	I can't handle it, I'm all alone, I'm a bad mom, I'm a failure for losing my temper	3 hours before I felt calm again. Guilt lingered longer

How was that? A worksheet like this can be profoundly helpful for you to identify what triggers you are experiencing regularly. You can eventually use this to track your progress as you work your way throughout this workbook (noticing insights, themes, or perhaps even changes in the time it takes you to recover after a trigger). It also can be helpful if you are working with a trauma therapist to follow your progress and notice what is coming up for you between your sessions.

Let's now help you learn additional skills to monitor the negative ways you might have been (even unconsciously) talking to yourself, and various ways to address this.

Self-talk

You have learned a lot in this chapter about how and why your brain has adapted to what you went through. Hopefully you have a greater understanding now of why you might have such negative thoughts, feel distracted and overwhelmed at times, easily triggered, or want to avoid thinking of what happened to you. You have learned some important ways of integrating mindfulness into your life, particularly to practice briefly tuning in or oscillating between your symptoms, thoughts, and the present.

As we wrap up this chapter on your mind, let's talk about the power of self-talk and when and how it can be useful to integrate into your trauma recovery journey. Remember earlier we talked about the intrusive and uncomfortable thoughts that can pop in about the future (e.g. what if this happens again if I try to have another baby?) or the past (e.g. what if I made a mistake in not being insistent on having a cesarean section earlier?). Even seemingly neutral events, such as hearing about loved ones who are pregnant, can bring up thoughts or fears about their pregnancy being safe. Mindfulness and self-talk practices can be useful to name and acknowledge these thoughts and return to the present of what you actually *do* know to be true. For example, "It makes a lot of sense that I'd be so scared about my friend being pregnant when I had such an awful thing happen to me, but right now, everything is going okay with her and she doesn't need to hear my fears." Notice how there are two crucial pieces here: 1) you are validating yourself and your emotions and thoughts by naming them; and 2) you are trying your best to redirect yourself back to what you do know is real and true right now. If you don't practice the first piece of self-validation, it can feel like you are lying to yourself and it won't help you feel better or feel even close to authentic. You are NOT trying to talk yourself out of what you are feeling; unfortunately that doesn't work.

Now let's have you practice this. First, name any worries, or distressing or uncomfortable thoughts that you are currently having that you feel okay writing down.

I've had a distressing/yucky/intrusive thought or fear about (e.g. my health, my baby's health, aspects of my experience(s) I wish hadn't happened, worries about my future):

_____

_____

_____

Now, let's practice a mindful redirection using this format of 1) self-validation of the emotion/thought, and 2) redirection back to the present. For example: "I keep beating myself up for not speaking up more to that doctor who made me feel so awful, and I also realize I did the best I could at the time in an awful situation. I am trying to be kind to myself." Or, "I am so worried about my baby and keep thinking about all the horrific things that might happen that I can't let her out of my sight, but it's helpful to know hypervigilance can be a symptom of trauma and this won't be forever." Or, "I get so angry that other people had an easier pregnancy and I feel guilty even thinking that, and I also know it's okay I feel that way given everything I've been through."

_____

_____

_____

If you feel stuck with this exercise, it's okay. Take some more time with it and return to this section over time. You can also think about how you would talk to someone else you love, as we are often more compassionate to others than we are to ourselves.

What might you say to a friend if they were telling you that this happened to them or that they were having this thought or fear?[14] For example, how might you support them if they were telling themselves they were a failure, were worried about their baby's health, or that what they went through was their fault?

_____

_____

_____

These practices are not going to make your trauma magically heal but they can be helpful tools to manage distressing thoughts in the moment, and return your attention to the present. Remember that you do not have to do this alone. If you are struggling with intrusive obsessive thoughts, images, and flashbacks (replaying events over in your mind), working with a therapist will be helpful to manage the intensity of those.

Mantras and positive self-talk

As we wrap up this chapter, let's talk a little about mantras. Perhaps you have learned a bit about mantras if you have taken hypnobirthing classes, yoga, meditation classes, or something similar. You may even have some mantras that you already like using. You can think of mantras as a self-soothing coach walking alongside you and saying supportive, wise, and kind things to you. Even better, the voice and wisdom are coming from inside of you. Mantras can be incredibly helpful in grounding and rooting you back to the present when it feels like your mind is being shot out of a cannon into full future catastrophic mode, or spinning, ruminating about the past. Some good times to practice are when you are being triggered, when you feel overwhelmed or incapable, or when you are in physical or emotional distress.

Mantras are also helpful by supplying your brain with the antidote for the poison of negative self-talk, and refocusing your mind away from the negative. Notice that these examples provided are in the same categorical themes of the negative beliefs we talked about earlier in this chapter.[15]

Some helpful self-talk mantras to use right now might be (check which ones resonate with you):

Responsibility themes:

☐ May I feel loved and supported

☐ I deserve healing and peace

☐ My needs are important and legitimate

☐ I am important

☐ I deserve to be seen and heard

☐ I am capable

☐ Another mantra I like with this theme is: _____

Safety themes:

☐ There is nothing bad happening right now

☐ What I'm feeling is distressing but not dangerous

☐ I am alive/okay now

☐ I am learning to safely show my emotions

☐ I can figure out how to assert myself

☐ Another mantra I like with this theme is: _____

Power/control themes:

☐ I have choices now that I didn't have before

☐ I am okay in this moment

☐ I can learn how (or who) to trust

☐ I am learning how to trust myself

☐ Another mantra I like with this theme is: _____

Notice which mantras positive self-talk phrases stood out for you. Take a moment to jot down the stand-outs in your phone, in your journal, or a visible place somewhere in your house so you can remind yourself of the importance of these words when you need them most. You have learned a lot of techniques in this chapter to help you on your healing. It's okay to be struggling right now. Your thoughts are often an indicator of what is below the surface. Keep practicing, keep showing up for yourself. This is hard work, and yet, you are doing it.

Chapter highlights

- As we talked about in the last chapter, trauma and chronic stress can cause structural changes to the brain, making us more emotionally reactive, and less rational and calm.

- Practices like mindfulness can reverse the changes to the brain caused by trauma and stress, and improve overall brain functioning.

- Mindfulness allows us to tolerate being in the present, improves our cognitive functioning and our mood symptoms. Practicing self-compassion is one important aspect of mindfulness.

- Trauma triggers can happen when your nervous system responds to any sensory stimuli that is reminiscent of the event(s) you have experienced, such as sounds, people, and places. Your own body can be a source of triggers.

- Mindful redirection, soothing self-talk and mantras can be useful to help you focus your mind when having negative thoughts and fears.

Notes

1 Kabat-Zinn, J. (1994). *Wherever You Go, There You Are: Mindfulness Meditation in Everyday Life*. Hyperion.
2 Treleaven, D. (2018). *Trauma-sensitive Mindfulness: Practices for Safe and Transformative Healing*. W.W. Norton & Company.
3 Davis, D.M., & Hayes, J.A. (2011). What are the benefits of mindfulness? A practice review of psychotherapy-related research. *Psychotherapy*, 48(2), 198– 208; Poli, A., Gemignani, A., Soldani, F., & Miccoli, M. (2021). A systematic review of a polyvagal perspective on embodied contemplative practices as promoters of cardiorespiratory coupling and traumatic stress recovery for PTSD and OCD: Research methodologies and state of the art. *International Journal of Environmental Research and Public Health*, 18(22), 11778. https://doi.org/10.3390/ijerph182211778; Scotland-Coogan, D., & Davis, E. (2016). Relaxation techniques for trauma. *Journal of Evidence-informed Social Work*, 13(5), 434–441. https://doi.org/10.1080/23761407.2016.1166845

4 Dick, A.M., Niles, B.L., Street, A.E., DiMartino, D.M., & Mitchell, K.S. (2014). Examining mechanisms of change in a yoga intervention for women: the influence of mindfulness, psychological flexibility, and emotion regulation on PTSD symptoms. *Journal of Clinical Psychology*, 70(12), 1170–1182. doi:10.1002/jclp.22104

5 Braehler, C., & Neff, K. (2020). Self-compassion in PTSD. In *Emotion in Posttraumatic Stress Disorder* (pp. 567–596). Academic Press.

6 Dahm, K.A., Meyer, E.C., Neff, K.D., Kimbrel, N.A., Gulliver, S.B., & Morissette, S.B. (2015). Mindfulness, self-compassion, posttraumatic stress disorder symptoms, and functional disability in US Iraq and Afghanistan war veterans. *Journal of Traumatic Stress*, 28(5), 460–464.

7 Neff, K. (2011). *Self-Compassion: The Proven Power of Being Kind to Yourself*. William Morrow.

8 Neff, K. (2019). The yin and yang of self-compassion (audio recording). Sounds True.

9 Shapiro, R. (2018). *Eye Movement Desensitization and Reprocessing (EMDR) Therapy* (3rd ed.). Guildford Press.

10 Shapiro, R. (2012). *Getting Past Your Past: Take Control of Your Life with Self-Help Techniques from EMDR Therapy*. Rodale Books.

11 Adapted from Laliotis, D. (2016, February). *Healing the Wounds of Attachment and Rebuilding Self* (Professional training); Shapiro, R. (2018). *Eye Movement Desensitization and Reprocessing (EMDR) Therapy* (3rd ed.). Guildford Press; Morgan, S. (2020). *Negative Cognition Options: Distorted, Maladaptive, Self-Refencing Beliefs: Training Materials* [PDF]. EMDR Precision Academy.

12 Shapiro, R. (2018). *Eye Movement Desensitization and Reprocessing (EMDR) Therapy* (3rd ed.). Guildford Press.

13 Adapted from Morgan, S. EMDR Precision Academy (2021) [EMDR Training Materials]; Leeds, A.M. (2017, August). Phase One: simplifying case formulation, history taking and target sequence. EMDR International Association Annual Conference, Bellevue, WA; Shapiro, F. (2018). *Eye Movement Desensitization and Reprocessing (EMDR) Therapy* (3rd ed.). Guildford Press; Parnell, L. (2013). *Attachment-focused EMDR: Healing Relational Trauma*. W.W. Norton & Company.

14 Adapted from Burns, D. (1999) *The Feeling Good Handbook*. Plume.

15 Adapted from Laliotis, D. (2016, February). *Healing the Wounds of Attachment and Rebuilding Self* (Professional training); Shapiro, R. (2018). *Eye Movement Desensitization and Reprocessing (EMDR) Therapy* (3rd ed.). Guildford Press; Morgan, S. (2020). *Negative Cognition Options: Distorted, Maladaptive, Self-Refencing Beliefs: Training Materials* [PDF]. EMDR Precision Academy.

Chapter 8

Support and telling your story: How to build and engage the village you need

Have you found that some of your relationships have changed since having a baby or having gone through your traumatizing experience? Maybe you feel like you have the support you've needed to be able to heal. Perhaps you have been able to comfortably talk about what happened to you, and get the validation that you are needing. Or maybe it has been hard to talk about your experience, and challenging to find the support from others you are hoping for right now.

What words from others have built you up and surrounded you with love? And which ones, even inadvertently, have pulled you down, made you feel even more alone, or sparked feelings of shame and guilt? We will talk in this chapter about what support you do have, what support you wish you'd had, and ideas to rally the support you need. We will also explore what messages you have received during your journey. Ultimately, you will be empowered with tools. You will learn communication skills to set boundaries when you're faced with unhelpful messages that hurt. You will learn to ask for what you do need, and engage with the support you have in ways that are helpful for your healing. It's hard enough healing from reproductive trauma; you deserve to do so with healthy support around you, even if that's just with a few safe people.

Telling your story

Do you ever find yourself telling your story to complete strangers, and then wish you hadn't? Or do you ever feel like you can't trust yourself to share parts (or all) of what happened to you, out of fear that you wouldn't be able to keep it together, or that it wouldn't feel safe to do so? Survivors of reproductive trauma find it challenging at times to tell their story in a way that feels safe. They might have difficulty finding what feels right, so they are often compelled to either overshare with others or feel shut down and avoid talking about it all together.

Perhaps those who tell their stories repeatedly, or feel like they have overshared without discernment, have done so in hopes of finding meaning, connection, and validation. These folks admit they will sometimes feel compelled to tell their stories to almost anyone who will listen to them talk. Or they might overshare personal details or tell their story again and again, as if they can't help themselves. Sometimes this leaves them feeling raw and exposed afterwards, regretting what they shared and worrying they will be judged. Some feel disappointed, recognizing that telling their story did not bring the satisfaction and relief they hoped it would. For the people who don't share at all, it can often be the opposite feeling. They avoid any discussion of what happened fearing it would feel unsafe, so they

DOI: 10.4324/9781003379973-10

shut it all down. Similarly, these people also often feel disappointed their story has been unheard and their pain was unwitnessed. Have you found yourself in either of these positions?

Recall what we talked about in Chapter 4 about the *window of tolerance*: if you are either *hyperaroused* or *hypoaroused*, you may find yourself feeling impulsive and without a filter at times, or shut down and numb. When coping with reproductive trauma, these trauma responses can make it hard to find discernment. In other words, it can be challenging to decide who to tell your story to, and how much you want to share.

The window of tolerance and common responses after a trauma[1]

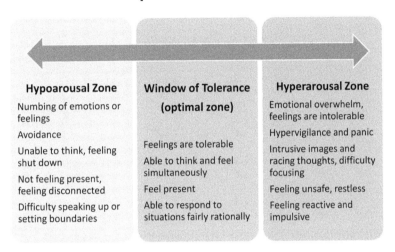

The confusion that can occur after trauma responses might be coupled with any additional confusion and disappointment that comes from interactions with your support around you. When you've been traumatized, you may have already been let down by providers, systems, and loved ones along the way. And now, perhaps you have people who aren't encouraging you to share what you've been through, or who become awkward and silent whenever you try to bring it up. Or maybe you have some people in your life who have responded in hurtful ways, such as minimizing what you experienced. All of this can highlight the importance of being surrounded by quality support as you continue to work on your posttraumatic recovery. While you are still actively working on grounding skills to stay within your *window of tolerance* more and process through what happened to you, it's also important that you have the support you need in order to heal.

The importance of support in healing

You're not alone or weak if you have been craving support throughout your journey. You're not crazy if you feel like you have been shouting into the void to feel heard and validated (yes, even from strangers). In fact, this desire to connect shows how healthy you are in wanting to heal. I notice that folks who have support around them tend to have a smoother road to recovery, and the opposite is true as well – that those without quality support seem to struggle even more. We see this in the research, too, with studies showing that having good quality support not only buffers people from developing PTSD, and those who do develop PTSD after traumatic experiences heal faster, respond well to treatment, and have less severe symptoms overall.[2] People with support by their sides also can experience fear and pain less intensely.[3] Unfortunately, those without good support are two to four times more likely to develop significant PTSD, depression, and anxiety symptoms following a traumatic event, and may have more prolonged recoveries.[4] People without validating support, such as those who receive negative responses or those who are not believed, may also turn inwards with self-blame, or even have maladaptive coping behaviors (like self-harming, addiction, etc.).[5] It makes sense, doesn't it? If you feel alone and without anyone else supporting your truth, it can be lonely and confusing. If this is resonating with you, I am so sorry. And yet, all is not lost. Let's continue to help you find and build your support system, and perhaps even capitalize on whatever support you do have. You deserve the support you need, and especially right now.

The impact of support on traumatic recovery

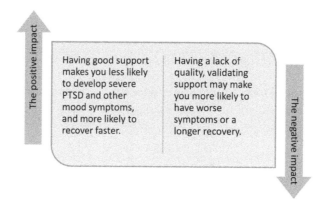

What stands out for you so far? As you think about your support system, have you felt like you have the support you have needed, or have you been craving more?

_____

_____

_____

How relationships can change when having a baby

You may have already noticed changes in your relationships on your journey towards becoming a parent, which can be even more pronounced when experiencing any sort of difficulty along the way. (The whole next chapter is devoted to your relationship with your partner, so stay tuned if this pertains to you, as we will explore that relationship even further.) For example, you may have been close with a certain group of friends and now find yourself feeling disconnected from them and grieving those relationships, or maybe even feeling jealous that they are still close. It can be hard to relate to people who aren't parents now or who didn't experience the same traumatic events that you did. In addition to disconnection, common feelings can also be jealousy of others, irritability, and disappointment your loved ones are not checking on you as you had hoped, and grief around your changing support system.

You may feel like your old life is so foreign, and your prior social support group may no longer feel like a good fit. It may be difficult to talk to certain people about your infertility or birth trauma, and as such, you might find yourself reaching out to them less. This can particularly be the case when also experiencing mental health issues. It takes effort to reach out to others, and many who are struggling with trauma symptoms (not to mention the physical aftermath of birth trauma recovery!) lack the motivation and energy to do so. This, coupled with any internal shame, can become a barrier to seeking and receiving support.

You're not alone if it feels like your friendships and relationships with loved ones are different.

It's common for relationships to change when becoming a parent, period.

This can be even more noticeable when going through difficult situations such as infertility, pregnancy complications, and birth trauma.

Regardless of the amount of support you do have, if you are noticing changes in your relationships, it can be common for this to bring about some fear. We talked about relationship changes being a common secondary loss after trauma in Chapter 4. These losses are really tough. It's scary enough to become a parent sometimes! But it's especially scary when there are already big changes in your life *and* you've been suffering. It makes sense that you don't want other things to change, such as your friend network. Perhaps these fears around things changing are coupled with some internal negative thoughts, such as "I'm alone, nobody knows what I'm going through," or "Nobody cares about me like I thought they did." And if you have been let down from loved ones during this time, this can amplify the feelings of isolation, loneliness, shame, and anger. Let's take stock of what support you *do* have right now, so we can help you form a plan to get the support you need.

Activity

These two circles represent your support system. This is called an Interpersonal Inventory, taken from the work of Interpersonal Psychotherapy.[6] You are represented by the dot at the center of the innermost circle. **Write down some of your support people in the two circles, such as family, friends, professionals in your life, people in your community, and whomever you consider to be in your support system.** Place each person in the circles by considering their proximity to the center dot (you) as a representation of your emotional closeness, the tangible support they provide, and how much trust you have in them, etc. You can place them outside of the outermost circle, if it seems appropriate. There is no right or wrong answer; this is an exploration for you.

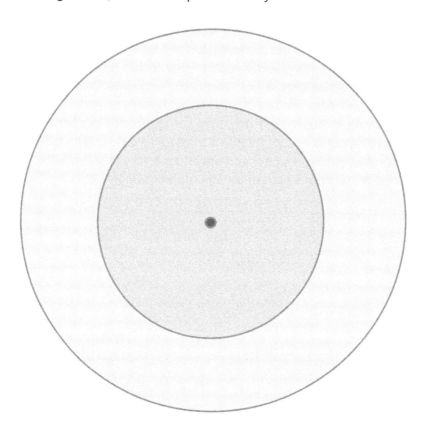

Now let's reflect on how you placed the people in the circles.

Who is placed the closest to you, and what function do they serve in your life? (For example, does someone provide emotional support? Tangible support? Professional support?)

_____

_____

_____

What might have changed in your support system over time? (Who might be missing from your inventory that used to be there? Were the changes more recent, and during your reproductive journey? Were they due to other reasons, such as a move, or a loss?)

_____

_____

_____

What was this experience like emotionally? For example, was there any sadness or regret about any of your support (were you closer to some friends before your infertility treatments, but you have since drifted apart)? Or, were there any insights that came up, such as realizing you already have the support you need in certain areas?

_____

_____

_____

Were there any surprises for you as you were placing people? Did you find that someone was closer to you because they have been more thoughtful and supportive of your birth story than you'd imagined? Or vice versa: did you not place someone close to you who is normally in your inner circle?

_____

_____

_____

I consider this to be one of the most helpful aspects of this exercise: were there any gaps in your support? For example, you might notice you need more hands-on support from people who can give you breaks, bring you food, or come to your house to help with your baby. Or perhaps you noticed you need more emotional support from people who are going through similar infertility journeys or whom you feel comfortable talking to about your birth trauma. Or maybe you noticed you have a great amount of emotional support, but they live farther away from you, and you could benefit from closer people in your community.

I noticed that I need more:

☐ Emotional support

☐ Tangible support

☐ Professional support

☐ Physical support

☐ Financial support

☐ I need more of this type of support:

_____

_____

_____

Lastly, of any potential support needs, and changes in your support system, what do you have within your capacity right now to address? This might mean that you noticed a close friend has drifted away and you could really use this person in your life right now. It might have been clear you could use more professional support around a specific aspect of your healing. Perhaps you noticed that you placed a certain family member further away because of some of the hurtful things they have recently said and you would like to eventually talk to them about this because you miss them. Do you have the energy to reach out to address any of these needs? What might help you do so?

_____

_____

_____

Where might you want to draw from to build on your support pod, if needed? Ideas might be as follows.

doulas	lactation consultants
night nurses	a new parent support group
members from your religious community	a new parent exercise class
an online or in-person support group	trauma-informed meditation classes
a trauma therapist	Mommy (or Daddy) and Me playgroup
physical therapists	social media connections

If you did notice that there are people missing from your circle, or they are outside of your inner circle and you would like to re-engage with them again (even if you're not sure how to do so in a way that feels comfortable), we will explore ways to reach out. First, let's think more about why some of these relationships may have changed (spoiler alert: it's not your fault, and some of it might actually be a normal, even painful part of becoming a parent!)

How roles change in becoming parents

You may not be feeling like yourself emotionally and physically because of what you have been through (as an understatement), but you also have probably noticed a change in your priorities and perspectives. The journey toward becoming a parent is a huge transition that includes tremendous emotional, physical, biological, and hormonal changes. Have you heard of the term *Matrescence*? This is a term originally coined by a medical anthropologist Dana Raphael in the 1970s (and since amplified by many in our field such as Dr. Aurélie Athan and Dr. Alexandra Sacks), to capture the transition and changes involved in becoming a mother.[7] Just as adolescence is the developmental period between childhood and adulthood packed with numerous biological, emotional, and physical changes, so too is this developmental shift. Because the transition to becoming a mother is such a significant one, matrescence can be a time of powerful feelings, and a time of deep reflection about life and priorities. There can be large ripple effects on relationships, your sense of self, and even how you interact with your partner and others. When you add reproductive trauma to the mix, these changes can feel quite amplified!

Becoming a parent is one of the biggest changes in life that you will ever go through. The term *matrescence* describes this transition to motherhood.

Matrescence occurs at a time of great emotional, biological, and hormonal shifts.

It's expected you would notice changes in your emotions and relationships as a result ... and particularly when you've been through something traumatic in this vulnerable time!

Roles can change in becoming a parent. For example, you may have previously been a fairly independent person, thank you very much, and now it feels vulnerable to be physically or emotionally reliant on others. You may have never before in your life needed to ask for help or permission in order to take a nap, for example. This shift can cause a lot of friction both internally and in relationships. Even changes in the household chore division can bring about some adjustment, not to mention larger role changes like grieving the loss (even temporarily) of your work self. You may also be grieving a loss of independence, and feel resentment about having to ask for things you think your partner or loved ones should instinctively be doing (and are not). If you are a single parent, it can often take even more intention and effort to secure support, which can be overwhelming.

In becoming a parent, so much of your life has changed. Some of the ways this can impact relationships are shown in the figure below.

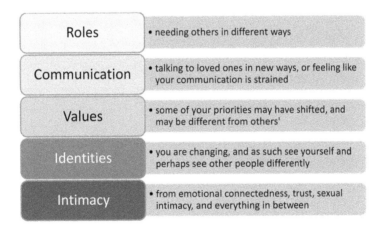

Reflection activity

As you read the prior section, you might have been thinking about all the changes you have noticed in your life recently. Particularly in experiencing trauma while becoming a new parent, what stands out to you? List some of the largest changes you have noticed in your life (e.g. changes in your physical functioning, loss or change in career, loss of independence, feeling like your friends don't understand you now, changes in communication with your partner, feeling responsible taking care of someone else, etc.):

_____

_____

_____

_____

_____

How was this activity? Was it any more or less difficult to name these changes than it was to address secondary losses back in Chapter 4? Recognizing some of these changes, particularly those impacting your relationship, can be hard. Facing these changes is a helpful way to begin to validate yourself with self-compassion for all that you have experienced.

Let's look at your strengths even as things are changing. During this time of great change, what are you noticing that you are capable of? Please know this is not a pass/fail activity nor an expectation for you to be checking off all the boxes. Instead, by encouraging you to reflect on your strengths, it can be helpful to balance the feelings of overwhelm that come with adjustment and change.

Examples of strengths or abilities might be **(put a checkmark next to the ones that resonate with you):**

☐ I am trying to take care of myself and feel better

☐ I am trying to learn about what I am feeling and needing

☐ I love my baby even though this is hard right now

☐ I'm trying to stick to a schedule

☐ I am taking care of my baby's basic needs

☐ I'm learning along the way

☐ I'm parenting differently than how I was parented

☐ I am using some of the good parenting skills I learned from my own parents

☐ I'm doing the best I can

☐ I'm figuring this out

☐ I'm learning how to ask for help

☐ I'm taking a shower sometimes

☐ I'm leaving the house occasionally

☐ I'm figuring out how to exercise or move my body

☐ I'm trying to eat throughout the day

☐ I've returned to work and I am learning how to manage my new schedule

☐ I am still recovering and have not returned to work; I'm trying to allow myself to take the time it takes to recover

☐ As a stay-at-home parent, I'm learning what I need in order to manage my new role while also healing

☐ As a stay-at-home parent, I'm proud of what I contribute to my family

☐ Another thing I am capable of is: _____

_____

As we've been exploring how you have been impacted by your journey towards parenthood, and particularly by your traumatic experience(s), let's turn back to the support you may have around you. Let's think about the people that you love, and why they might be responding in the ways that they are.

Friends and family

First, the good stuff

Before we dive back into the things that your loved ones are saying or doing that might be perplexing, painful or downright unhelpful, let's first think about what *is* working. **As you completed your support inventory, and thought about what support you have, what did you notice that was good?** For example, where have you found validating messages or helpful support? Or, who has become a closer part of your support pod and someone you are relying on more?

_____

_____

_____

This can be an important reminder as we start thinking now about what isn't working for you along your healing journey, and what parts of your support have been painful or unhelpful. Why might your loved ones be responding in those ways?

Secondary and vicarious traumatization

What happens when those around you are also impacted by what you went through? Whether your loved ones walked with you through your infertility procedures, were supportive and present during your losses, or were with you in your delivery room, some of them have also been affected by your trauma. I'm certainly not comparing what they're feeling with what you have endured. Rather, it's the idea of being curious why some of the people you love dearly might be responding in such confusing and hurtful ways. Why might your close girlfriend be pulling away, suddenly, or your aunt who is normally supportive be acting like you should "get over it"?

Witnessing or hearing about someone's traumatic birth or other distressing events, such as a pregnancy loss, can be traumatic. Partners and loved ones can also be impacted by others' traumatic events and develop PTSD symptoms *even if they were not there*. That may be strange or difficult for you to hear, because you were the one in it. You were the one impacted, and your life has been changed as a result. Vicarious and secondary traumatization is just that: the idea that people can suffer the consequences of trauma just by witnessing or hearing about it. I find that, as humans, we will do whatever we can to avoid suffering. We're quite good at it, actually. Many of the hurtful messages and actions that survivors inadvertently receive from loved ones will often come from this exact intention: folks wanting to avoid suffering themselves, and wanting to prevent the survivor from suffering. And yet it doesn't work! Telling a survivor of birth trauma, a mother of a precious stillborn baby, or an infertility warrior, to "just focus on the positive" never, ever works. In fact, it will ultimately make the person feel more alone, right? Trying to tiptoe around the elephant in the room (or worse, ghosting the person entirely) not only doesn't work; it causes harm.

> Secondary traumatization can occur when another person (such as your loved one or partner) witnesses or hears about the traumatizing event.
>
> Healthcare workers (like birth workers) are susceptible to secondary traumatization, too.
>
> Around 35% of Labor and Delivery and OB nurses report moderate to severe levels of secondary traumatic distress and 26% had PTSD symptoms.[8]
>
> OB nurses also reported moral injuries such as feeling guilt and self-condemnation.[9]
>
> Almost 40% of ObGyns reported high PTSD symptoms in the early part of the pandemic.[10]

Even if the reason your loved ones are acting weird is not because of their own trauma response, it might be chalked up to plain old awkwardness around the subject matter. Remember in Chapter 4 when we talked about *disenfranchised grief*? Unfortunately, difficult subjects can make people uncomfortable, and talking about these topics can bring out their most awkward selves.

Messages from others

It's not just the behavior of others that can be confusing and hurtful sometimes; it's also the statements they say following traumatic events. As you have been sorting through all the complexity of your emotions, how have others supported you, or the opposite, potentially contributed to what you were feeling?

When it came to your reproductive journey, and particularly the traumatic aspects, how did interactions with others help you to feel validated and supported? Which ones in particular were helpful? (You can flip back to the end of Chapter 4 if you need reminders of what you filled out previously, or perhaps there have been some new ones since then that have come up.)

_____

_____

_____

_____

On the flip side, what conversations did you come away from feeling even more lonely, isolated, or invalidated? Which statements or questions were unhelpful?

_____

_____

_____

_____

Let's talk now about some ways you can address these more unhelpful messages.

Communication skills to deal with well-meaning but hurtful comments and unwanted advice:

You are working hard on your recovery, both physically and emotionally. I recognize it can take a lot of effort to learn new things right now. Even practicing your grounding and self-soothing skills you've learned in this book takes effort because it's new, you're not feeling your best, and your life is really busy right now. Whew, that's a lot. So, suffice it to say that we're not about to do a deep dive into communication skill building to revamp your communication patterns. Let's keep it simple and give you some ideas for how to manage challenging scenarios you might be up against. Toward the end of the chapter, there will be a section that you can actually just hand off to loved ones if it's easier.

If you're finding yourself fatigued by those "at least" statements, feeling like your experience or emotions are being minimized, or that you can't tell your story in a safe way, here are some ideas for you. These use a similar format: naming the situation while also identifying what you need instead, all while setting a boundary. You can also use these when you are getting unwanted advice or feeling judged.

See which of these you could try out and practice:

☐ I know you're trying to help but what I actually need right now is (e.g. a listening ear; a space to vent about what happened to me; a shoulder to cry on; some space to figure this out with my treatment team):

_____

☐ Do you think you can do that for me?

☐ I appreciate your concern and love, but it's hard for me when (e.g. I hear advice, I feel guilty when I hear what I _should_ be doing instead of what I am doing right). Instead, I could really use your help with (e.g. tangible support, can you please come help me as I'm sorting through all this laundry?):

_____

☐ Would you be able to help me with that?

☐ Thank you for thinking of us, and the thing I'm learning about myself right now is (e.g. I need some space to process what happened and I'll reach out when I'm able; I need you to please keep checking on me, don't give up on me even though I'm not my normal self; I don't want to talk yet but I could use some fresh air, will you walk with me?):

_____

☐ Thank you for understanding where I am in this healing journey.

☐ Sounds like you have some ideas of what might be helpful but I'm pretty overwhelmed with options right now. I'll reach back out if I need some additional ideas, thank you.

☐ I could see how that helped you. I'm glad it did. I'm still trying to figure out what works for me and find my own way.

☐ Any other communication ideas either that you have been practicing or that you are now inspired to try?

_____

_____

Notice how many of these options graciously but firmly set a boundary by saying what is *not* working for you, and establish what you need instead. Even if you do not yet know what you need, you likely have a sense of what you don't need, or what does not feel good.

Who might you want to practice these with? Would it be easier to do it by text first? In person? Email? Think about when and how you will try these out, and consider writing your favorite one down in your phone or somewhere visible to have it close by.

_____

_____

Another good basic communication skill that is helpful in expressing your needs directly is called an "I" statement.[11]

The basic premise is:

"I feel _____ (emotion) when _____ (objective description of event) happened, and what I need instead is _____(direct expression of need).

> Here is an example of an "I" statement:
>
> "I feel frustrated when I talk about my infertility experiences and you tell me I should be happy and just focus on my baby (that it's all over now). I AM happy and yet those years were so hard. If I can talk about my journey leading up to being a mom *and* what it's like to be a mom now, it will help me feel more supported. Can you help me with that?"

Are there any "I" statements you would like to practice right now? It can be helpful to write them down first to practice:

_____

_____

Social media

While it might seem strange to include social media as we talk about expanding and building your social support, I would be remiss not to mention it as part of today's modern village of support for many of us. There can be many positive and negative aspects of social media in general, but particularly those that can come up during the vulnerable time of infertility, conception, pregnancy, and parenthood. On the positive front, it can be helpful to use social media to find connection with others across the globe, and seek validation and commonality, particularly when struggling or feeling lonely. As you have been healing from reproductive trauma, perhaps you have found certain accounts helpful that provide information, resources, and reassurance you are not alone. For many, it can feel like a lifeline during what can otherwise feel like such a lonely time of life. As your identity and world has so drastically changed in becoming a parent, it can feel reassuring to surround yourself with other parents, experts, and advice. It's certainly not wrong to seek out connection in this way, and the busier we have become and more separated we are from family and physical support, it can be wonderful to have additional means of finding support.

At the same time, modern parenthood can already be a virtual minefield of comparison and judgment from others. The pressure from society on parents and particularly on moms is relentless! Social media can amplify this, unfortunately, as conversations often lack nuance and posts can't show the full picture of someone's real life. The downside of social media can also be the negative feelings that can pop up regularly during scrolling, such as comparison to others and thoughts of what you *should* be feeling and doing. It's the idea of comparing your insides to someone else's outsides; it's difficult to be feeling low and seeing other people's beautifully cultivated photos portraying a curated glimpse of their lives. Distorted thoughts can creep up, such as believing perfection or happiness exists for everyone else except you, particularly if you are suffering. Triggers can lurk around any corner. Think about it this way: if I were about to tell you some bad news, you could mentally brace yourself or tell me that you're not in a good space to hear it. But as you are scrolling, there is no way to guard your heart and mind against what is coming next. You might be seeing within mere seconds a beautiful photo that elicits a happy response for you, an ad (annoyance or neutral response), an adorable puppy (back to a happy, warm response), a friend's baby (a mix of warm and jealous response), and a heated political post from an acquaintance (annoyance and anger response). Whew! That can be a lot for our brains to take in, and as such, we might start to numb out, potentially leading us to feel *less* connected, rather than more.

Again, social media is not all bad or all good; it's truly a tool that you can learn to use in different ways depending on the season of life that you are in. As you have been learning about *mindfulness*, I encourage you to apply these practices as you are scrolling and following certain accounts.

Some questions you can ask yourself are (check which appeal to you):

☐ How does it feel in your body as you are reading certain posts or following specific accounts?

☐ Do you notice certain *negative beliefs* about yourself (such as those you learned about in the last chapter) pop up more when you are on social media or when following certain accounts?

☐ Does looking at certain posts elicit a certain emotion?

☐ As you follow a certain person or account, think about "how does this serve me?"

☐ Is a particular account helping you feel more or less alone? More or less supported? More or less validated?

☐ Do you need to mute or unfollow any accounts right now?

☐ Are there particular times that you find scrolling through social media more or less helpful (e.g. do you find yourself more vulnerable to comparison and self-judgment when going online in the middle of the night during feeds, around major holidays, or when going through an IVF cycle)?

☐ What other questions might you ask yourself right now as you tune into your social media use?

☐ _____

What was that like for you? Did that make you think about what you need more of, or less of? Did any thoughts come up around changes to the way you want to engage with social media?

_____

_____

Let's now turn our gaze to the support you do have around you so you can engage help from them as much as possible.

A section for loved ones

This section is specifically for friends and family who are looking to help you, and who may have said things to you like, "Let me know if you need anything", or "I'm here for you." If you know that they care for you but may not know how exactly to support you right now, this is the section for them. You can use ideas from it and adapt it to the people in your life, since you know them best, and what might work (and what might not work). You are also welcome to give this section to loved ones and colleagues (perhaps highlighting pertinent sections that apply to you). This section is designed to take the burden off you and help empower and involve your loved ones to support you in ways that you might need.

A note to friends, family, and coworkers

I am so glad that you are reading this. Thank you for supporting your loved one by being here for them and being open and curious to their needs after everything that they have experienced. Going through reproductive trauma is incredibly difficult, and people in grief and/or crisis often do not have the bandwidth to reach out to ask for help. Perhaps you have asked how you can help, and I applaud your willingness to be there for them. I will be suggesting some things that have been very helpful to the trauma survivors I have worked with over the years. These suggestions for things to say and offers to help (and recommendations of what not to say) are just that – suggestions. Many of these are prompts to start a conversation, if your loved one desires it, and encourages you to be in the listener role. Practicing listening can be harder than it sounds, and I hope that these ideas can bring you some inspiration. Regardless of how you show up for your loved one, it's great you're wanting to be there for them.

Things that can be very helpful to say to people following a reproductive trauma (these are just ideas to get started and this list is by no means exhaustive):

☐ I am so sorry this happened to you

☐ I love you

☐ I'd like to be here for you but I'm not sure what you need. Can I check back in with you next week?

☐ I'm here for you; would you like to talk?

☐ Is there anything about your experience (birth, infertility journey, your baby being in the NICU, etc.) that you would like to share with me?

☐ Would you like company right now?

☐ Can I bring you a meal this week? I can just drop it off if you're not ready for a visit.

☐ Is it okay if I call (or text) you later? If you don't pick up, that's okay.

☐ Would it be okay if I brought you some groceries?

☐ What do you think you need the most right now? I'd like to help if I can.

☐ Is there any information that I can relay to others on your behalf?

☐ If these inspired you, any additional ideas: _____

_____

Then, on the other hand, there are things that we might say, with good intentions, that do not feel good to the one receiving it. For example, we've all been guilty of saying things like, "Let me know if you need anything," which unfortunately puts the burden on the person suffering with not only coming up with a suggestion, but then also reaching back out to you (neither of which is very likely). When we do that, we may think we're offering ourselves up in service and being available, but it can actually do the opposite and *burden the burdened*, so to speak. Similarly, giving advice or your own interpretation of what happened is often not welcomed, and should be kept as an internal thought (or processed with someone else). I do want to release you from the fear of trying to find the perfect thing to say, though, and encourage you to practice listening more than talking and not adding your own narrative.

That being said, if it would help to have some suggestions of things to avoid, I would recommend NOT to say any of the following things. Even with good intentions these can be received as invalidating and diminishing of the suffering a person is experiencing. Even if there is some partial truth to these statements, it's not the whole truth of a person's experience. For example, I recommend avoiding any comments about their body or comments that they look tired (because they probably are). Your concerns about them not eating or sleeping enough are probably quite valid and coming from an abundance of love and concern, and yet offering to help with tangible support in these areas is going to be better received than comments about their appearance. Similarly, with belief-based thoughts, while your beliefs may be very important to you, they may not be shared by the person receiving them and might be received as minimizing of their suffering. Some of these may seem obvious to you, and some might be eye-opening. Survivors of reproductive trauma have often shared that these messages are to be avoided:

- At least you can try again

- At least you know you can actually conceive

- Let's focus on the baby (or the positive, or the future)

- Thankfully you're healthy now and it's all behind you

- At least you're all home now

- Everything happens for a reason

- You look tired

- You look so skinny (or you look like you're still pregnant, etc.)

- God does not give you more than you can handle

- You don't have to go back to work yet; you still have time, so focus on that

- The baby's fine; let's not talk about those awful moments

- You know what I think you should do? _____

- You should have done ___ instead.

As we mentioned, offering help is wonderful, and offering tangible help is even better so the survivor does not have to come up with a task or reach back out to you.

Tangible things that are usually helpful for people following a reproductive trauma:

- Offering help with food such as delivering groceries, a meal drop-off, or organizing a meal train with loved ones, if the person is open to it.

- Offering to help with the person's pets or other children, if applicable, such as driving to school and sports, walking the dog, etc.

- Depending on your relationship, offering household support such as doing laundry, tidying up, supporting their sleep, etc.

- Continuing to check on the person routinely to let them know you are thinking of them

- Offering to drive them to appointments

☐ Inviting them to low-key social events (e.g. brunch or coffee) to let them know they are still included and missed, even if they are not up for it yet

☐ What else might you add? _____

Thank you so much for reading this section, and for supporting your loved one. I hope you have some inspiration now for ideas of how to further help them.

As we wrap up this chapter, let's have you think about what themes you noticed when it comes to communication, relationships, and support.

Reflection activity

Where can you use your voice right now? Ideas might be using an "I" statement, addressing your loved one's statements that have been causing you hurt, telling your partner what you need, reaching out to a friend you have missed, etc.

_____

_____

_____

_____

Where can you use more support? Ideas might be finding an online birth trauma support group from resources at the end of this book, sharing the "Family and Friends" section with people, considering getting professional support, or seeking help from someone in your community, etc.

_____

_____

_____

_____

Building your support network as an expecting or new parent takes time, and particularly when you are struggling. It's hard enough just getting through the day, much less reaching out to others. Give yourself credit for what you are doing, and keep noticing what you need as you work to expand your village around you.

Chapter highlights

- It's very normal to grieve the loss of your old self even if you are happy being a parent. Becoming a parent is a major change in your life, as is healing from trauma.

- These changes in your new identity as a parent can impact the relationships you have, and how you communicate with your support system.

- This can be an important time to evaluate who is already on your support team so that you can better meet your needs. You can also consider who else you need to bring in to your pod (postpartum doulas, birth trauma support groups, a therapist, etc.).

- If you are not receiving the support you need, or are finding that you need to have a challenging conversation, communication skills and suggestions are provided to help you navigate these discussions.

- Social media can also be a part of a modern support network. Survivors of reproductive trauma may find both positive and negative aspects of social media and learn mindful ways to navigate this resource.

- Giving loved ones a section of this chapter to read can be one way of enhancing your support by providing tangible suggestions of ways to help you.

Notes

1 Ogden, P., Minton, K., & Pain, C. (2006). *Trauma and the Body: A Sensorimotor Approach to Psychotherapy*. Norton.
2 Price, M., Lancaster, C.L., Gros, D.F., Legrand, A.C., van Stolk-Cooke, K., & Acierno, R. (2018). An examination of social support and PTSD treatment response during prolonged exposure. *Psychiatry*, 81(3), 258–270. https://doi.org/10.1080/00332747.2017.1402569; Shnaider, P., Sijercic, I., Wanklyn, S.G., Suvak, M.K., & Monson, C.M. (2017). The role of social support in cognitive-behavioral conjoint therapy for posttraumatic stress disorder. *Behavior Therapy*, 48(3), 285–294. https://doi.org/10.1016/j.beth.2016.05.003
3 Coan, J.A., Schaefer, H.S., & Davidson, R.J. (2006). Lending a hand: social regulation of the neural response to threat. *Psychological Science*, 17(12), 1032–1039. https://doi.org/10.1111/j.1467-9280.2006.01832.x; Graff, T.C., Fitzgerald, J.R., Luke, S.G., & Birmingham, W.C. (2021). Spousal emotional support and relationship quality buffers pupillary response to horror movies. *PloS ONE*, 16(9), e0256823. https://doi.org/10.1371/journal.pone.0256823
4 van der Velden, P.G., Contino, C., Marchand, M., Das, M., & Schut, H. (2020). Does pre-event lack of emotional support increase the risk of post-event PTSD, anxiety, depression symptoms and lack of support? A comparative population-based study among victims of threat and violence. *Journal of Anxiety Disorders*, 75, 102269. https://doi.org/10.1016/j.janxdis.2020.102269
5 Ullman, S.E., & Relyea, M. (2016). Social support, coping, and posttraumatic stress symptoms in female sexual assault survivors: a longitudinal analysis. *Journal of Traumatic Stress*, 29(6), 500–506. https://doi.org/10.1002/jts.22143; Ullman, S.E., Townsend, S.M., Filipas, H.H., & Starzynski, L.L. (2007). Structural models of the relations of assault severity, social support, avoidance coping, self-blame, and PTSD among sexual assault survivors. *Psychology of Women Quarterly*, 31(1), 23–37.
6 Stuart, S., & Robertson, M. *(2012). Interpersonal Psychotherapy: A Clinician's Guide* (2nd ed.). CRC Press.
7 Athan, A.M. (2020). Reproductive identity: an emerging concept. *American Psychologist*, 75(4), 445–456; Raphael, D. (1975). *Being Female: Reproduction, Power, and Change*. De Gruyter Mouton; Sacks, A. (2017, May 8). The birth of a mother. *The New York Times*. https://www.nytimes.com/2017/05/08/well/family/the-birth-of-a-mother.html
8 Beck, C.T., & Gable, R.K. (2012). A mixed methods study of secondary traumatic stress in labor and delivery nurses. *Journal of Obstetric, Gynecologic, and Neonatal Nursing*, 41(6), 747–760. https://doi.org/10.1111/j.1552-6909.2012.01386.x
9 Beck C.T. (2022). Secondary qualitative analysis of moral injury in obstetric and neonatal nurses. *Journal of Obstetric, Gynecologic, and Neonatal Nursing*, 51(2), 166–176. https://doi.org/10.1016/j.jogn.2021.12.003
10 Kiefer, M.K., Mehl, R.R., Venkatesh, K.K., Costantine, M.M., & Rood, K.M. (2021). High frequency of posttraumatic stress symptoms among US obstetrical and gynecologic providers during the coronavirus disease 2019 pandemic. *American Journal of Obstetrics and Gynecology*, 224(4), 410–413. https://doi.org/10.1016/j.ajog.2020.12.1211
11 Adapted from Markman, H. J., Floyd, F., Stanley, S., & Lewis, H. (1986). Prevention. In N. Jacobson & A. Gurman (eds.), *Clinical Handbook of Marital Therapy* (pp. 173–195). Guilford Press.

Chapter 9

The impact of reproductive trauma on partners and relationships: How are you and your partner doing?

Real talk here. I don't know anyone who hasn't been through infertility treatments, pregnancy complications, a traumatic birth, or a pregnancy loss, and which hasn't had an impact on their relationship, to some degree. Some couples feel isolated, lonely, and resentful, and others can eventually feel much closer after everything they have been through. Even when you both experience the ripple effects differently, it's important to highlight that you two have been through this together. It can be common, though, after everything that you've endured, that you might be looking at each other through new lenses, and interacting in new ways. To add to that, your partner may also be dealing with their own fallout from the journey. They may be struggling with the adjustment to parenthood, too, and even going through their own mental health battles. This can cause some couples to cling to each other, and cause others to feel more isolated and alone in their healing.

Regardless of how you feel, and whatever the impact on your relationship, what you are experiencing is not abnormal. This chapter will help you explore, first, what your partner might be feeling as a result of going through this experience. We will then identify some of the ways your relationship may have been impacted by what you went through, and then we will talk about some tangible things you can do together to address these challenges. First, a few suggestions on how to use this chapter. You can read it by yourself or with your partner. You may want to hand parts of this chapter over to your partner to read if it feels like too much to focus on both your own healing and your partner's needs right now. You might not have the bandwidth to consider your relationship right now either. If that's the case, it's okay to return to this chapter if and when you're ready.

> Parenthood can be a difficult time for most couples to navigate initially, period!
>
> Upwards of 67% of couples report marital dissatisfaction after having a baby,[1] and that's even when things went relatively "smoothly."
>
> Imagine the potential impact on the relationship when there are trauma and challenges throughout the reproductive journey.
>
> In other words, you are not alone if you've noticed a change in your relationship!

DOI: 10.4324/9781003379973-11

Partners can experience Perinatal Mental Health changes, too

Has your partner or spouse been withdrawing more than normal, or been more angry and irritable? Do they seem to be leaning on you emotionally, when you feel like you have nothing extra to give? Even though it's not talked about as much, partners can experience Perinatal Mood and Anxiety Disorders, too. Anywhere between 2% and 18% of men will have an anxiety disorder when becoming a parent.[2] And about 1 in 10 fathers and same-sex partners will experience depression during this time and are at risk for developing other mental health disorders like OCD and Bipolar Disorder, among others.[3] Similarly, partners can also experience Posttraumatic Stress Disorder (PTSD) following the birthing person's traumatic birth, as well as symptoms that linger but may not bloom into a full disorder (but that can still be quite impactful). Secondary traumatization is very real in partners. However, it is not often effectively addressed by others surrounding the couple, and the partner is often overlooked.

> Research shows that up to 26% of men develop PTSD after their partner's traumatic delivery.[4]
>
> Some partners can have PTSD symptoms for years without being screened, or without seeking their own treatment.[5]
>
> Your partner can benefit from reading this book, too, to learn about trauma, and take the PCL-5 themselves in Chapter 3 to monitor their own symptoms.

It may feel overwhelming to consider that your partner may be struggling with their mental health when you are too. And yet, it's common that you both may be impacted since you both have been through significant life events. Even though you and your partner may share some lived experiences, you may be dealing with your mental health in completely different ways. For example, it is common for men experiencing depression after having a baby to pour themselves into their work, start experimenting with riskier activities, have new or worsening addictions (gaming, gambling, drinking, etc.), and withdraw from others. To add to the differences in how you might be coping, you also might be noticing differences in how the two of you are being treated by your support systems. How often are you asked how you are doing, and how often are people checking in on your partner? As a society, we typically don't do a great job of checking in on partners.

What was your partner's experience like for them?

Whether we are talking about difficult infertility procedures, pregnancy or postpartum complications, traumatic losses, birth trauma, or scary interventions that happened with the baby, your partner may have been impacted by what you went through as well. Partners often share several common themes to describe their experiences. Partners will often describe **(check any that your partner may have experienced):**[6]

☐ Feeling anxious, helpless, hopeless

☐ Having PTSD symptoms such nightmares, flashbacks, and intrusive thoughts

☐ Feeling unprepared for what happened

- ☐ Feeling excluded from the events, feeling like they were an invisible observer
- ☐ That nobody asked how they were doing, either during or afterwards
- ☐ They did not know what was happening with their partner or their baby for long periods of time
- ☐ Feeling afraid for their partner or baby's lives
- ☐ That the event impacted them for a significant amount of time afterwards
- ☐ That the event has an impact on their relationship over time
- ☐ I noticed my partner experienced: _____

Men of color, in particular, have reported additional themes such as **(check any that your partner may have experienced):**[7]

- ☐ Feeling mistrust of the system and providers
- ☐ Not getting the information they needed, feeling left out of the conversation
- ☐ Feeling like they have to defend themselves and their partner
- ☐ Feeling unheard yet feeling like they had to be the voice for their partner
- ☐ Feeling guarded due to previous experiences of discrimination
- ☐ I noticed my partner experienced: _____

Do any of these sound familiar? Has your partner shared any of these experiences? Are any additional insights standing out for you?

_____

_____

There can be a lot of pressure on partners, and men in particular, to be strong during traumatic experiences. This can be challenging when partners are suffering and impacted by the distress of what they went through.

> Some men (and male identifying people) may have difficulty identifying and discussing what they are feeling during this time.
>
> This can be a common time when men may stuff down their emotions and not seek outside support. This may lead to isolation and feeling resentment that their partner is not present enough for them, and vice versa – fatigue from their partner who is also struggling!
>
> Same-sex partners might be going through some of these similar challenges in addition to feeling left out of the conversation, bias from providers, and other systemic barriers.
>
> In other words, both you _and_ your partner deserve and need quality support during this time. It is virtually impossible to hold each other up without outside support.

Risk factors in partners

If your partner is struggling right now (or just acting *off* and not like their normal self), there are probably a lot of reasons for that. Just like you, so much has changed for them in preparing to become, or becoming, a parent. (It just might have changed in different ways than it did for you.) As we talked about before, they have likely been with you throughout your traumatic experience(s) and may be dealing with vicarious traumatization themselves, to some degree. Your partner also might be feeling a lot of pressure to keep it all together for you and feel like they have to support you. Or perhaps they're worried about you and wondering when they're going to get *you* back (you've probably wondered that sometimes, too).

> There is a lot of pressure on partners to be the *strong* one and to support you.
>
> While certainly their support role is important, they can also be impacted by trauma, and experience mental health symptoms as well.
>
> One of the ways your partner can support you and the baby is to be their healthiest version of themselves. Yet, recognizing their own needs, or reaching out for help, may feel selfish or strange for them (and your support team may not instinctively think to help them with this).

Just like how various factors may have put you at higher risk for developing PTSD, your partner, too, may have been at higher risk for posttraumatic symptoms. Studies show that partners with their own prior histories of PTSD and depression are at higher risk for developing worsening (or reoccurrence of) symptoms after their partner's birth, *even if the birth was uncomplicated and non-life-threatening!*[8] Similar studies of heterosexual couples found that men who become dads when they are older, and those whose partners had depression or PTSD, are more likely to have these symptoms themselves. Men tend to be more prone towards anxiety and hypervigilance in parenthood when they feel unprepared for fatherhood or are nervous about the delivery.[9] Dads whose babies are in the NICU are at significantly higher risk for PTSD and stress than other fathers.[10] In other words, there may be a number of reasons why your partner may be struggling right now. As always, there is a need for more studies with same-sex partners and partners of color to validate what we are seeing in our practices.

Reflection activity

How are you doing as you are reading this information? It might feel overwhelming to consider that your partner is, well, overwhelmed too. You might even be annoyed to think of them struggling when you are at your absolute breaking point. I get it. A relationship can face a lot of strain when both partners are hurting, and many people in relationships after a reproductive trauma (particularly when a new baby also comes on the scene) can feel like everything is about to combust. You may have very limited bandwidth; and yet, just as it is not your partner's job to fix everything or hold you up through the storm, it is also not your job to fix them. Being supportive of each other might look different at various times of your partnership. In crisis, support will certainly look different than it does when things are smooth sailing.

If this section has been difficult to read, this is a good time for a check-in.

What has been particularly difficult (e.g. "It's been hard to read things that remind me that things actually aren't so great in my relationship," or "I don't have the energy to deal with my own stuff right now much less her emotions," or "The thought of him struggling makes me feel scared")?

_____

_____

_____

What strengths would you like to recognize about your relationship or partner right now (e.g. "I see that he's struggling but he's also reaching out to his family for support and I'm thankful for that," or "We certainly have our issues and I'm thankful she isn't struggling with her mental health," or "This has been hard but I see that there are some things going ok with us")?

_____

_____

_____

A common trap many couples fall into is when a dad/partner tries to get all of their emotional needs met from their partner in general, and particularly after having a baby. This can increase resentment and fatigue, especially after reproductive trauma. While it can be hard for partners to reach outside of the relationship for their own support (it can feel like dating again!), it's also important the two of you are not each other's only support. **If this resonates with you, is there anything you would like your partner to know about your need for them to have additional support that isn't you? As a reminder, ideas for both of you for support are in the Resources and support chapter.**

_____

_____

_____

Are you noticing any negative thoughts coming up as you think about your partner or relationship? (You can look at examples from page 91 if needed, such as "I'm unlovable," "I can't handle it," "It's all my fault.") If so, note them here so you can keep working to address your triggers with the skills you're learning and perhaps with a therapist.

_____

_____

_____

Whatever has been coming up in this section, check in with your body and your emotional state. Are you inside of your *window of tolerance*, or activated or numbed out? Could you benefit from using one of your grounding skills from Chapter 5 or 6? Practice it here and note how that was for you.

_____

_____

_____

_____

The impact of reproductive trauma on relationships

What has this all meant for your relationship?

As we explored a bit in the prior chapter, you are probably feeling *off,* to say the least. This can mean that not only are you not feeling and acting like you normally would, but you are also probably interacting with those around you in different ways. It would make sense that this would include your romantic partner. As you are healing physically and emotionally, and perhaps still in crisis mode, this is going to have an impact on your relationship, and the way you both see each other and talk to one another.

Not only have your roles potentially changed, as we addressed previously, but you may need each other in new ways, which can be uncomfortable, and even scary. Before in your relationship, you probably did not have to ask for such basic needs (such as help getting sleep, eating, or reassurance that you are safe), but you likely do now. You might feel vulnerable needing someone in this way, and you might get easily frustrated when they are not responding immediately with rescue or relief. Particularly if you are out of your *window of tolerance*, relief cannot come soon enough, and it is common for people to become upset when their partner does not respond in the way they were expecting or needing.

You might also be noticing that you are coping differently with this challenging time. It can be common for couples to have stress around communication or values during a crisis. For example, perhaps one of you wants to talk about what happened, to process through it for shared understanding. But maybe the other finds talking about it uncomfortable and wants to simply move on. Do you two seem to be focused on different things right now? Perhaps you are focused on safety (yours, the baby's, or both) and your partner seems more keen to return to work and a normal routine. It can be so frustrating to feel like you are prioritizing different things or that you are on different planets. It makes sense that when one or either partner has PTSD or other mental health symptoms, it can have large ripple effects on the relationship and on parenting. The positive news is this all can change. For example, we see frequently that when one or both partners receive professional treatment, there are not only improvements in mental health, there are improvements in the relationship, and the bond with the baby.[11] There has also been promising research to show that when a couple gets support for their relationship with a trauma-focused and attachment lens (specifically Emotionally Focused Therapy, or EFT, in this study), the couple's PTSD and depressive symptoms reduced as their relationship distress did![12] If you are not in a space to address your relationship at this time, that is okay. This is merely to highlight how interconnected we can be as couples.

To add to challenges of connecting with each other in new ways while you are struggling, you might also be resentful of having to ask for things that you think your partner should just intuitively figure out. It can be hard to be patient, understanding that they are also learning to become a parent (and will be doing things differently than you sometimes!). Their way of taking care of the baby will likely be quite different than yours, sometimes, and this can be a big source of conflict. You may also be grieving or adjusting to a major change in connection with each other. Let's talk a little more about this.

> Remember that earlier statistic about 67% of couples reporting marital dissatisfaction after having a baby? It's not all doom and gloom!
>
> What can we learn from the 33% of couples who felt content? They felt the same stressors of parenthood and then learned to navigate them together as a team.[13] What are some ways you can do this as you are struggling and healing?

The impact that trauma can have on your intimacy

Perhaps you saw this subheading and thought "oh yikes, yes that's us." Or maybe you wanted to (or did) skip right over it because the thought of addressing intimacy feels like too much right now. It's okay, as I keep saying; not everyone's experience is the same, and it's important to take your journey at your speed. Here's the thing: reproductive trauma can have a very real impact on a couple's intimacy.[14] Beyond even the changes in sex drive, communication, closeness, or connection that some might expect to see in their relationship during pregnancy or post-baby, trauma can also pack a large punch. Perhaps the thought of sex, or even physical touch, is beyond laughable when you are in survival mode and just trying to get through each day. Or maybe you are holding resentments and anger, feeling emotionally distant from each other. Some people describe feeling cold and detached from their partners during this time.[15] Perhaps your trauma reactions, such as discomfort in your body, flashbacks, and difficulties staying within your *window of tolerance* also make physical closeness challenging.

As this is a time of great biological, hormonal, emotional, and physical changes, it is understandable that becoming a parent may have impacted your sex drive.[16] To add to that, you may have had physical trauma (such as discomfort from infertility treatments, pelvic floor pain, etc.) that you are still healing from in addition to your emotional healing from trauma. Postpartum feeding challenges, feeling exhausted and depleted, and being in pain can also all pile onto this challenging time. Some people describe that they feel like their bodies are not even theirs anymore. Having a loss of libido is quite common after having a baby, actually, and particularly after reproductive trauma,[17] and it can have ripple effects on the relationship.

> Remember how we talked about your sympathetic nervous system being activated right now?
>
> If you were being chased by a bear and in survival mode, the last thing you would be interested in would be sex. Right?
>
> To add to that might be that you are recovering physically and/or in pain, which of course can impact the desire for intimacy (or the lack thereof).

Some aspects of intimacy that survivors of reproductive trauma find challenging are (check which ones might feel familiar to you, if it feels safe to do so):

☐ Feeling over-touched or overstimulated easily

☐ Feeling unsafe in your own body

☐ Not wanting to be looked at while naked

☐ Dissociating when being intimate or being touched

☐ Going outside of your *window of tolerance*

☐ Your partner feeling cautious of touching you

☐ Your partner is dealing with their own trauma responses, and/or anxiety and fears

☐ Still healing physically (or hurting/uncomfortable)

☐ Not feeling comfortable with silence, lights off, or any of the environmental cues of intimacy

☐ Not feeling safe in the bedroom, feeling anxious around bedtime or having insomnia

☐ Feeling resentful or angry at your partner

☐ Aspects of intimacy reminding you of awful experiences during birth or prior procedures

☐ Not feeling emotionally connected

☐ Feeling exhausted

☐ Not having privacy

☐ Hypervigilance to your baby's needs and cues (e.g. worrying your baby might cry)

☐ Being afraid of becoming pregnant again

☐ Other ways that your intimacy has been impacted are: _____

_____

What did you notice? Any themes?

_____

_____

It's important as we talk about this to think about a few crucial points. One is that the concept of intimacy does not just equal sexual intimacy and the full act of sex. Intimacy also includes emotional intimacy and feeling safe and trusting with each other. For some couples at this stage, it feels more feasible to address trust, teamwork, and connection again before sexual intimacy is even on the radar. We also have to take into account your relationship prior to your baby as well, and any challenges you were already dealing with as a couple, such as communication patterns or conflict avoidance. The other thing to point out is that physical intimacy can also include so many other activities outside of sex, particularly as you are physically and emotionally healing, and rebuilding connection with your partner. This can include sitting close to each other, snuggling, hand holding, spooning, kissing, and so much more. And the biggest thing to know: just because you got clearance from your ObGyn or midwife to resume sexual intimacy, it does not mean that you feel ready for it. It can take time to recover physically and emotionally, and for couples to start feeling reconnected. You have to take this at your own time, and having choice and a voice is crucial, particularly after what you've been through. Let's talk a bit more about what that can look like.

> It is common for intimacy to be impacted on the journey towards parenthood and particularly after reproductive trauma.
>
> Feeling disconnected or unsupported by each other can make physical intimacy that much more difficult.
>
> There can be a lot of pressure to resume sexual intimacy, and it's totally okay if you are not ready yet.

The "ladder" of intimacy, or gently returning back to each other

When I am working with a client with OCD helping them manage their intrusive, obsessive thoughts and compulsive behaviors, we start slowly. They learn to build a hierarchy ladder of tasks they will work towards, starting small, rather than flooding them by jumping straight to the hardest and most distressing challenge. They slowly build up to more challenging activities so there is a sense of mastery and accomplishment. This also minimizes the likelihood of becoming flooded, overwhelmed, or discouraged. As the two of you are working together to build back intimacy and connection, you could use a similar concept of slowly working up to more challenging steps, too. Certainly you could use a "rip the bandage off" approach and dive right back into emotional or sexual intimacy, but for many trauma survivors, that both sounds and feels overwhelming, and can have unintentional and negative consequences on the relationship, with partners feeling ashamed, disappointed, or not wanting to try again.

This might look like having a conversation together about what you both have been missing in your relationship and what you are both comfortable with trying right now. It can be helpful, as mentioned previously, to start small, such as intentionally being near each other physically, or touching non-sexually (on the couch, holding hands, etc.) without any expectation of sex. Until it feels comfortable to progress to another level of closeness, such as more intimate touch (kissing, shoulder massage, etc.), it's important to practice this physical closeness and emotional intimacy with some regularity.

> You can use your Trigger Worksheet from Chapter 7 (page 97) to notice what comes up for you as you're working on addressing intimacy and closeness with your partner.

This would also be an excellent time to work with a couples' therapist, and particularly one who works with sexual intimacy and trauma survivors. Physical and occupational therapists that specialize in the pelvic floor can also be excellent resources both during the pregnancy and for postpartum healing and recovery.

Activity

Here is an idea for rebuilding intimacy together with some sections filled in with examples. It can be useful for some people to have something tangible to help them feel like they are working together again as a team. This may not fit for you, though – right now, or at all. You may not yet be in a space to address your intimacy, or even any part of your relationship. This activity is here for you to use as you see fit.

Some key aspects are for you to name your mutually agreed-upon goal(s) together, and to work on filling in the steps of the ladder as a team. Your goal does *not* have to be sexual intercourse if you are not ready for that yet. If you find yourself disagreeing about the goals, the speed at which you want to proceed, or the steps, that's okay. This requires some patience and time (and again, professional support is helpful).

GOALS	10	
	9	
	8	
MIDDLE	7	
	6	
	5	
START	4	
		Asking for a hug when either one of us is upset
	3	
		Intentionally sharing about our day as we get ready for bed
	2	
		Holding hands on our walk
	1	
		Time spent together on the couch side by side, watching TV

Coming together as a team

Whether or not the two of you are in a space to address your intimacy right now, let's finish out this chapter by helping identify the changes in your relationship and thinking of a few other ways that you can come together as a team again. This can be especially helpful if you have been feeling disconnected.

As you have been reading this chapter, in what ways have you noticed trauma has influenced your relationship?

_____

_____

_____

As a reminder, some of the common changes experienced in a relationship are found in the figure below.

Roles	• needing others in different ways
Communication	• talking to loved ones in new ways, or feeling like your communication is strained
Values	• some of your priorities may have shifted, and may be different from others'
Identities	• you are changing, and as such see yourself and perhaps see other people differently
Intimacy	• from emotional connectedness, trust, sexual intimacy, and everything in between

We all know it's much easier to be working with each other than it is to be working against each other, so why is it so difficult to do this when in crisis? People tend to forget about their internal and external resources when in crisis. (We're not always in our logical brains when we're having a trauma response and often out of our *window of tolerance*.) It's common to forget to soothe and ground yourself, which is why I'm repetitive when reminding you about the skills you're learning here. It's also common to not reach out to loved ones in these moments, even though we don't heal well in isolation. People who have support from their spouse have faster healing from their PTSD than people without spousal support.[18] In other words, including partners in your treatment can improve the efficacy and speed of trauma treatment. People who have support from their partners also experience pain and fear less intensely.[19] One way to come together as a team might be to involve your partner in your emotional and/or physical healing. What might that look like? From giving your partner this book (or chapter) to read and discuss highlighted sections together, to asking them to join you for some of your therapy or doctor's appointments, how else might you include them in your healing? **How might you engage your partner as an active supporter (or vice versa, if they, too, need some encouragement?)**

_____

_____

_____

Ideas to practice coming together as a team are (check any that you are willing to try):

☐ Ask your partner to join you at an appointment or share with them how your appointment went

☐ Ask your partner to read a specific section of this book you felt was helpful or that described what you were feeling

- ☐ Tell your partner when you are triggered (even after the fact)

- ☐ Ask your partner to practice a grounding skill with you (such as meditating with you before bed)

- ☐ Spend some quality (even brief) time together after the baby goes to sleep

- ☐ Talk with your partner about various practices of your childhood that were important to you that you would like to incorporate into your parenting (and ask about theirs)

- ☐ Ask your partner to help you do one of the challenging goals you are working on (practicing setting a boundary with a loved one, maintaining regular hygiene, creating a nighttime schedule together to protect your sleep, etc.)

- ☐ Help your partner build confidence with the baby by encouraging them to have alone time together (or gradually building up to that, if either of you find this overwhelming initially)

- ☐ Get exercise or sunlight together (going on walks together, etc.)

- ☐ Try some of the sleep ideas together from Chapter 5

- ☐ Another idea you have for connecting as a team is: _____

_____

Ways to explore your shifting roles, values and identities as a couple:
Another way you and your partner can practice working together is to start addressing some of the other aspects of your relationship that have changed, such as your roles, values, and identities (from page 132). Some ways you can do this are to intentionally bring up these conversations while on walks with the baby or during meals together, or to purposefully set aside time to ask each other these questions. There are no right or wrong answers; these prompts are there to help you learn more about what your partner is experiencing in becoming a parent, and vice versa: helping them learn more about you.

Some ideas include:

- ☐ How has your life shifted since becoming a parent?

- ☐ Since we went through _____, what feels more important to you than it did previously? What feels less important to you?

- ☐ What relationships of yours have changed since our experience of _____?

- ☐ What support do you wish we had more of?

- ☐ How do you think your identity has changed since becoming a parent?

- ☐ What has helped you cope when things get particularly challenging?

- ☐ What has been the hardest part of this for you? The most surprising?

- ☐ What are you most missing about our prior life, or hoping that you can do again at some point in the future?

- ☐ What do you wish I knew about what this has been like for you?

- ☐ How have you coped with this experience? What are you most proud of, or most regretful about?

- ☐ Another question I would like to bring up to my partner is: _____

Keep at it. Becoming parents is no small feat, and you are both experiencing major changes in your lives. Coupled with that is the experience of surviving trauma, and the impact that this has had on you, both individually and as a couple.

Chapter highlights

- Partners can experience mental health disorders such as PTSD during the journey of parenthood, too.

- Certain risk factors may make a partner more likely to develop PTSD during the reproductive period, yet partners are often less likely to be asked about how they are doing.

- Going through reproductive trauma can have a significant impact on the relationship, from strains on communication patterns to changes in roles and values.

- Intimacy can be significantly impacted after having a baby, and particularly after surviving trauma. Resuming intimacy can be done at your speed and whenever you are ready with a focus on emotional relatedness to help rebuild a feeling of safety and connection.

- Connecting as a team can help you both recover faster from trauma and feel more supported through your healing journey.

Notes

1 Gottman, J.M., Gottman, J.S. (2007). *And Baby Makes Three: The Six-Step Plan for Preserving Marital Intimacy and Rekindling Romance After Baby Arrives*. Harmony Books.

2 Leach, L.S., Poyser, C., Cooklin, A.R., & Giallo, R. (2016). Prevalence and course of anxiety disorders (and symptom levels) in men across the perinatal period: a systematic review. *Journal of Affective Disorders*, 190, 675–686. https://doi.org/10.1016/j.jad.2015.09.063; Leiferman, J.A., Farewell, C.V., Jewell, J., Lacy, R., Walls, J., Harnke, B., & Paulson, J.F. (2021). Anxiety among fathers during the prenatal and postpartum period: a meta-analysis. *Journal of Psychosomatic Obstetrics and Gynaecology*, 42(2), 152–161. https://doi.org/10.1080; Philpott, L.F., Savage, E., FitzGerald, S., & Leahy-Warren, P. (2019). Anxiety in fathers in the perinatal period: a systematic review. *Midwifery*, 76, 54–101. https://doi.org/10.1016/j.midw.2019.05.013

3 Paulson, J.F., & Bazemore S.D. (2010). Prenatal and postpartum depression in fathers and its association with maternal depression. *JAMA*, 303(19), 1961–1969; O'Brien, A.P., McNeil, K.A., Fletcher, R., Conrad, A., Wilson, A.J., Jones, D., & Chan, S.W. (2017). New fathers' perinatal depression and anxiety-treatment options: an integrative review. *American Journal of Men's Health*, 11(4), 863–876. https://doi.org/10.1177/1557988316669047

4 Susan, A., Harris, R., Sawyer, A., Parfitt, Y., & Ford, E. (2009). Posttraumatic stress disorder after childbirth: analysis of symptom presentation and sampling. *Journal of Affective Disorders*, 119(1–3), 200–204. https://doi.org/10.1016/j.jad.2009.02.029; Bradley, R., Slade, P., & Leviston, A. (2008). Low rates of PTSD in men attending childbirth: a preliminary study. *The British Journal of Clinical Psychology*, 47(Pt 3), 295–302. https://doi.org/10.1348/014466508X279495; Webb, R., Smith, A.M., Ayers, S., Wright, D.B., & Thornton, A. (2021). Development and validation of a measure of birth-related PTSD for fathers and birth partners: the city birth trauma scale (partner version). *Frontiers in Psychology*, 12, 596779. https://doi.org/10.3389/fpsyg.2021.596779

5 Hinton, L., Locock, L., & Knight, M. (2014). Partner experiences of "near-miss" events in pregnancy and childbirth in the UK: a qualitative study. *PloS ONE*, 9(4), e91735. https://doi.org/10.1371/journal.pone.0091735

6 Daniels, E., Arden-Close, E., & Mayers, A. (2020). Be quiet and man up: a qualitative questionnaire study into fathers who witnessed their Partner's birth trauma. *BMC Pregnancy and Childbirth*, 20(1), 236. https://doi.org/10.1186/s12884-020-02902-2; Elmir, R., & Schmied, V. (2022). A qualitative study of the impact of adverse birth experiences on fathers. *Women and Birth: Journal of the Australian College of Midwives*, 35(1), e41–e48. https://doi.org/10.1016/j.wombi.2021.01.005

7 Edwards, B.N., McLemore, M.R., Baltzell, K., Hodgkin, A., Nunez, O., & Franck, L.S. (2020). What about the men? Perinatal experiences of men of color whose partners were at risk for preterm birth, a qualitative study. *BMC Pregnancy and Childbirth*, 20(1), 91. https://doi.org/10.1186/s12884-020-2785-6; Olukotun, O. (2021). Black fathers who experienced the birth of their baby as traumatic: a qualitative study [Doctoral Thesis, University of Essex]. http://repository.essex.ac.uk/id/eprint/31266

8 Stramrood, C.A.I., Doornbos, B., Wessel, I., van Geenen, M., Aarnoudse, J.G., van den Berg, P.P.,. . . van Pampus, M.G. (2013). Fathers with PTSD and depression in pregnancies complicated by preterm preeclampsia or PPROM. *Archives of Gynecology and Obstetrics*, 287, 653–661. http://dx.doi.org/10.1007/s00404-012-2611-0

9 Bradley, R., Slade, P., & Leviston, A. (2008). Low rates of PTSD in men attending childbirth: a preliminary study. *The British Journal of Clinical Psychology*, 47(Pt 3), 295–302. https://doi.org/10.1348/014466508X279495

10 Prouhet P.M., Gregory M.R., Russell C.L., Yaeger, L.H. (2018). Fathers' stress in the neonatal intensive care unit: a systematic review. *Advances in Neonatal Care*, 18(2), 105–120. doi:10.1097/ANC.0000000000000472

11 Garthus-Niegel, S., Horsch, A., Handtke, E., von Soest, T., Ayers, S., Weidner, K., & Eberhard-Gran, M. (2018). The impact of postpartum posttraumatic stress and depression symptoms on couples' relationship satisfaction: a population-based prospective study. *Frontiers in Psychology*, 9, 1728. https://doi.org/10.3389/fpsyg.2018.01728

12 Ganz, M.B., Rasmussen, H.F., McDougall, T.V., Corner, G.W., Black, T.T., & De Los Santos, H.F. (2022). Emotionally focused couple therapy within VA healthcare: reductions in relationship distress, PTSD, and depressive symptoms as a function of attachment-based couple treatment. *Couple and Family Psychology: Research and Practice*, 11(1), 15–32. https://doi.org/10.1037/cfp0000210

13 Gottman, J.M., & Gottman, J.S. (2007). *And Baby Makes Three: The Six-Step Plan for Preserving Marital Intimacy and Rekindling Romance After Baby Arrives*. Harmony Books.

14 Beck, C.T. (2015). Middle range theory of traumatic childbirth: the ever-widening ripple effect. *Global Qualitative Nursing Research*, 2. doi:10.1177/2333393615575313; Nicholls, K., & Ayers, S. (2007). Childbirth-related post-traumatic stress disorder in couples: a qualitative study. *Brit J health Psychol*, 12(Pt 4), 491–509. doi:10.1348/135910706X120627

15 Bailham, D., & Joseph, S. (2003). Post-traumatic stress following childbirth: a review of the emerging literature and directions for research and practice. *Psychology, Health & Medicine*, 8(2), 159–168.

16 Rupp, H.A., James, T.W., Ketterson, E.D., Sengelaub, D.R., Ditzen, B., & Heiman, J.R. (2013). Lower sexual interest in postpartum women: relationship to amygdala activation and intranasal oxytocin. *Hormones and Behavior*, 63(1), 114–121. https://doi.org/10.1016/j.yhbeh.2012.10.007

17 Rathfisch, G., Dikencik, B.K., Kizilkaya Beji, N., Comert, N., Tekirdag, A.I., & Kadioglu, A. (2010). Effects of perineal trauma on postpartum sexual function. *Journal of Advanced Nursing*, 66(12), 2640–2649. https://doi.org/10.1111/j.1365-2648.2010.05428.x

18 Shnaider, P., Sijercic, I., Wanklyn, S.G., Suvak, M.K., & Monson, C.M. (2017). The role of social support in cognitive-behavioral conjoint therapy for posttraumatic stress disorder. *Behavior Therapy*, 48(3), 285–294. https://doi.org/10.1016/j.beth.2016.05.003

19 Coan, J.A., Schaefer, H.S., & Davidson, R.J. (2006). Lending a hand: social regulation of the neural response to threat. *Psychological Science*, 17(12), 1032–1039. https://doi.org/10.1111/j.1467-9280.2006.01832.x; Graff, T.C., Fitzgerald, J.R., Luke, S.G., & Birmingham, W.C. (2021). Spousal emotional support and relationship quality buffers pupillary response to horror movies. *PloS ONE*, 16(9), e0256823. https://doi.org/10.1371/journal.pone.0256823

Chapter 10

You are your baby's best parent (even if you're struggling)

There is a lot of expectation that you will feel a bond with your baby from the onset, right? From social media, movies, and TV portrayals, there are so many images that portray it all as picture-perfect. Many parents don't feel safe openly sharing their less-than-ideal experiences around meeting, and bonding with their baby, and, as such, there remain more glorified portrayals about this process than there are realistic ones. So when a person has challenging experiences during conception and pregnancy, and struggles to bond with their baby, there is a chance they may feel alone in their experience. Yet, it is quite common to experience challenges around bonding after reproductive trauma. In this chapter, we will explore the potential impact your traumatic journey may have had on your developing bond with your baby, why it is normal, and what you can do to strengthen the bond (and build self-compassion for yourself along the way!).

Perhaps you are feeling a lot of pressure to bond with your baby due to your own childhood experiences, and want to parent differently than how you were parented. Or maybe, because of everything you went through on your reproductive journey, you have struggled to connect with your baby in the ways that you thought you would and are feeling bad about that. Maybe you feel disconnected from your baby at times, or so hypervigilant and anxious that it's hard to settle into quiet connection. Whatever you are experiencing, this chapter is here to help support your growing bond with your baby. We will help point out what you are likely already doing well, and talk about ways to help enhance the connection you already have with your baby. Whether you feel like you have a solid connection with your baby and are wanting to improve it, or feel like you are on shaky ground and this was not the experience you thought it would be as a parent, you are not alone.

> To bond is a verb; it is an action.
>
> It is a process that develops over time as you provide care for your baby.
>
> Even if you are struggling, your attachment will continue to grow.

What are bonding and attachment?

Attachment is a result of how primary caregivers respond to their baby's needs. It is the relationship that the baby and caregivers form after the baby is born. The bonding process with a baby begins in pregnancy, and includes the attunement between parent and baby.[1] When a caregiver/parent is

DOI: 10.4324/9781003379973-12

available and responds to their infant's needs, the child is ultimately able to grow a developing sense of security. The child learns that the caregiver/parent is dependable, which helps create a sense of internal safety for the child to start exploring the world. Becoming securely attached to your baby means learning how to become attuned to their needs over time, feel emotionally connected, and respond to their cues. And like any relationship, it truly takes time. I frequently remind clients that to bond is a verb, and that bonding with a baby unfolds with the process of caregiving. It is not an immediate event, like a light switch that flips on when you have a baby.

> You can *feel* like you're messing up and not doing it right as a parent AND still be connected with your baby.
>
> Continuing to show up, trying to learn your baby's cues and care for them contributes to a secure bond over time.

As you've been reading this information, what comes up for you? What expectations did you have about how you would feel upon learning you were having a baby or meeting them?

_____

_____

_____

_____

What feelings have been coming up as you're starting this chapter? Any sense of validation, relief, shame, or something else? Are you surprised by any of your feelings?

_____

_____

_____

_____

Toward the end of this chapter, you will learn some simple but helpful ways that you can use to keep enhancing your connection with your baby. But first, real talk. It's not possible to be a perfect parent; such a phenomenon does not exist. It's literally impossible to respond to all of your baby's cues at all times, or to feel nothing but calm, sunny patience. Yet, even basic things like practicing eye contact with your baby or talking to them are important practices in helping them feel safe and connected to you. Even holding them lays the groundwork for their growing sense of self and identity.[2] These basic activities may not seem like much, but they truly lay the foundation for them forming secure attachments in relationships throughout their lives. In other words, the small things you're probably already doing are making a large impact.

Here are some other reasons why growing your attachment with your baby is important. **Developing a secure attachment over time with a child enables them to:[3]**

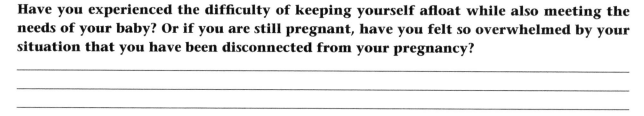

learn to imitate you and eventually build the crucial skill of empathy

develop healthy physiological well-being. When your baby is in sync with you, it's reflected in their steady heartbeat, their breathing slows, and they have low stress hormone levels

learn to self-regulate through their emotions (learn to self-soothe and tolerate difficult emotions)

read others' cues (it's a two-way feedback loop – as you respond to your baby, they learn to eventually respond to you)

set the tone for their relationships with others by teaching them what to expect from interactions

create an internal locus of control (ability to learn what makes them feel good or bad, how they have choices in their responses)

The potential impact of reproductive trauma on attachment

How might your traumatic experience(s) come into play when it comes to attachment to your baby? Let me first normalize something. Many new parents don't immediately feel connected to their baby. Some feel detached like they are going through the motions of caregiving long before the emotional connection starts to develop. This is particularly the case for parents who are struggling with perinatal mental health symptoms. It makes sense, right? If you are already feeling like you're in survival mode and just trying to make it through the day, forming a new relationship with *anyone* is hard, much less a baby that requires a lot of care. It's as if you were just trying to stay afloat in the middle of the ocean, treading water, and then someone hands you a baby. It would be exhausting to keep you both afloat *and* simultaneously tend to their needs (and feel gooey and loving while doing it), right? It may seem like an extreme comparison, and yet, that's similar to what you're going through as a survivor of reproductive trauma while trying to recover *and* care for a little one.

Have you experienced the difficulty of keeping yourself afloat while also meeting the needs of your baby? Or if you are still pregnant, have you felt so overwhelmed by your situation that you have been disconnected from your pregnancy?

_____

_____

_____

_____

> You can love your baby while simultaneously hating parts (or all) of your birth experience.
>
> You are also likely still recovering physically and emotionally from what you went through while also actively trying to forge a relationship with this new little stranger.
>
> This adds to why some parents find parenting a complicated experience layered with a mix of emotions.

Hopefully you are seeing that not everyone feels an instantaneous, miraculous, clouds-parting-angels-singing-movie-version of a bond with their baby, and that many parents take time to develop and grow their bond. Survivors of reproductive trauma, in particular, can sometimes struggle with connecting with their babies. Many feel like they had no connection at all during their pregnancy or initially after birth. Others had a delayed connection and bond, taking months for an attachment to start to develop.[4] Some admit they initially felt negative feelings towards their baby, or had a gut-level rejection response, resulting in shame and feeling they could not talk about it openly with others.[5] And some admit they just felt fairly neutral about their baby, like they were going through the motions of parenthood, doing what they had to in caretaking, yet not feeling a sense of fondness or warm connection.

Do any of these scenarios resonate with you? Have you experienced those negative or neutral thoughts and feelings? You are not alone. Some common statements I hear from parents who are struggling are: "I regret becoming a mom," "I love my baby but I'm ashamed I get annoyed at him sometimes," "I just don't feel like my baby likes me," "I feel anxious taking care of my baby," etc. What has come up for you?

_____

_____

_____

_____

> ### Other common parenting triggers for survivors of reproductive trauma
>
> - Anniversaries of events (infertility procedures like egg retrievals, milestone experiences in the NICU, etc.)
>
> - Birthdates can be a reminder of both the joy of your baby and everything you went through during your journey
>
> - Due dates from prior losses
>
> - Feeling out of control with parenting is very common and especially hard for trauma survivors, with themes of powerlessness
>
> - Touch, closeness, and the intensity of the baby's noises can be particularly hard for survivors of trauma still feeling easily reactive.

How might your mental health come into play as a parent?

Whether you are still pregnant or are in your postpartum recovery, mood symptoms can unfortunately have an impact on attachment. Let me acknowledge that you might already be feeling quite anxious about this and judging yourself throughout your experiences. I _know_ that you want to do your very best as a parent. You might already be feeling guilty about what happened to you and feeling robbed of the experience you thought you'd have. Let me remind you again that what happened to you AND how you're feeling is not your fault. You've also picked up this book, which shows that you're wanting to address your emotions and feelings (and probably recognizing that you're not feeling like your normal self.) What matters is you are being intentional with your healing. Reassuringly, it is also not guaranteed that having trauma or perinatal mood symptoms will negatively impact your bond with your baby, and the great news is that it's never too late to work to repair any potential negative impacts on attachment and bonding.

With those caveats, let's talk about how your mood symptoms *might* impact the bond with your baby. No parent is trying to allow their mental health symptoms to get in the way of bonding with their baby; these symptoms can be overwhelming sometimes, right? It is exhausting to deal with intrusive thoughts coming at you constantly throughout the day or to brace against the hypervigilance of anxiety, feeling like you are constantly warding off doom and catastrophe. It is tiring to fight against trauma responses and triggers when they pop up unexpectedly and at the most inconvenient of times. You might also be battling a lack of motivation, low energy, irritability, and the brain fog that comes with depression and anxiety.

Parents may sometimes not even know they are out of tune with their babies and miss relevant cues if they are preoccupied. Once these challenges start, it can be easy to get caught in negative cycles that can impact the connection with your baby. A cycle of disconnection can occur if you continually reach out to your baby for engagement and it feels like you are unable to soothe them effectively or connect with them.[6] I often hear this feeling of frustration and self-blame from parents, this feeling of failure, or thoughts their baby does not like them or prefers the other parent. When there are patterns of difficult interactions, it can be easy to either think it's your fault: "I'm a bad mother" or, instead, project this on to your baby: "my baby is difficult," or "my baby doesn't like me." We know that how we talk to ourselves can influence how we feel, so yes, of course your mood can have an impact on attachment with your baby even when you love them fiercely and have wanted to be a parent.

> If you or your partner find yourself easily frustrated or disconnected from your baby, *you are not alone!*
>
> You will learn skills in this chapter to keep connecting with your baby and help strengthen and support your bond over time.
>
> New parent support groups can also be helpful to receive validation from other parents during this time.
>
> Support and coaching from a perinatal mental health therapist can help you gain insight and learn parenting skills to connect with your baby as well as get help to heal from your own symptoms.

Studies show us that women with *untreated* depression in the postpartum period can struggle with bonding and connecting with their babies. They can feel less confident as parents, and, as such, may engage less with their babies. They tend to read and talk less to their babies, have difficulty following routines, and are less likely to breastfeed[7] (though breastfeeding is certainly not required to form a solid bond with a baby). Let's face it – battling mental health symptoms and recovering from trauma is so hard.

How has this information about mental health connected with you? How has your mental health informed aspects of your parenting thus far? For example, do you notice yourself being more hypervigilant towards your baby or having difficulty reading their cues sometimes? Do you find yourself having difficulty with their cry and feeling irritable when unable to soothe them? Is it hard to connect when you are feeling preoccupied with your own trauma responses? Do you tend to blame yourself when things aren't going smoothly?

_____

_____

_____

_____

The good news

Any challenges you have connecting with your baby are temporary and can be addressed. While interacting with your baby and providing care to them, you are slowly becoming attached. While reproductive trauma can certainly be tremendously challenging and may cause difficulties with bonding initially, a parent's trauma symptoms are not often associated with the bond with their baby even six months later.[8] Usually the issues that continue to have an impact on the bond are things like a parent's own attachment style and/or untreated mental health symptoms, both of which can then be the focus of supportive mental health treatment. In other words, parents who are still struggling to make a connection with their babies can benefit from support and coaching, particularly if they did not have positive models from their own childhood growing up.

I continually see in my practice that as parents address their mood and anxiety symptoms, this can have a tremendously positive impact on their connection with their babies[9]. As they start to feel better themselves, they feel more confident as caregivers and have more resilience, patience, and capability to turn towards their infants. It's reassuring that attachment can be a learned skill, just like the other skills you have been learning throughout this book. If for whatever reason parenting and connection do not come easy initially, it is absolutely okay. You can keep working on your connection with your baby as you work on your healing.

> **Some positive news:**
>
> Even when struggling with depression, women who get treatment and work on attachment skill building find that their bonding with their babies improves.[10]
>
> Regardless of their childhood experiences, parents can learn new ways of parenting and break multigenerational patterns.
>
> Growing a connection with your baby takes time and learning skills to enhance your bond can help. It's never too late!

Self-doubt and self-blame

I notice that many of my clients who have been through distressing experiences in becoming a parent can often second-guess and judge their bond with their babies. It's possible that reading the last few sections have brought up some of these thoughts and feelings. It's similar to what we were talking about in Chapter 4 with all the jumbled, complex emotions you're often holding as a survivor of reproductive trauma. Perhaps you've been through reproductive losses, and/or years of infertility, and are now incredibly grateful and relieved to be a parent. This may create pressure as you evaluate your connection with your baby. Many parents will question themselves: "Am I bonded *enough?*" Or they might compare themselves to others: "I feel connected to my baby, but I don't look at my baby the way my friend does." Remember how, in Chapter 7, we talked about negative beliefs that can be triggered when you are distressed? You may be blaming yourself for anything you think you are doing wrong as a parent. It may feel as if this is yet another example that you have failed (when you haven't), or yet another time you feel like you are defective (when you aren't), or not deserving (when you absolutely are). Self-blame can happen especially when challenging situations come up, such as the more mundane parts of parenting, or the early stages when the relationship is more one-sided. Perhaps you're not noticing much of a connection initially and questioning whether that says something negative about your abilities and qualities as a parent. After all, you've worked really hard to be here. Shouldn't that mean that you feel grateful and joyous most of the time? Absolutely not.

> Parents can bond differently with their children at different ages.
>
> It is common for one parent to enjoy the infancy stage, for example, whereas their partner might not feel bonded with their child until the toddler stage when they have more interaction and feedback.

Reflection activity

Here are some common negative thoughts and experiences survivors of reproductive trauma will share about their connections with their babies. This will help you explore what you might be feeling as a parent. We will use the same negative thoughts list from Chapter 7, modified now specifically with parenting and bonding.[11]

In the figure below, circle which ones feel familiar, if it feels okay to do so.

Responsibility / Defectiveness	Safety / Vulnerability	Power / Control / Choice
I am a failure as a parent	I cannot protect my baby	I'm powerless / helpless
I'm worthless / inadequate (as a mom, etc.)	I can't trust anyone (to help me, etc.)	I can't handle parenthood (or this stage of their life)
I am permanently damaged (and unable to bond with my baby, etc.)	I am still not safe (including baby's health, etc.)	I can't trust my judgment as a parent
I am a disappointment as a parent	My baby is not safe or could be harmed	I can't let my feelings out (or handle my baby's)
I should have done something	I have to _ in order to be safe	I have no control
I did something wrong as a parent	My baby is in danger	I can't get what I want
I should have known better	I cannot trust myself (as a parent)	I have to be perfect as a parent
I do not deserve ____(love from my baby, etc.)	It's not safe for me to____	I'm unable to soothe my baby
My body is ___ (negative) (e.g. with breast/chestfeeding, etc.)	People will let me down (are not supporting me, etc.)	I have no voice (as a dad, etc.)
I was not meant to be a parent	My baby is still vulnerable	I can't succeed as a parent
Others:		

I always like to say "name your dragon so you can slay your dragon."[12] Once you bring any negative thoughts to the conscious level, then you can do something about it. Perhaps you will notice a theme of beliefs that you frequently have about yourself as a parent, and this can then be a focus of your work with your therapist. Or you might notice that you have not previously admitted these thoughts to yourself, and it feels like a relief to do so now that you know it's normal, and it's something you can address.

What did you notice as you were circling the various beliefs you may have? Did you notice similar or different themes from those that you identified before in Chapter 7?

_____

_____

_____

Now, let's do the opposite. If your baby could thank you for something you are doing for them right now, what would that be? (Check all that apply.)

☐ Doing your best to figure out what their cry means

☐ Feeding them

☐ Holding them when they cry

☐ Bathing them

☐ Showing up for them even when you are struggling

☐ Changing their diapers

☐ Working on eye contact

☐ Talking to them

☐ Doing your best right now

☐ Helping them feel safe

☐ Going through tough situations together

☐ Trying to learn about parenting

☐ Something else they might thank me for would be: _____

_____

What positive, supportive, or self-compassionate statements might you say to yourself right now about your parenting, bond, or connection with your baby?

☐ I'm doing the best I can

☐ I'm learning as I go

☐ I'm figuring this out

☐ I feel capable sometimes

☐ I am not the only parent feeling this way; it helps me to read that it takes time to bond with babies

☐ I may not feel good, but I keep showing up, and that says something

☐ My anxiety is hard to deal with but I'm going to try not to allow it to get in the way of taking care of my baby

☐ I've never done something so hard; I'm proving to myself what I'm capable of

☐ I don't have to be perfect; it's okay to make mistakes

☐ I'm slowly learning how to trust myself as a parent

☐ This is hard and I'm learning how to manage it

☐ Another self-compassionate statement that I can say to myself is:

_____

_____

Self-compassion and parenting

That activity we just did together was important. It may have been hard. In fact, it is for most parents who are struggling. It's so much easier to speak kindly to and praise others when they are in the thick of it, rather than turn this kindness towards yourself. Yet, as you learned in Chapter 7, self-compassion can be helpful in building resilience, and it's profoundly impactful with parenting as well. Research early in the pandemic showed that practicing self-compassion and mindfulness helped parents cope with the stress of parenting, and helped mediate perinatal mood symptoms (like depression and anxiety).[13] This is particularly the case with parents with anxiety who are hypervigilant with their babies (checking on them repeatedly throughout the night to the detriment of their own sleep) or avoidant of activities (not leaving the house or isolating from their social network). When parents practice mindfulness and self-compassion, they build resilience and notice a reduction in their symptoms. Parents who practice these skills also feel more bonded with their babies, and have an easier time responding to their children's emotions.[14]

This is such a big deal as you might be learning to parent differently than how you were raised and breaking multigenerational patterns. Learning to respond in helpful and healthy ways to your baby is a superpower and a skill that can be honed. You can learn how to build emotional resilience to respond better to your child's cues and emotions. As a reminder, here are the key components of self-compassion. As you review them, try to do so now through the lens of bonding with your baby. How might self-compassion help you with whatever you are experiencing?

The key components of self-compassion

Based on the self-compassion prompts that you created for yourself in Chapter 7, let's help you add in connecting with your baby. Some ideas might be:

- "I feel guilty that my birth trauma has impacted not just me but also my baby, and it helps me to know I'm not alone in this and can keep growing my bond with her. I'm going to keep working on that; it's something concrete I can do."

- "I'm angry that I got robbed of the postpartum experience I thought I would have because of my scary delivery and time we spent in the NICU. I'm learning how to connect with my baby now without all the hospital staff's help."

- "It's hard to raise another human and I know I'm not alone if I lose my temper or if I sometimes feel like a bad parent."

_____

_____

_____

_____

How does how you were raised influence your connection with your baby?

Parents can be influenced by a number of factors in how they instinctively tend to parent. For example, attachment can also be impacted by both a parent's mental health AND their attachment styles.[15] How you were raised and the modeling of the parenting you received can inform your own parenting style. Numerous attachment theory psychologists have noticed that a parent's own childhood experiences around nurturing will then shape their own parenting style.[16] There can be *multigenerational patterns* in which there are repetitions of parenting patterns from one generation to the next.[17] For some people, this can be a mixed bag of both positive examples of parenting and some negative experiences they are trying to heal from. You may or may not be trying to parent differently than how you were raised. A quote that I love from author Alexandra Elle captures this concept so nicely: "our parents do the best they can with what they have, and sometimes their best isn't supportive of our healing in the way that we want or need. I've grown to know starting from scratch so well that, like baking, it feels restorative now, rather than draining."[18] When there were healthy or positive interactions to draw from, this can be such a gift. Yet, when there are dysfunctional, harmful, or negative interactions you are healing from, it can be hard now as a parent breaking new ground on your own with your new little one. The great thing to know is these multigenerational patterns can be changed.[19] This is some of my favorite work with clients: helping them heal from some of their own childhood attachment wounds, while simultaneously supporting them in becoming the best parent they can be. I like to think of it as learning to honor the past to guide the direction of the future. While healing from any unresolved pain from your childhood, this not only positively affects you but also benefits your new baby.

Exploring the impact of your own attachment

Learning about our attachment experiences from childhood can help us think about what has worked and not worked for us to feel safe and secure in the world with relationships. This stems from our own experiences being parented and cared for early in life. Here is an over-simplified (but I think that can be helpful sometimes) explanation of attachment wounds and attachment styles. You can think of trauma wounds as the difficult things that happened to us, and attachment wounds as the important things that did not happen when we were children. When our physical and emotional needs are regularly met, we can become securely attached over time. When our needs are consistently unmet by parents who were misattuned or even harmful, we can develop ways of connecting to people that are rooted in anxious, insecure, or distrustful attachment patterns.[20]. Generally speaking, the more attuned a caregiver is to their child's needs, the more secure the attachment. That is not to say that perfect attunement is attainable or even necessary, but chronic misattunement can lead to feeling less secure and safe in the world, and less capable of managing the range and intensity of emotions that come up.

Some examples of chronic misattunement over time that can have lasting impacts are when caregivers are continually:

unresponsive	rejecting
judgmental	unable to manage their own emotions
not good with their own boundaries	distant or dismissive
unable to repair after conflict	emotionally volatile or labile
emotionally unavailable or cold	unable to soothe child's emotions

or when caregivers are unable to provide:

safety	nurturing
guidance	protection

Maybe some of this resonates with your childhood experiences, or maybe you are concerned some of your own parenting is reflected in these examples. That's okay. It's common when learning about attachment or when looking backwards at your own childhood to then immediately rotate the spotlight towards yourself as a parent and instantly feel guilty or worried. Let me remind you that you are still learning and growing as a parent. Any unhealthy patterns can be addressed, and healthy behaviors can be enhanced. Plus, there is no such thing as perfection. When we are talking about any potential attachment wounds or unmet needs from your own childhood, we are not talking about the occasional times that caregivers had regrettable moments (because literally every caregiver does), but about pervasive patterns of caregiving that were not what you needed. A child who does not have a secure attachment in childhood might erroneously "learn" that they are unlovable or defective, or feel like their parent's confusing behaviors are their fault. They might be continually looking to a parent for safety, soothing, and stability – and not finding it. Or there might be a temperament mismatch between a child and their parent, with a child reaching out for warm reassuring words or touch and not getting the comfort they needed. There might be shame that develops around certain emotions and feelings, and some children may lack the ability to tolerate and move through their emotional states without great distress.

When you think about your childhood and learning that how you were parented can inform aspects of your parenting style, what are some of the initial thoughts that come to mind for you?

As you think back to your childhood, perhaps you were given a fair number of the tools you need now as a parent, so you can focus on the challenge of healing from your trauma and connecting with your baby. Or maybe you are at times grieving the parents you needed and did not have, while also simultaneously trying to be that parent now for your new little one. In doing so, you are also reparenting yourself. For example, if it was not comfortable or safe to express big emotions in your house (perhaps a parent would become angry or violent, openly mock you, or you could sense they "couldn't handle" your feelings), it's a big deal every time you soothe your baby when they are upset, or are becoming attuned to their needs. You're also helping yourself learn that it's okay to be soothed, and it's okay to get your needs met, too. This is continued practice of building the emotional regulation skills you needed as a child. By parenting your little one, you're also parenting your little YOU. It's profound work you are doing in addition to healing, which is no small feat.

> You have been building and growing your emotional regulation skills all the way through this book!
>
> Mindfulness and breathing practices, for example, can help improve emotional regulation.[21]
>
> Every time you're practicing your 5 senses, meditations, self-compassion mantras, or doing any mindful movements (like yoga or stretching), you are developing better emotional regulation skills.

Your attachment system is like your underlying operating system that you may not even be aware is influencing you, and yet it shapes your response in relationships. So, if you are noticing that you are struggling with connection with your baby, and/or your response to their emotions and needs, and this is not changing as much as you hoped over time, then it can be helpful to go deeper and address your attachment patterns through therapy. Doing attachment work takes time and can be a tremendous gift to both yourself and your child. There are additional resources for inspiration at the end of this book.

Reflection activity

I've just given you a lot to think about, and looking back at your childhood (or perhaps thinking about the bond with your baby) can sometimes bring up some tender spots. This would be a good time to do a check-in with yourself. How are you doing? What might you need right now? Perhaps you could use some calming breath work, or a walk to practice mindfully tuning into your emotions.

When you think about how you were raised, how have those relationships influenced the way you interact with people now (both positively and negatively)?[22]

_____

_____

_____

When you think back to your childhood, how would others respond when you were upset?

_____

_____

_____

When you were sick or injured, how would others respond to you?

_____

_____

_____

As a child, how comfortable were the people around you with closeness, and how comfortable are you with closeness now? Has that changed since your reproductive journey?[23]

_____

_____

_____

There's no right or wrong here, no all or nothing. How can you honor your heritage and forge your own way? As you think about becoming a parent, what are some ways you were raised that you would like to honor and incorporate into your parenting style, and some things that you would like to release, and thereby do differently?

_____

_____

_____

You have practiced some important work of looking back at how you were parented while also tuning into you as a parent presently. Maybe this chapter has inspired you to do more exploration with your own attachment styles and maybe even your own family of origin to find some additional repair and healing. Perhaps this hasn't resonated with you or felt like a fit right now, and that's okay too. We will now discuss some concrete ways to strengthen your connection to your baby that you can implement today.

Strengthening the bond with your baby

You may be wondering how to foster a stronger connection to your baby, even if you are struggling. Here are some small, tangible ideas you can start incorporating today. These are broken down into two sections, one for those who are still pregnant or expecting and wanting to strengthen their bond with their developing baby, and the next section for those who have already met their baby.

How can you enhance your bond if you are expecting?

While pregnant, some people feel able to comfortably tune into and connect with their pregnancy and developing baby for the most part. For other people, this is not the case, particularly those who have experienced losses, gone through infertility, or had challenging early pregnancies. Perhaps you are trying to protect yourself from any potential distress so you are not wanting to talk about your pregnancy (or have others talk about it). Maybe you are feeling disconnected and dissociated from your changing body. Or maybe the opposite is true, that you feel such a heightened sense of anxiety that you feel hyper-attuned and aware. Perhaps every movement or sensation brings about great fear, and you frequently worry about the outcome of this pregnancy. It might also be hard for you to comfortably connect with your pregnancy (in a different way), and as such, you too might not feel a comfortable developing bond yet. People who have experienced pregnancy losses and infertility journeys often say things like, "Once I hit the second trimester I'll start to feel better," "I won't connect with this baby until we have the 20 week anatomy scan," "There's no way I'm having a baby shower, it'll jinx me," "I won't think of it as my baby until it's in my arms," or similar sentiments. With these experiences, it makes sense that you might try to wall off your heart and mind from your pregnancy and prevent yourself from feeling pain in the chance that this does not result in a good ending. However, the opposite is often true. By trying to fight against thinking about the baby or feeling any emotional connection, you might be feeling *more* anxious and fearful.

The interesting thing is that as bonding and connection with your baby during the pregnancy increases, so does the connection with your baby once they are born.[24] The opposite happens as well; unresolved trauma throughout the pregnancy can have a negative impact on the postpartum bonding experience with the baby.[25] This is again why it's admirable that you're looking for healing; there can be positive ripple effects as a result. Let's help you find some small ways to connect with your pregnancy, even if it's for brief bits at a time (that concept of *oscillation*). This can be particularly helpful if you experienced challenges in conceiving, have had prior losses, or are having a challenging pregnancy and are finding it hard to be present right now.

Activity for pregnant or expecting parents

Here are some ideas to help promote attachment and connection with your developing baby while you are pregnant or expecting. Your partner (or another loved one) can join you in these practices. If you are having a baby via surrogate or adoption, you can amend some of these to use with the person carrying the baby – get creative! **Choose one or more from the list to regularly practice.** Spending a few minutes every day practicing any of these moments of connection is a great start. Some of these may seem overly simple, yet it's okay to start small, especially if you have realized you have been trying to protect yourself emotionally. You can even use the *ladder* concept we talked about in the last chapter to build up to eventually tolerate actions that might at first feel overwhelming.

☐ **Talk about your pregnancy.** Find a scheduled time of day to talk about your pregnancy with your partner or loved one. Even a brief 1–2-minute check-in can be a good way to start practicing bringing this pregnancy into your realm of reality and putting *oscillation* into practice.

☐ **Talk to your baby/belly.** If it feels easier, you can talk while you are doing another activity, like driving or walking, and simply describe what you are doing. Practice getting used to talking to your baby, as they are listening to you and enjoy hearing your voice.

☐ **Practice touching or rubbing your belly, even briefly.** You can use your breathing exercises you are practicing from Chapters 5 and 6 to help calm and ground yourself if this is uncomfortable.

☐ **Incorporate grounding skills and mindful practices as you are tuning into your baby's movement and kicks.** Using the skills you have learned from Chapter 6, such as the 5 Senses, mindful movement, breath skills, body scan, and more, notice what it is like to pay attention to your baby's movements and your belly as a part of any mindfulness or self-soothing practice. If this becomes difficult to tolerate for longer periods of time, you can start with 30-second practices.

☐ **Play quiet music for your baby.** Whether you use headphones or a speaker nearby, having some of your favorite music playing can be a great way to intentionally focus on your belly and your developing baby. Think about what it will be like to play this for your baby when you are eventually with them. Or if those thoughts become too challenging, practice being present for small blocks of time using your mindfulness skills.

☐ **Think about the story you will tell of this time.** Whether you use a baby book, a personal journal that is just for you, or audio recordings on your phone, how do you want to remember this experience? What would you like your baby to know that you learned about yourself, even when things got hard? You can incorporate skills you are learning here such as your mantras, self-compassion statements, or any of the insights you have noticed along the way.

☐ **Buy one baby item.** Even if you do not show anyone and this is just for you, this can be an important step for many parents to start feeling connected to their baby and to make this feel "real."

☐ **If you are having a baby via adoption or surrogate, record your voices to have played for the baby.** Think about what you want to say, even if it feels embarrassing or silly.

☐ **Another idea to build a connection with your growing baby is:**

_____

_____

Activity for postpartum parents

Here are some simple ideas to help promote attachment and connection with your baby if you have already met them. If you are in a relationship, your partner (or another loved one) can join you in these practices as well. **Choose one or more from the list to regularly practice.** Spending a few minutes every day practicing any of these moments of connection is sufficient and a great start. It is not expected for you to do these 100% of the time, particularly if closeness or eye contact is challenging or uncomfortable. Instead, by slowly incorporating these into your interactions with your baby, this will help you get to know them more, and practice feeling more comfortable and confident in your connection with them.

☐ **Look into your baby's eyes and smile.** This can be challenging for some parents who are feeling depressed. Notice what happens as you smile at your baby when they are calm. Are they old enough that they are able to look back at you yet? Do they look at you and then look away? What little noises do they make? Can you mimic their sounds or talk back to them? By tuning into them and smiling for a bit, you are strengthening your connection.

☐ **Talk to your baby.** It honestly doesn't matter what you are talking about because your baby *loves* the sound of your voice. If it feels weird to talk to your baby at this point and you have trouble coming up with something to say, you can simply describe what you are doing, what you are thinking about, etc. Notice if they turn towards you, get more energized, sleepy, etc. This promotes connection with your baby, as your baby wants to hear *your voice* no matter what you're saying.

☐ **Tune into yourself.** As you have been learning, mindfulness is a practice of noticing how you are feeling in any given moment. Try to catch yourself during various parenting moments. Do you tend to face your baby away from you or towards you if you are feeling sad? Do you tend to zone out when they cry or when you're feeding them? Here's the thing: every parent needs mental (and literal) breaks. Parenting is exhausting. There can also be opportunities to check in to try something different sometimes: facing your baby towards you for purposeful interactions, intentionally talking to them during their bath time, etc.

☐ **Read to your baby.** You can read an actual baby book, a blog or social media post you're into, or something else entirely. Your baby gets a lot out of hearing your voice and you can practice noticing how they respond when you talk to them. Notice how your baby responds if you change your voice (a silly voice to go with the characters in the book, or a more soothing and quiet voice if your baby is sleepy).

☐ **Wear your baby.** By using a sling, wrap, or whatever you prefer, your baby will get the benefit of hearing your heartbeat, smelling you, and feeling close to you, all of which promote bonding and attachment (and also frees your arms up to do other stuff, which is a huge bonus!). The benefits for you both are numerous, including your baby getting relief from pain and crying less in addition to improving your connection.[26] This can be especially useful with colicky babies and those with other health challenges! While the research around babywearing may be newer, I find such comfort that wise ancestors had this figured out long before science did. Babywearing harkens back to African and Asian cultures, and close attachment to babies has deep roots going back centuries with indigenous cultures. If touch is still difficult to tolerate in your trauma healing, you can practice small amounts of time doing this, or notice which different types of babywearing gear feels less restrictive.

☐ **Have some baby spa time.** A lot of babies love getting massaged (ditto here). Whether you use a soothing lotion after bath time, or massage them over their clothes as you're hanging out together on the floor, this can be a good time to connect to your baby.

☐ **Do some skin-to-skin time.** Place your baby on your chest for a few minutes (or however long feels tolerable) and talk to them softly. You can even wrap both of you up loosely in something cozy and soft, if it feels okay. Notice their breathing patterns and your own, how they smell, the softness of their skin, and notice any changes in you. (Are you more or less tense? Is your breathing slow or fast?) Skin to skin, or "kangaroo care," is practiced in NICUs with premature babies to help stabilize them, and even with full-term infants. The benefits are numerous, as it helps improve your bond with your baby, and helps them regulate their temperature, heartrate, and circadian rhythm (improving their sleep, huzzah![27]). And this close contact helps lower their stress hormones, creating an improved sense of safety for them. If this is not yet comfortable for you, it's okay to work towards this, or perhaps even encourage your partner or loved one to do this first.

☐ **Practice your self-soothing skills when your baby is fussy.** Practice tuning into your needs and then back to your baby's needs. Maybe you need your slowed breathing skills because you feel frazzled when feeding them, for example. Or as you are going about tasks (changing a diaper, walking up and down your hallway holding your baby), try noticing where you are feeling tension in your body and focus your breath there. This one will take practice.

☐ **Build in quiet interactions.** When your child is having a quiet moment, use those moments to mirror their calm. It can be great to build in positive interactions during those times, particularly with babies prone to upset tummies and fussiness. By tuning in and getting in sync with each other's rhythms, this is how you grow *attunement*. If their eyes are averted from yours, notice this cue might mean "I need a little break" so you can check in with them occasionally. If they look at you, notice this cue might mean "I'm checking in" so you can try speaking warmly, quieting again when they look away.

☐ **Watch for indicators that your baby is interested in playing or engaging.** This is another good practice of *attunement* and getting in sync. If your baby is smiling and kicking their legs, get on their level to talk and play with them. You can use toys and animated language, smile and mirror any of their expressions (tongue out, etc.). As they grow, they will learn to mirror your expressions!

☐ **Watch for indicators that your baby is overstimulated.** I wish babies came with an owner's manual, but learning how to read their cues is the next best thing. By learning what cues your baby gives you that they need to take a break, this again is a good practice of *attunement*. They may keep their eyes averted, be more fussy, or show other signs like arching their back. Please be reassured – you are likely to miss these cues sometimes and they might get more peevish by something you just did; you are a good parent, you are learning, and this is part of becoming in sync over time.

Of all of the suggestions listed, notice which ones you checked that you want to start practicing now (or that you are already doing and want to try more intentionally). When might be optimal times in the day for you to practice (e.g. just after feeding or before bedtime)?

It's okay if some (or all) of these are uncomfortable or challenging for you for some of the reasons we've talked about before (your own traumatic experiences from your reproductive journey, the way you were raised, etc.).

You can use your Trigger Worksheet from Chapter 7 (page 97) to notice what comes up for you as you're working on strengthening your bond with your baby.

Parenthood is hard no matter what, especially these first years. It is exponentially harder when you are struggling with perinatal mental health symptoms and recovering from trauma. This is a super tough job, and yet, here you are doing it. As you work on your healing and strengthening your connection with your baby, both things will improve. It takes time to develop a connection with your baby and learn their cues. While your own symptoms may be taking some (okay, a lot) of your attention and energy, you are addressing them and that is important. Whether you are healing physically or emotionally from your trauma and/or reproductive journey (or all of it!), you are still doing your very best to take care of your baby even if you are not the parent you would like to be yet.

Even if you feel like you are faking it sometimes as a parent, or just going through the motions of caregiving, what is one (or more) thing that you think you are doing to tend to your baby's needs?

_____

_____

_____

The things you just named *are* what connects you with your baby and grows your bond. Tending to some of your baby's needs is a way for you to connect even if you don't feel that strong bond yet. You are doing a good job during a really challenging time.

Chapter highlights

- You may be struggling with feeling attached to your baby after everything that you just have experienced.

- Please remember that bonding is a verb and is a process that takes time.

- Secure attachment with your baby will help them learn amazing skills that will set them up for a lifetime, such as self-regulation, self-control, and empathy.

- How you were raised can inform how you are now bonding with and parenting your child. You can continue to grow and learn and break multigenerational patterns.

- Whether you are pregnant, or postpartum and recovering both physically and emotionally, you can continue to strengthen your connection and bond with your baby.

- Everything you are already doing is important, and you can keep learning skills to connect and bond with your baby.

Notes

1 Bowlby, J. (1979). On knowing what you are not supposed to know and feeling what you are not supposed to feel. *The Canadian Journal of Psychiatry*, 24(5), 403–408. https://doi.org/10.1177/070674377902400506; de Cock, E.S., Henrichs, J., Vreeswijk, C.M., Maas, A.J., Rijk, C.H., & van Bakel, H.J. (2016). Continuous feelings of love? The parental bond from pregnancy to toddlerhood. *J Fam Psychol*, 30(1), 125.; Dubber, S., Reck, C., Muller, M., & Gawlik, S. (2015). Postpartum bonding: the role of perinatal depression, anxiety and maternal-fetal bonding during pregnancy. *Archives of Women's Mental Health*, 18, 187–195. https://doi.org/10.1007/s00737-014-0445-4; Hairston, I., Handelzaltz, J., Lehman-Inbar, T., & Kovo, M. (2019). Mother-infant bonding is not associated with feeding type: a community study sample. *BMC Pregnancy Childbirth*, 19(125). https://doi.org/10.1186/s12884-019-2264-0

2 Winnicott, D.W. (1971). *Playing and Reality*. Psychology Press.

3 Gopnik, A., Meltzoff, A.N., & Kuhl, P.K. (2009). *The Scientist in the Crib: Minds, Brains, and How Children Learn*. HarperCollins; Main, M. (1996). Overview of the field of attachment. *Journal of Consulting and Clinical*

Psychology, 64(2), 237–243; Tronick, E.Z. (1989). Emotions and emotional communication in infants. *American Psychologist*, 44(2), 112; Tronick, E., & Beeghley, M. (2011). Infants' meaning-making and the development of mental health problems. *American Psychologist*, 66(2), 107–119.

4 Ayers, S., Eagle, A., & Waring, H. (2006). The effects of childbirth-related post-traumatic stress disorder on women and their relationships: a qualitative study. *Psychology, Health & Medicine*, 11(4), 389–398. https://doi.org/10.1080/13548500600708409; Dekel, S., Thiel, F., Dishy, G., & Ashenfarb, A.L. (2019). Is childbirth-induced PTSD associated with low maternal attachment? *Archives of Women's Mental Health*, 22(1), 119–122. https://doi.org/10.1007/s00737-018-0853-y; Nicholls, K., & Ayers, S. (2007). Childbirth-related post-traumatic stress disorder in couples: a qualitative study. *British Journal of Health Psychology*, 12(Pt 4), 491–509.

5 Porter, M., van Teijlingen, E., Chi Ying Yip, L., & Bhattacharya, S. (2007). Satisfaction with cesarean section: qualitative analysis of open-ended questions in a large postal survey. *Birth (Berkeley, Calif.)*, 34(2), 148–154. https://doi.org/10.1111/j.1523-536X.2007.00161.x; Svanberg, E., & Boutaleb, J. (2020). Difficult beginnings: how birth trauma impacts parent-infant relationships. *International Journal of Birth and Parent Education*, 7(5); Taghizadeh, Z., Irajpour, A., & Arbabi, M. (2013). Mothers' response to psychological birth trauma: a qualitative study. *Iranian Red Crescent Medical Journal*, 15(10), e10572. https://doi.org/10.5812/ircmj.10572

6 Van der Kolk, B. (2015). *The Body Keeps the Score: Brain, Mind, and Body in the Healing of Trauma*. Penguin Books.

7 McLearn, K.T., Minkovitz, C.S., Strobino, D.M., Marks E., & Hou, W. (2006). Maternal depressive symptoms at 2 to 4 months postpartum and early parenting practices. *Archives of Pediatric and Adolescent Medicine*, 160, 279–284; Murray, L., Fiori-Cowley, A., & Hooper, R. (1996). The impact of postnatal depression and associated adversity on early mother-infant interactions and later infant outcome. *Child Development*, 67(5), 2512–2526.

8 Handelzalts, J.E., Levy, S., Molmen-Lichter, M., Ayers, S., Krissi, H., Wiznitzer, A., & Peled, Y. (2021). The association of attachment style, postpartum PTSD and depression with bonding – a longitudinal path analysis model, from childbirth to six months. *Journal of Affective Disorders*, 280(Pt A), 17–25. https://doi.org/10.1016/j.jad.2020.10.068; Radoš, S.N., Matijaš, M., Anđelinović, M., Čartolovni, A., & Ayers, S. (2020). The role of posttraumatic stress and depression symptoms in mother-infant bonding. *Journal of Affective Disorders*, 268, 134–140. https://doi.org/10.1016/j.jad.2020.03.006

9 Mulcahy, R., Reay, R.E., Wilkinson, R.B., & Owen, C. (2010). A randomised control trial for the effectiveness of group interpersonal psychotherapy for postnatal depression. *Arch Women's Mental Health*, 13, 125–139. https://doi.org/10.1007/s00737-009-0101-6

10 Jung, V., Short, R., Letourneau, N., & Andrews, D. (2007). Interventions with depressed mothers and their infants: modifying interactive behaviours. *Journal of Affective Disorders*, 98(3), 199–205. https://doi.org/10.1016/j.jad.2006.07.014

11 Adapted from Laliotis, D. (2016, February). *Healing the Wounds of Attachment and Rebuilding Self* (Professional training); Shapiro, F. (2018). *Eye Movement Desensitization and Reprocessing, Basic Principles, Protocols and Procedures* (3rd ed.). Guilford Press; Morgan, S. (2020). *Negative Cognition Options: Distorted, Maladaptive, Self-Refencing Beliefs: Training Materials* [PDF]. EMDR Precision Academy.

12 Warren, B., & Creager Berger, B. (2021). *The Pregnancy and Postpartum Mood Workbook: The Guide to Surviving Your Emotions When Having a Baby*. Routledge.

13 Fernandes, D.V., Canavarro, M.C., & Moreira, H. (2021). The role of mothers' self-compassion on mother-infant bonding during the COVID-19 pandemic: a longitudinal study exploring the mediating role of mindful parenting and parenting stress in the postpartum period. *Infant Mental Health Journal*, 42(5), 621–635. https://doi.org/10.1002/imhj.21942; Fonseca, A., & Canavarro, M.C. (2018). Exploring the paths between dysfunctional attitudes towards motherhood and postpartum depressive symptoms: the moderating role of self-compassion. *Clinical Psychology & Psychotherapy*, 25(1), e96–e106. https://doi.org/10.1002/cpp.2145; Moreira, H., Carona, C., Silva, N., Nunes, J., & Canavarro, M.C. (2016). Exploring the link between maternal attachment-related anxiety and avoidance and mindful parenting: the mediating role of self-compassion. *Psychology and Psychotherapy*, 89(4), 369–384. https://doi.org/10.1111/papt.12082

14 Lathren, C., Bluth, K., & Zvara, B. (2020). Parent self-compassion and supportive responses to child difficult emotion: an intergenerational theoretical model rooted in attachment. *Journal of Family Theory & Review*, 12(3), 368–381. https://doi.org/10.1111/jftr.12388

15 Hairston, S.I., Handelzalts, E.J., Assis, C., & Kovo, M. (2018). Postpartum bonding difficulties and adult attachment styles: the mediating role of postpartum depression and childbirth-related PTSD. *Infant Mental Health Journal*, 39(2), 198–208. https://doi.org/10.1002/imhj.21695

16 Bowlby, J. (1979). On knowing what you are not supposed to know and feeling what you are not supposed to feel. *The Canadian Journal of Psychiatry*, 24(5), 403–408. https://doi.org/10.1177/070674377902400506; Fraiberg, S. (1980). *Clinical Studies in Infant Mental Health: The First Year of Life*. Basic Books, Inc.; Sansone, A. (2018). When the breast says no – the missing link: a case study. *Journal of Prenatal & Perinatal Psychology & Health*, 32(4), 318–338; Winnicott, D.W. (1971). *Playing and Reality*. Psychology Press.

17 Bowen, M. (1976). *Family Therapy: Theory and Practice Therapy*. Gardner Press.

18 Elle, A. (2020). *How We Heal: Uncover Your Power and Set Yourself Free*. Chronicle Books.

19 Cortizo, R. (2020). Hidden trauma, dissociation and prenatal assessment within the calming womb model. *Journal of Prenatal and Perinatal Psychology and Health*, 34(6), 469–481; Cortizo, R. (2021). Prenatal broken bonds: trauma, dissociation and the calming womb model. *Journal of Trauma and Dissociation*, 22(1), 1–10.

20 Ainsworth, M.D.S., & Bell, S.M. (1970). Attachment, exploration, and separation: illustrated by the behavior of one-year-olds in a strange situation. *Child Development*, 41(1), 49–67; Baumeister, R.F., & Leary, M.R. (1995). The need to belong: desire for interpersonal attachments as a fundamental human motivation. *Psychological*

Bulletin, 117(3), 497–529; Bowlby J. (1958). The nature of the child's tie to his mother. *International Journal of Psychoanalysis, 39*, 350–371; Bowlby, J. (1982). *Attachment and Loss: Volume 1 Attachment* (2nd ed.). Basic Books; Mikulincer, M., & Shaver, P.R. (2007). *Attachment in Adulthood: Structure, Dynamics, and Change.* Guilford Press.

21 Iani, L., Lauriola, M., Chiesa, A., & Cafaro, V. (2019). Associations between mindfulness and emotion regulation: the key role of describing and nonreactivity. *Mindfulness*, 10, 366–375. https://doi.org/10.1007/s12671-018-0981-5

22 Adapted from George, C., Kaplan, N., & Main, M. (1985). The adult attachment interview. Unpublished manuscript, University of California at Berkley; Morgan, S. (2020). *Attachment Based Family History: Training Materials* [PDF]. EMDR Precision Academy.

23 Adapted from Fisher, J. (2021). *Transforming the Living Legacy of Trauma.* PESI, Inc.

24 Daglar, G., & Nur, N. (2018). Level of mother-baby bonding and influencing factors during pregnancy and postpartum period. *Psychiatria Danubina*, 30(4), 433–440. https://doi.org/10.24869/psyd.2018.433

25 Klaus, H., Kennell, J., & Klaus, P. (1996). *Bonding: Building the Foundations of Secure Attachment and Independence.* Addison-Wesley.

26 Reynolds-Miller R.L. (2016). Potential therapeutic benefits of babywearing. *Creative Nursing*, 22(1), 17–23. https://doi.org/10.1891/1078-4535.22.1.17

27 Bigelow, A.E., & Power, M. (2020). Mother-infant skin-to-skin contact: short- and long-term effects for mothers and their children born full-term. *Frontiers in Psychology*, 11, 1921. https://doi.org/10.3389/fpsyg.2020.01921

Part III

The future, complicated decisions, and making plans again:
A path toward healing

Chapter 11

Looking towards the future: Finding your way through complex decisions and subsequent pregnancies

I want to recognize that even in reading the title of this chapter, you may have felt like you were not yet ready for this conversation. If so, you can skim sections of this chapter to normalize and validate what complicated emotions you might be feeling right now about having another baby (especially if you are feeling pressure from other people). You can then put it aside until you're ready to explore some of these ideas in more depth yourself. You may want to skip this chapter entirely and go to the next chapter, and that's fine too, because – please let me say – if nobody else has said it to you yet: you do not need to have another baby in order to heal from a traumatic reproductive experience. I'll say it another way. Your healing journey does not need to result in another pregnancy or baby in order to complete your healing process. Every healing path is unique and different, and how you walk along yours is the right way for you. Some people feel empowered by eventually choosing not to have another child and grieving/holding space for that decision. Or perhaps having another child is not an option for you for whatever reason, or you feel too overwhelmed at this time to go into another pregnancy with so many unknown variables. I get it. If these thoughts and feelings are coming up for you, then this chapter can provide some help in working through this complexity.

When I was writing this book, I debated about whether to end the book with this chapter, with the chapter about growth preceding it, or leave it where I did. Ultimately, I thought it was important to place it here, because I did not want to imply that your healing journey (thus the end of the book) needed to result in having another pregnancy or finding resolution in this decision for yourself. Healing from your experience is separate from wanting to have another baby. In fact, many survivors may feel internal conflict around thinking about having another baby, and may feel stuck in their healing journey as they try to solve that conundrum. Some continue working on this ambivalence and uncertainty for quite a while. And some, tragically, don't have this option at all, such as if they had emergency hysterectomies or other pelvic floor injuries. You are giving yourself a tremendous gift of focusing on your healing, and the more distance you get from being in frequent *fight/flight/freeze/fawn* mode, the more clarity I hope you will find in making any big decision, but particularly these big decisions about your future. Remember that it's virtually impossible to make rational decisions while activated (think: outside of your *window of tolerance*), so no wonder this can be such a tremendously overwhelming decision, and especially one layered with such nuance. It's like you've been burned by a hot stove. Your internal warning bells are trying to keep you from being burned again, while you might simultaneously be yearning to reach out. While certainly having a different experience the next time around can be

DOI: 10.4324/9781003379973-14

incredibly repairing, I know it also can be terrifying to have so many unknowns and no guarantees that all will go well.

In this chapter, we will help you unpack some of the complex emotions and thoughts you may be having about having another baby. Whether you feel even remotely close to making this decision or not, exploring your underlying emotional distress can be beneficial in reducing anything looming over your head and help bring you back into the present. This can be an active practice in mindfulness. We will help you focus on what you can and cannot control at this time in order to create a plan for what you need right now. And finally, we will help you create a trauma-informed individualized pregnancy and postpartum plan you can return to, if you decide to conceive at any point in the future.

> You do not have to have another baby to prove to yourself or to anyone else that you have healed.
>
> While some people want to have a corrective experience by hoping for a different outcome, many understandably do not want to go through the process of pregnancy or birth again, given everything that they went through.
>
> It can be hard knowing that so much uncertainty exists in the future while you are already living in the uncertainty and unpredictability of trauma recovery.

How your trauma may be impacting your decision

You are not alone if even the idea of another pregnancy is overwhelming, much less if you find yourself facing "analysis paralysis" once you come closer to having this conversation. This comes up in therapy sessions with almost every client who has survived reproductive trauma and loss. Research shows us this as well. Studies highlight that women who have experienced reproductive trauma such as high-risk pregnancies and birth trauma may fear having another, choose not to have another baby entirely, or may delay their decision for quite a while.[1] The likelihood of parents having another baby is greatly reduced, particularly if they did not receive treatment and support.[2] To me it speaks volumes about the importance of having a safe space to sort through all the complexity of emotions that are swirling about this decision while also being able to heal.

I continually see the benefits of people having had a chance to process their reproductive trauma, and we see this echoed in the research. We'll talk more about what healing can look like in more depth in the next chapter, including what options you have for mental health treatment. Women who have experienced trauma treatment like EMDR therapy to process their traumatic birth experiences are more likely to have a reduction in their PTSD symptoms and are more likely to have less fear about an upcoming birth.[3] The phenomenal thing is that they often have more positive birth experiences the next time, even when there are birth complications and challenges the next time around.[4] For those who choose not to have another child, there can be more clarity when the past feels more resolved and is less painful.

Let's give you some space to jot down some of your current thoughts you might be having about the future, or with regard to another pregnancy. If it feels comfortable doing so, can you name any of your hopes, goals or dreams for the future? These do not have to be specific about having another child but can also be about your continued healing journey, your identity, any goals for your work, relationships, etc.

_____

_____

_____

_____

_____

What are any of your concerns, fears or worries about the future? These might be specifically about having another child, or about other aspects of your life to come.

_____

_____

_____

_____

_____

Do you need to make any decisions right now? Or, are you able to pause decision making? For example, you might need to decide whether or not to extend your embryo or sperm storage fees for another year, you might want another appointment with your doctor to discuss your risks and timing if you do conceive again, or you may like to seek a second opinion to discuss delivery options to help you feel more reassured.

_____

_____

_____

_____

_____

You may have identified that you are able to pause or set aside some decisions for now, and that things are not as urgent as you had initially thought. It's common when healing from trauma that a number of things feel urgent, and part of healing can be practicing returning to the present, and within your window of tolerance. Even if you don't need to make any decisions, what options and choices do you have right now, or do you want to address?

What do we know about preventing reproductive trauma?

We have highlighted that reproductive trauma is more than just what happened to you; it's how things made you feel.[5] In other words, it's not just an emergent intervention (like an urgent cesarean section or a baby going to the NICU) that can be traumatic; it can also happen when a person feels demeaned, powerless, or terrified. So, while some aspects of having another baby are beyond your control, what is important to you if choosing to go down this path again? At the end of this chapter, you will have help creating a pregnancy and postpartum plan. For now, let's have you start thinking about what you can address, and what options you have to help mitigate any risks.

You can go back and review the risk factors for reproductive trauma that you circled in Chapter 2. Have any of these changed since you circled them, e.g. risk factors that can be addressed like having untreated depression during pregnancy, or having little or no support? Have you been able to address any of the factors that are within your control? If not, this gives you an idea of some options that are within your domain to address when you have the bandwidth. Other risk factors such as your age or your history of trauma may obviously be outside of your control.

Which of your risk factors stand out for you now that you can address (either now, or at some point in the future)?

_____

_____

_____

> As we talk about risk factors that may be beyond your control, we have acknowledged that there need to be significant systemic changes to reduce reproductive trauma.
>
> As I mentioned before, there are wonderful organizations doing important work to address these issues with advocacy, policy, and lobbying efforts. Knowing what we know about the disproportionate impact of reproductive trauma on people of color, implicit bias, and medical maltreatment cases in healthcare, big changes are needed on a larger scale. If you are interested, I have included a few in the Resources and support chapter at the end of the book.
>
> Some people find that this can be a helpful part of their healing journey in feeling they are contributing to positive change, even in small ways. While this certainly is not a part of everyone's journey, it can be helpful to think about what you might be interested in.

As we address what is within your control, it is vital to ensure you have a supportive, trauma-informed team of providers. Whether you are nearing making a decision, or just contemplating your options, this can be a helpful step for a lot of traumatized parents. As we keep talking about reproductive trauma, the interactions with and level of support from hospital staff can have an important impact on a parent's emotional experience (both negatively and positively). For example, supportive care during birth increases a parent's perceived control and helps them feel less anxious overall, while the opposite is also true: that negative interactions can become part of a traumatic experience.[6] The rates of birth trauma drop significantly when there is a focus on ongoing informed consent and a supportive and nurturing environment for the birther (and partner).[7] What might your partner need as they walk with you through this journey? It's vital for your partner to have the support they need as well. Think back to what we talked about in Chapter 9 of partners' experiences feeling like observers, and how terrifying it was to feel powerless themselves. Encouraging partners to be involved and getting support from providers can help mitigate any potential sense of helplessness and fear.[8] While certainly you can't control who all will be involved in your care, what ideas might you have to surround yourself with a trauma-informed team?

Some ideas for resources for providers you could involve in your team next time include (doulas, midwives, acupuncturists, physical and occupational therapists, trauma-informed mental health providers, providers who you feel more represented by, etc.):

_____

_____

_____

What does it mean to be a trauma-informed provider?

As you interview providers, it's helpful to inquire about their training and experience around trauma. Being _trauma-informed_ means that your provider is communicating with you throughout your procedures (or pregnancy, etc.) and letting you know what to expect. Obtaining _informed consent_ is more than a piece of paper that you sign indicating that you understand your rights, but, instead, a constant ongoing conversation to ensure you understand what is happening and are okay with proceeding. Trauma-informed care is respectful and creates an environment of safety, ensuring that you have agency, which helps decrease anxiety and powerlessness (key risk factors in trauma). Providers working through this lens involve you in the plan and inquire about your questions and preferences, giving choices, even during emergencies if possible. The mental walk-through before procedures, check-ins throughout, and follow-up afterwards are also vital, even during urgent situations.

> **Trauma-informed care is:**
>
> • respectful
>
> • collaborative
>
> • focused on agency and choices
>
> • explaining procedures ahead of time, during and providing debriefing afterwards
>
> • culturally sensitive
>
> All of these factors can help reduce the likelihood of experiencing an event as traumatic.
>
> People are less likely to experience birth trauma when the birther delivers in a supportive environment that involves ongoing consent.[9]

While we're talking about what is within your control, let's also talk about your mental health and what you can address. We've talked about how fear of childbirth and unresolved, untreated PTSD and mood symptoms are also risk factors for a traumatic birth and postpartum PTSD. At the same time, when one or either partner receives professional help, mood symptoms are relieved, the relationship improves, as do the interactions with the child.[10]

In the pregnancy and postpartum planning we will discuss ideas for addressing your mental health during a subsequent pregnancy, if that is a path you decide to take. Regardless of whether or not you try for another pregnancy, is there anything that you feel is currently lacking when it comes to how your mental health is being addressed right now?

_____

_____

_____

_____

_____

_____

What you named is important, because whether or not you move forward with another pregnancy, addressing your mental health promotes further stability. If you are thinking you may want to eventually have another baby, then what a gift to yourself to keep healing your mental health. If you decide not to have another baby, then what a gift to yourself to keep addressing your mental wellbeing.

Let's do a check-in, because I know this topic can sometimes bring up a lot of distress and a feeling of urgency to solve the decision about whether or not to have another baby in the future. Perhaps you could give yourself permission to take a break for a while before you return to the next section, or draw on one of your grounding skills, like some of your breath practices, to help remind yourself that you are present in the here and now. You can return whenever you're ready.

How are you talking to yourself about this decision?

Whether are you are feeling internal or external pressure to make a decision about having another baby after reproductive trauma, noticing how you are talking to yourself about it can be a great place to start. This would be a good time to revisit the negative belief list in Chapter 7 to highlight what you're thinking about trying again. Are there underlying fears of safety, powerlessness, or self-blame with feeling responsible or defective? Tracking your anxious thoughts and how often they come up can be useful with your Trigger Tracking Worksheet on page 97. Working with a therapist on this can be a great gift for yourself in your continued healing journey; no matter what you decide, it's how you _feel_ about it that is important.

Practicing self-compassion can also be useful to name whatever suffering you are experiencing, recognize you are not alone in this pain, and then practice the self-kindness you are learning. Here are some examples you can draw from for inspiration, and you can also create your own.

☐ It's normal I would be scared given everything I've been through. Anyone else in my shoes would probably be afraid to try again. I'm learning to be open to the possibility this is a different pregnancy with a different outcome.

☐ I feel so many mixed emotions about whether or not to have another baby, I feel like I need to hear from other people who know what this is like. Otherwise, I'm surrounded by friends and family for whom it seems the decision was easy. I'm going to seek out a birth trauma support group online to get some validation.

☐ I notice every time I think about having another baby, a wave of paralyzing anxiety hits me, and I feel afraid for my life. That tells me that I'm not ready to move forward until I address that. I deserve more healing.

☐ I'm not able to carry my own baby next time and that brings up so much anger, grief, and resentment. I think I need more time to heal and work through those feelings until I'm able to explore options. To do this I need _____

☐ I'm realizing it's okay not to try again and still work on healing with the family that I do have.

☐ A statement of self-compassion that works for you as you think about this decision is:

_____

_____

_____

_____

Whatever statements you create are really important. Keep these somewhere close to you, or somewhere that will be visible. You can update them over time, and notice how they help you.

Pregnancy and postpartum planning

Let's now turn to some additional, tangible options that you have as you look towards the future. Whether you just skim these now and return to them at some point in the future, or spend some time filling out some ideas, you can keep working on this. This plan is one way of finding empowerment and control by working on your needs and preferences if you choose to try for another baby.

While I know that the unknown can be uncomfortable, the positive thing about having your lived experience is that you are learning so much about yourself, and what is working for you (and certainly, what isn't!). You are working hard to identify what triggers you (such as certain touch or physical exams without being told what to expect in advance), and what support you needed (and didn't have). You're identifying what you could have used more of (like more people who were validating of your story) and less of (isolation or an expectation to return to normal right away). You are also learning what helps you feel better. Let's help you now start to create a pregnancy and postpartum plan using your own lived experience and internal wisdom. This particular plan is roughly inspired by the one used in my prior book and you will be able to update it to fit your specific needs.[11] Let's work together to help you think about your needs and your family's needs during this important time. If you need some ideas for additional support, you can find help in the Resources and support chapter.

Activity

As you think back to your reproductive journey, and particularly the distressing and traumatic parts, what are some of the crucial things you were lacking? Ideas might be emotional support, a better fit with a trauma-informed provider, breastfeeding support, professional support during your vital "fourth trimester" recovery, support at night for sleep, meals from others, mental health resources, etc.

_____

_____

_____

_____

_____

As you think back to your reproductive journey, and particularly the distressing and traumatic parts, what are some of the major themes? For example, as you are working through this workbook, perhaps you're recognizing strong themes of feeling powerless, are often blaming yourself, or recognizing you had a poor fit with your providers.

_____

_____

_____

_____

_____

As you notice the overall picture and themes of your journey as well as the needs you have had (that perhaps went unmet), pay attention to those as we go step by step through some common planning topics and see what is relevant for you. Let's make sure that your needs are all named by the end of this exercise. Not all of these topics will pertain to you, but it can be empowering knowing numerous options are available.

> **I suggest pregnancy/postpartum plans include (if appropriate):**
>
> - Mental health
> - Safety
> - Sleep
> - Coping skills
> - Eating
> - Feeding your baby
> - Support
> - Other children
> - Relationship

1. How will you address your mental health next time? As you think back to your experience(s) and mental health symptoms, what do you wish you had known? Perhaps you had difficulty identifying that something was wrong for quite a while. Or maybe it was hard speaking up and reaching out to others for help, or maybe your symptoms were missed by some of your providers.

Even though every pregnancy experience can be quite different, it can be helpful to think about how you might know you were feeling *off*. Let's think about your mental health warning signs.

How might you notice if you were struggling (e.g. "It would be a red flag if I was isolating from others," "If I was jumpy again and short-fused with my spouse," "If I wasn't sleeping at night when the baby was sleeping," "If I had any awful intrusive thoughts or images," or "If I was struggling to take care of myself in addition to the baby")?

_____

_____

_____

_____

What would you do to address those challenges (e.g. "If I were noticing any mental health symptoms next time, I would seek out therapy," "I would start medication right away and not wait," "I would tell someone about my thoughts earlier next time," or "If I were struggling with sleep, I would ask for help from a family member, hire a postpartum doula, or start a sleep swap schedule with my partner")?

_____

_____

_____

_____

If you start noticing specific fears, such as fears about your upcoming delivery, or worrying about attaching to your developing baby, how might you address them? Remember how you learned in the last chapter that connecting with this pregnancy and addressing your fears of childbirth will help your growing positive connection with your baby after delivery?[12] Ideas might be taking a pregnancy yoga class, practicing mindfulness and self-compassionate skills you learned in this workbook, and/or seeking out a perinatal mental health therapist who specializes in reproductive trauma.

_____

_____

_____

_____

What are some of the triggers you have noticed throughout your journey? This is not necessarily for you to be able to avoid all of these triggers but to keep bringing awareness to them and keep working through your trauma healing. For example, if pelvic exams are triggering, how can you talk with your provider about creating more safety and predictability with exams? Or, if seeing pregnant people is triggering, how can you keep working on your trauma response?

_____

_____

_____

_____

Who are the support people that you would reach out to if you felt *off* next time? Who have you learned is in your village?(e.g. your partner, your doula, a neighbor, a good friend)?

_____

_____

_____

_____

As you have been working your way through this workbook, you may have also been building a treatment team around you. List those people here so that for your next pregnancy you can easily remember who you can reach out to for help, if needed. **Given what you have been through, I recommend at least a few visits with a mental health provider throughout your pregnancy and at least 2–3 visits in the early postpartum period, if not more** (from the standpoint of support and checking in). Remember, with treatment you will get better, and you are not alone!

The people on my mental health team who I can go to for professional treatment, planning, or support include (and if you have not yet developed a professional treatment team, this might be a need you are noticing here):

_____

_____

_____

_____

2. What might help you feel more empowered and/or safe next time? This can be a tricky one because some resources and tools built to provide reassurance, when used well, can help provide relief. On the other hand, some equipment such as home dopplers and blood pressure cuffs used during pregnancy, or frequent checking of pregnancy tests to ensure a viable pregnancy earlier on, can feel self-protective but might actually add to an anxious and hypervigilant response. It's not the resource itself that is problematic, but the way it is used. Can you think of what might help you feel more protected and empowered, and how you might want to use resources to avoid repetitive or anxious checking behaviors? You might request more frequent appointments with your provider or change to a different one from last time. Maybe you need more frequent contact with loved ones. What else can you think of? If nothing comes to mind right now, that's okay, and you can return to this section if inspiration strikes in the future.

_____

_____

_____

_____

3. How can you address your sleep next time? As you have likely learned, new parents need extra help to ensure they get as much rest and sleep as possible, and this is even more important when battling mental health symptoms while your body is in recovery mode. Your sleep was likely affected by your mood symptoms, or vice versa. Perhaps you felt like there was no amount of sleep that would be adequate to address your exhaustion. After feeding your baby, you may have had trouble falling back asleep due to a wired brain or body. However issues presented for you, your sleep was probably a focus of your recovery.

Whether or not you experience challenges again, sleep support can be useful. Having supportive people available during the day for naps and at night for optimal sleep can be life-changing. You can always schedule out for several weeks postpartum and cancel if you find you don't want or need that assistance after all.

The following people might be good supports for rest (choose which you have called upon to help or would like to):

☐ Postpartum night doulas

☐ Family members

☐ Sleep coaches

☐ Friends

☐ Neighbors

☐ Members of your religious community

☐ Other support people:

_____

A protected sleep schedule you can try next time would be: (e.g. you could do the last feeding of the night, your partner does the middle feeling and you get up early in the morning; or you might aim for longer blocks of sleep for yourself on the weekend if a loved one can provide the nighttime care):

_____

_____

4. How will you practice self-soothing and grounding practices next time? As you have likely learned by working through this workbook, you are seeing the benefits of practicing regular self-soothing skills. Whether you are tuning into your breath more and using square/box breathing throughout the day, practicing mindful movement or self-compassion (or all of the above), what are you liking best to help you feel more emotionally regulated? What is helping you stay within your *window of tolerance*? Whether or not you experience something challenging next time, it can be beneficial for both you and a developing baby to have reduced stress, and the skills to manage your distress when it spikes.[13]

The following are skills that you can practice regularly (check any that you are already doing or plan to do):

☐ Square/box breathing (page 69)

☐ Diaphragmatic breathing (page 70)

☐ Sip breathing (page 70)

☐ 4–7–8 breathing (page 70)

☐ Meditation using an app, or going to a class

☐ Body scan meditation (page 74–75)

☐ Muscle relaxation exercises like Progressive Muscle Relaxation (page 77)

☐ Mindfulness such as mini check-ins (page 87)

☐ Mindful self-compassion prompts (written or verbal to yourself) (page 85)

☐ 5 senses (page 86)

☐ Mindful movement or yoga (page 87–88, 76)

☐ Mantras (page 99–100)

The following are additional tools you learned that you can use (check any you are already using or plan to use):

☐ Trigger Tracking Worksheet (page 97)

☐ Negative thoughts lists (page 91, 143)

☐ Communication skills (page 113–114)

☐ Interpersonal Inventory (page 106)

☐ Another skill I've learned that I will use is: _____

5. How are you going to ensure you are eating and staying hydrated? Whether it was due to an upset, anxious stomach, or the forgetfulness that comes with being overwhelmed and busy, how often did you find yourself missing meals altogether, or eating snacks on the fly? Eating regular, healthy meals and staying hydrated are important to help keep your mood, not to mention your blood sugar, stable. Preparing ahead of time can help you avoid skipping meals, plus involving your village in this task can empower them to help you in the ways you need.

Things you can do to ensure you are eating throughout the day:

☐ When people ask you "what do you need?" or "what can I do?", accept help by letting them know what foods you like or what specific meals would be helpful in your recovery.

☐ Ask friends, family, neighbors, or community members to bring you meals.

☐ If people ask for ideas, let loved ones know a meal train, a food delivery gift card, or prepared meal delivery service would be a helpful baby shower gift.

☐ Prepare frozen meals before you deliver.

☐ Compile a list of your favorite take-out and delivery options.

☐ Have snack and drink stations prepared throughout the house, such as jars of nuts or easy-to-grab bottles of water in plain sight.

☐ Other options:

_____

6. How might you ensure you are getting the support you need when feeding your baby? Whether or not feeding your baby contributed to your distress, or was a big aspect of your trauma, it's likely you have already thought about how you would like to feed another baby, or if you make the decision to try again. Whether you hope to breastfeed/chestfeed exclusively, bottle-feed using formula or pumped milk, or using a combination, you've likely put a lot of thought into this. Planning out your support team now can take the mental effort out of the decision if/when you need to call upon your help.

What was your experience around feeding your baby this time (check any feeding struggles you may have encountered if breastfeeding/chestfeeding):

☐ Any distress or trauma around nursing

☐ Sore nipples or pain

☐ Triggers when feeding or experiencing closeness with your baby

☐ Mastitis or other health challenges around nursing

☐ Low milk supply

☐ Baby's low birthweight and/or fears around their health

☐ Judgment from others

☐ Guilt about the amount of time you breast-/chestfed

☐ Difficulty latching

☐ Baby had torticollis, tongue and/or lip-tie

☐ Exclusively pumping

☐ Triggers when pumping

☐ Other: _____

If you bottle-fed, pumped, cup- or tube-fed your baby, or used another means of feeding your baby, check any struggles you may have encountered:

☐ Trauma or distress around feeding methods or baby's health

☐ Difficulty with baby's allergies

☐ Difficulty with milk supply

☐ Judgment or comments from others

☐ Challenges finding the right formula or donor source

☐ Baby's low birthweight and/or fears around their health

☐ Triggers when experiencing closeness with your baby

☐ Other: _____

You may have had challenges and distress around feeding your baby; it is a common source of reproductive trauma. As you may have explored throughout the book, such as in Chapter 7, parents can internalize these difficulties ("I can't handle it," "I've failed") with intense feelings of shame and guilt. However you feed your baby next time, it can be helpful to seek out support to help you through this, such as lactation consultants, pediatric OTs and PTs, doulas, supportive friends, aunts, etc.

The following friends, professionals, or relatives are supportive of your feeding preferences for your baby, and are good sources of support when there are challenges:

_____

_____

_____

_____

_____

7. Who is in your village, and who else might you want to add to your support team? As you have been working your way through this book, you have likely been identifying how important it is to have quality support surrounding you. People who can empathize with your experience or validate what you're feeling can make any distress all that more bearable.

These people already make up part of your support team (as you identified in Chapter 8):

_____

_____

_____

_____

If you are still developing your community and trying to find your people, some ideas for further building your support network include the following (suggestions can also be found in the Resources and support chapter):

☐ Postpartum support groups (online or in person)

☐ Birth trauma support groups

☐ NICU support groups (and/or groups specific to your baby's medical or health issues)

☐ Trauma-informed yoga, mindfulness, or meditation classes

☐ Childbirth education classes

☐ New baby music classes

☐ Prenatal/postnatal fitness classes

☐ Breastfeeding support groups

☐ Friends of friends

☐ Family members with children

☐ Other ideas for support can include: _____

8. What are some ways you can support your other child(ren) with their adjustment?
You might be worried about the impact another baby would have on your current or older children, and potentially scared to rock the boat. I hear this a lot from my clients as they consider adding to their families, but particularly those who have gone through hell during their path towards parenthood. A lot of parents are worried that they will never love another baby like they did their first, or scared they will "mess everything up" by introducing another baby to the mix. These fears are so common! All of you in your family will experience an adjustment when a new baby comes home, but that does not mean it's a bad thing, or that you can't do things to help support the transition.

Ways you can help ease the transition of your older child(ren) might include (check all that might apply):

☐ Try to spend some regular one-on-one time together (even if it's just ten minutes or so). You can enlist loved ones to help with the baby, if it feels comfortable for you, or you can wear your baby to have your hands free to read a book or play a game with your older child.

☐ Maintain their routine for them as much as possible. Enlist others to help with this, if possible, such as for pickup and drop-off at sports or childcare.

☐ Ask your friends or family to spend special one-on-one time with your older child.

☐ Acknowledge your child's feelings and help them feel safe when they are having tough times. They may feel anxious, regress a bit with behaviors, or even have amplified emotions. This may be great practice for you in *reparenting yourself*, like we talked about in the last chapter, by validating your child's feelings.

☐ Similarly, praise your child frequently for any times they practice cooperation, patience, or empathy. This is a big time of adjustment for them and, as such, it can be reassuring for them to hear they're doing their best to be helpful (even if it means they're trying to "love the baby so hard").

☐ A small gift from the new baby to the older sibling is something that can also help your older sibling feel excited by the addition of the new baby (some people might call this bribery, but I definitely don't).

☐ Ask for friends or family to give you breaks by providing tangible help (such as driving your children to school, etc.).

☐ Other things you can do:

_____

9. How might you want to protect your relationship with your partner: As you have likely experienced, having a baby can change a relationship, period, and particularly when one or both partners have been impacted by trauma. The relationship you have with your partner can be foundational to your well-being, and when there are stressors in the relationship, this can amplify whatever else you are going through. The nice thing to know, though, is the opposite is also true. If you are struggling, any sense of stability and safety in your relationship can bring a sense of calm. Your relationship and the lack of quality time with each other may have been a source of stress for you with your first baby and contributed to your symptoms. Hopefully with time and effort, this has become more of a safe haven (or you both are continuing to work on this).

Ways that you are learning to safely reconnect include (check all that apply or that you want to start incorporating into your relationship):

☐ Working on your intimacy ladder from page 131

☐ Connecting with small gestures of touch throughout the day

☐ Maintaining small rituals together that are still feasible as new parents (such as watching your favorite TV show at night or taking walks with the baby)

☐ Going out together with the baby, or working towards going out together without the baby

☐ Similarly, asking friends, professionals or family for breaks so you have more time together (whether or not you stay at home)

☐ Telling your partner things that you appreciate about them in general, and as a parent in particular

☐ Texting or calling them to touch base and connecting through the day when you are apart

☐ Other activities that are relatively easy to do as new parents:

_____

10. As you review this chapter, and think about some of the crucial things you were lacking throughout your experience, what else is missing from your pregnancy and postpartum plan? Ideas might be hiring a doula well versed in trauma, ensuring that you have a trauma-sensitive provider next time, interviewing a few providers to ensure you have a good fit, etc. The options are limitless. Write your initial ideas here and you can keep coming back to it whenever you think of another option or if you hear something that inspires you. This plan is tailored just for you and can continue to be updated over time.

_____
_____
_____
_____
_____
_____
_____
_____
_____
_____

Chapter highlights

- The decision of whether or not to have another baby can be overwhelming for most survivors of reproductive trauma.

- In fact, many people will delay the decision for quite a while. Some will choose not to have another baby.

- Having another baby is a personal and individual decision and is not a required step of healing.

- In order to give yourself what you need to make your decision in a non-pressured way, it can be useful to think about what options you have control over.

- Reviewing your risk factors and what you need can be a useful way to focus your energy and determine what is within your control.

- If you do decide to move forward, a pregnancy and postpartum plan can be useful to consider what you needed last time (and didn't have), what you were triggered by, and as such, what you would need differently next time.

- Gathering a supportive team in advance can be empowering.

Notes

1 Gottvall K., & Waldenström, U. (2002). Does a traumatic birth experience have an impact on future reproduction? *BJOG: An International Journal of Obstetrics and Gynaecology*, 109(3), 254–260; Placheck, I.S., Dulitzky, M., Margolis-Dorfman, L., & Simchen, M.J. (2015). A simple model for prediction postpartum PTSD in high-risk pregnancies. *Archives of Women's Mental Health*, 19(3), 483–490. https://doi.org/10.1007/s00737-015-0582-4

2 Skari, H., Skreden, M., Malt, U.F., Dalholt, M., Ostensen, A.B., Egeland, T., & Emblem, R. (2002). Comparative levels of psychological distress, stress symptoms, depression and anxiety after childbirth – a prospective population-based study of mothers and fathers. *BJOG: An International Journal of Obstetrics and Gynaecology*, 109(10), 1154–1163. https://doi.org/10.1111/j.1471-0528.2002.00468.x

3 Baas, M.A.M., van Pampus, M.G., Stramrood, C.A.I., Dijksman L.M., Vanhommerig, J.W., & de Jongh, A. (2022). Treatment of pregnant women with fear of childbirth using EMDR therapy: Results of a multi-center randomized controlled trial. *Front Psychiatry*, 12, 798249. doi:10.3389/fpsyt.2021.798249

4 Stramrood, C.A.I., van der Velde, J., Doornbos, B., Paarlberg, K.M., Weijmar Schultz, W.C.M., & van Pampus, M.G. (2012). The patient observer: eye-movement desensitization and reprocessing for the treatment of posttraumatic stress following childbirth. *Birth-Issues in Perinatal Care*, 39(1), 70–76. https://doi.org/(...)23-536X.2011.00517.x

5 Creedy, D.K., Shochet, I.M., & Horsfall, J. (2000). Childbirth and the development of acute trauma symptoms: incidence and contributing factors. *Birth (Berkeley, Calif.)*, 27(2), 104–111. https://doi.org/10.1046/j.1523-536x.2000.00104.x; Grekin, R., & O'Hara, M.W. (2014). Prevalence and risk factors of postpartum posttraumatic stress disorder: a meta-analysis. *Clinical Psychology Review*, 34(5), 389–401. https://doi.org/10.1016/j.cpr.2014.05.003; Dekel, S., Stuebe, C., & Dishy, G. (2017). Childbirth induced posttraumatic stress syndrome: a systematic review of prevalence and risk factors. *Frontiers in Psychology*, 8, 560. https://doi.org/10.3389/fpsyg.2017.00560

6 Ayers, S., Radoš, S.N., & Balouch, S. (2015). Narratives of traumatic birth: quality and changes over time. *Psychological Trauma: Theory, Research, Practice, and Policy*, 7(3), 234–242. https://doi.org/10.1037/a0039044; Ford, E., & Ayers, S. (2009). Stressful events and support during birth: the effect on anxiety, mood and perceived control. *Journal of Anxiety Disorders*, 23(2), 260–268. https://doi.org/10.1016/j.janxdis.2008.07.009

7 Baptie, G., Andrade, J., Bacon., A., & Norman, A. (2020). Birth trauma: the mediating effects of perceived support. *British Journal of Midwifery*, 28(10). https://doi.org/10.12968/bjom.2020.28.10.724

8 Elmir, R., & Schmied, V. (2022). A qualitative study of the impact of adverse birth experiences on fathers. *Women and Birth: Journal of the Australian College of Midwives*, 35(1), e41–e48. https://doi.org/10.1016/j.wombi.2021.01.005

9 Baptie, G., Andrade, J., Bacon, A.M., & Norman, A. (2020). Birth trauma: the mediating effects of perceived support. *The British Journal of Midwifery*, 28, 724–730.

10 Garthus-Niegel, S., Horsch, A., Handtke, E., von Soest, T., Ayers, S., Weidner, K., & Eberhard-Gran, M. (2018). The impact of postpartum posttraumatic stress and depression symptoms on couples' relationship satisfaction: a population-based prospective study. *Frontiers in Psychology*, 9, 1728. https://doi.org/10.3389/fpsyg.2018.01728

11 DONA.org Postpartum Plan Retrieved from https://www.dona.org/wp-content/uploads/2016/12/postpartum-plan-template.pdf; Warren, B., & Creager Berger, B. (2021). *The Pregnancy and Postpartum Mood Workbook: The Guide to Surviving Your Emotions When Having a Baby*. Routledge.

12 Daglar, G., & Nur, N. (2018). Level of mother-baby bonding and influencing factors during pregnancy and postpartum period. *Psychiatria Danubina*, 30(4), 433–440. https://doi.org/10.24869/psyd.2018.433; Klabbers, G., van Bakel, H., van den Heuvel, M., & Vingerhoets, A. (2016). Severe fear of childbirth: its features, assessment, prevalence, determinants, consequences and possible treatments. *Psychological Topics*, 25(1), 107–127.

13 Zietlow, A-L., Nonnenmacher, N., Reck, C., Ditzen, B., & Müller, M. (2019). Emotional stress during pregnancy – associations with maternal anxiety disorders, infant cortisol reactivity, and mother-child interaction at preschool age. *Frontiers in Psychology*, 25(9). https://doi.org/10.3389/fpsyg.2019.02179

Chapter 12

A path towards healing: Hope, resiliency, and growth

Notice how far you've come in your healing journey! I know this is hard work and I hope you keep going. Whether you still feel like you are at the very beginning of healing or are noticing significant progress, it can help to think about what you might need next. As we near the end of the book, let's review what you have learned so far and help you discover additional treatment options. A reminder first that healing from reproductive trauma is possible. I've mentioned this throughout the book – not all healing experiences look the same, but change is possible and there is hope.

> Notice how far you've come on your journey in reading this book!
>
> Healing is a process that takes time and you are still exactly where you need to be.
>
> As there can be pain and struggle, there can also be joy found in healing at times.

What can healing look like after reproductive trauma?

Living inside your traumatized body and being impacted on a daily basis can be so hard. This is why I think it's vital to know that hope is not only possible, but real. We will talk about treatment options in a bit, but for now let's talk about what this can look like. There are no absolutes with healing. For example, forgiveness is not a necessary step of healing, nor is having another baby, as we talked about in the previous chapter. I want to plant a seed of hope that wherever you are right now in your healing journey is okay. While some people who have experienced reproductive trauma and traumatic grief may feel stuck afterwards, or have major impacts on their mental health and functioning, most people, particularly those who get professional treatment, eventually find healing and change.

Healing from reproductive trauma will look different for everyone. Certainly, it can look like transformation and change. Some people in treatment will have a reduction in triggers, reduction in mental health symptoms, and an improvement in overall functioning (such as fewer flashbacks and eventually resuming intimacy comfortably). Using skills and techniques learned, people will be able to return to their lives and move through their worlds safely and feel more comfortable in their own skin. What is especially an honor is to see people heal from their reproductive distress and be able to recall their experiences with more distance (rather than still living in *trauma time*), have fewer negative

DOI: 10.4324/9781003379973-15

beliefs about themselves, and have more positive and adaptive thoughts (such as: "Look at what I went through, I am capable"). Some people feel like they can talk about their stories with more discernment and safety, when and to whom they choose. Some survivors are able to find meaning from their stories, like something beautiful coming from something awful.

Posttraumatic growth after reproductive trauma

Posttraumatic growth (PTG) is a process that refers to experiencing a significant psychological change as a result of dealing with a challenging life circumstance. It is the process of finding meaning from trauma and growing from it.[1] It is not a toxic positivity slant that implies that what you went through was for a reason, or that you were *supposed to* go through what you did. That feels wrong to imply and simply isn't true. Instead, people who experience PTG feel like they are changing or becoming a new person as a result of their traumatic event, or are noticing new possibilities and new priorities. They are allowing themselves to feel all of their emotions around their event, move through the trauma, and are eventually able to notice some positive aspects in their lives. You can think about PTG as this awful thing that happened to you that you never would have wanted, yet there may have been some positive changes in your life that might have happened as a result. Remarkably, about two-thirds of people who experience trauma will eventually experience PTG. Specifically with reproductive trauma, more than half of women who had a traumatic birth eventually experience posttraumatic growth![2] For example, some people who experienced a traumatic birth where they felt silenced and overpowered learned through their healing to find their voice in more situations and became more of a self-advocate. Others may have found that their lives changed so drastically by what they went through in becoming a parent that their priorities and values shifted, such as making healthy changes in their careers to become more protective of their time and mental health. Some notice spiritual insights, or a sense they are stronger than they ever thought they could be. Others may relate to people in new ways, such as letting go of some relationships that no longer serve them or even feeling more empathetic or tolerant at times. Remember the positive changes to the brain that can happen over time?

Positive benefits to the brain by practicing calming and self-soothing skills like yoga, slow breathing, meditation, or mindfulness:[3]

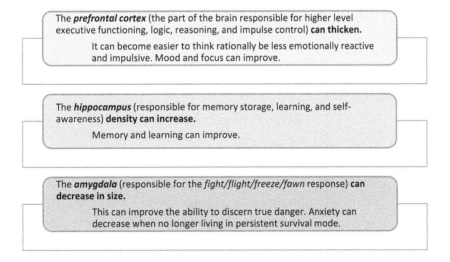

The *prefrontal cortex* (the part of the brain responsible for higher level executive functioning, logic, reasoning, and impulse control) **can thicken.**

It can become easier to think rationally be less emotionally reactive and impulsive. Mood and focus can improve.

The *hippocampus* (responsible for memory storage, learning, and self-awareness) **density can increase.**

Memory and learning can improve.

The *amygdala* (responsible for the *fight/flight/freeze/fawn* response) **can decrease in size.**

This can improve the ability to discern true danger. Anxiety can decrease when no longer living in persistent survival mode.

I do want to share that while posttraumatic growth is common, it is not a universal experience for all survivors of reproductive trauma. There is absolutely no shame if you do not feel like a "better, more improved version" of yourself right now. You likely picked up this book because you are struggling. Please know this isn't to put additional pressure on you to now become a better person on top of what you went through. This is instead to share that change continues to be possible. Hope is possible. In fact, the reason I'm including this information here is not to place it as a measuring stick of your growth, but instead to plant a seed of hope that you can continue to heal and your experience will continue to change. I'm speaking especially to those of you who are not where you would like to be yet, or who may have skipped to reading the last chapter of the book first to see what experiences of healing from reproductive trauma can look like. I get it. I'm notorious for Googling "does the dog die in ...?" before watching movies. I can't stand the suspense as an animal softie, and you, too, may have wanted to skip to the end first. Your healing will not look like someone else's, and trauma healing is not a competitive sport. It is possible to keep healing while still struggling at times, and yet notice overall progress. Even if the idea of posttraumatic growth does not resonate with your experience, it is okay. It is important to share this so that survivors of reproductive trauma don't only equate trauma with permanent suffering. What you went through matters and there is hope and change.

> Posttraumatic growth is the concept of growing and changing as a result of a traumatic event.
>
> It does NOT mean that this happened for a reason.
>
> Birth workers can experience PTG after working with birth trauma and traumatic loss, too, if surrounded by helpful support.[4]

Real talk here. You do NOT have to do something meaningful with your trauma in order to heal. You don't have to fund a nonprofit, testify to Congress, scale a mountain, or shave your head in order for this to have changed your life. It has already changed your life. You get to find the meaning and purpose your life takes now, and for anyone else to tell you what that looks like is just wrong. I like to think of healing, and specifically about posttraumatic growth, when I wear a cuff bracelet that I bought traveling in Cambodia. On the surface, this appears to be a simple, bronze cuff with some etchings in it. What I love so much about it, though, is that it is made from the shrapnel of a landmine (and made from a local artist whose community has been devastated by the impact of landmines, which makes it even more of a testament to the power of this piece). Talk about transformation from something awful.

> There are no rules with your healing journey.
>
> Everyone's process will look different.
>
> Forgiveness is not a requirement at any stage of your journey, for example.
>
> This might be an important reminder if anyone has suggested that you have to "forgive and forget" in order to heal, such as if you experienced mistreatment, harm, violence, racism, or other similar situations during your journey.

Reflection activity

Let's take an opportunity to reflect on any growth or change you have noticed along your way. While posttraumatic growth is not the goal, perhaps some of the concepts we have talked about have resonated with you.

What have you noticed, if anything, is different in the way you look at your life since your trauma?

_____
_____
_____
_____
_____
_____

Have any of your values or priorities shifted since your experience(s)?

_____
_____
_____
_____
_____

Resiliency and strength

Part of healing is building resilience as well as learning how to deal with adversity and challenges. You've actually been building resilience this whole time! By learning how to feel your feelings, tune into your body, and manage your triggers and distress, you have been building resiliency. As you're learning, resilience can be taught by practicing your skills. It is not an innate quality we either have or do not have. The other lovely thing is that resiliency can be enhanced when people have support. By building your village you are reaping even one more benefit: building more resiliency to help you weather these storms.[5] There has been some interesting research about resiliency. For example, two doctors spent decades working with numerous trauma survivors, including prisoners of war, and compiled their research findings of what they learned about those who have managed to overcome seemingly impossible situations.[6] They honed in on several resilience factors that these folks all had in common, and these factors can be incorporated into your healing journey, too.

Check which resilience practices you are currently working on, and place a "?" on which you might want to keep attending to.

☐ Having a positive attitude (the idea that optimism can also be learned and taught)

☐ Cognitive flexibility (re-evaluating your experience and meaning of the event with adaptable perspectives)

☐ Embracing a personal moral compass (developing solid core beliefs and values)

☐ Finding a resilient role model to emulate

☐ Facing your fears (practicing your skills and building self-esteem)

☐ Developing active coping skills

☐ Establishing and nurturing a supportive social network

☐ Attending to your physical well-being (which has positive effects on your mental health)

What stands out for you? Had you ever thought of any of these practices as building resilience before?

_____

_____

Many of these are concepts you have already been working on throughout this book, and I hope that you keep at it!

Healing and goals for the future

Part of what helps us heal and move through difficult situations is practicing attending to our present needs while simultaneously looking towards the future and where we want to go. Having goals can be important when we've lost all hope or a sense of control. Learning to live with present difficulties while also moving forward can be a learned skill and part of the transformative nature of healing. One of the only choices you may have sometimes is to think about your view on life and how you would like to steer your healing journey.

Reflection activity

What are you striving towards in your healing journey? Is there a goal (or goals) that you are working towards? If it is hard to think of something off the top of your head, that's okay. Trauma can be all encompassing and getting your bearings can be useful. Where are you headed? What are you hoping for? For example, are you working in physical therapy to repair your pelvic floor injury with the goal of lessened pain and improved functioning? Are you actively addressing how you are feeding your baby with the hopes of increasing your confidence and decreasing your anxiety and distress? Are you working in therapy to manage and reduce your overall trauma triggers and symptoms? Are you hoping to eventually be less reactive and on edge?

_____

_____

_____

_____

_____

How would you would like to think about your traumatic experience(s) years down the road? It's okay if this is a tough one to answer right now, and you can skip this, or return to it at any point.

_____

_____

Continuing your healing with treatment

My hope for you as you take what you've learned from this book is that you continue your healing journey, whatever that looks like. If you have not connected with professional care already, let's talk about what options are possible. These are suggestions based on my own professional experience of working with reproductive trauma, as well as what research has shown to be effective in helping survivors heal. This is by no means an exhaustive list. I'm grateful that treatment for reproductive trauma and perinatal mental health is a constantly changing and growing field, and there is more attention and research being devoted to this population than there was when I started my career over two decades ago. We are continually learning new ways to support grieving and traumatized parents through their journeys.

As you consider various treatment options, I strongly encourage you to seek out providers with perinatal mental health experience AND those who have trauma expertise. One of the greatest goals of trauma-informed care is, as trauma therapist Babette Rothschild beautifully puts it, to "relieve, not intensify, suffering."[7] Being a trauma-informed provider means that they are focused on providing:[8]

- Trustworthiness and transparency in their treatment approach

- Collaboration in their space (you might also hear the concept of providing client-centered care)

- Empowerment and a sense of agency to their clients/patients

- Informed consent that is ongoing throughout treatment

- Choices whenever possible

- A sense of safety

- A practice built on respect and culture, ability, and gender awareness

What else might you add that is important to you, and that you believe makes a provider trauma-sensitive or informed? What qualities have your favorite providers shown that embody safety, transparency, empowerment, and trauma-sensitive treatment in your care?

Activity

We talked about this a bit in the prior chapter but let's go into more depth here. When you are talking to a potential provider (mental health, birth worker, physical therapist, acupuncturist, yoga instructor, etc.), it can be helpful to have an idea of some potential questions that you can ask so that you can learn about them, and, as such, feel more safe and empowered. This is not an exhaustive list, and please add whatever questions feel important to you that pertain specifically to your situation. Here are some prompts to get you started:

☐ What is your experience in working with people who have had reproductive trauma?

☐ What is your experience working with people with my situation (cultural background, diagnosis, etc.)?

☐ How long have you worked in this field?

☐ What is it like to be a patient/client of yours?

☐ What is your experience working towards being a trauma-informed (anti-racist, culturally sensitive, etc.) provider?

☐ What have you done to work on your implicit bias (cultural sensitivity, trauma sensitivity, etc.)?

☐ What are some of your thoughts on how we might work together to address my concerns or situation?

☐ What else might you add that is important for you to ask your provider?

Additional considerations when working with providers after trauma

In addition to finding professionals who have experience working with trauma, and who approach treatment with a trauma-informed lens, there are some other treatment options that you can think about as a trauma survivor. Here are just a few ideas, but of course, you are an expert on you and what you need.

• Your providers, with a signed release, can collaborate together so that you do not have to share your story repeatedly. Ideally, your care can also be coordinated by one primary provider so that everyone is clear on your treatment plan, there can be avoidance of potential triggers, and they can focus on ways to support you.

• Other ways of finding agency and feeling protective of yourself are to think about your body and permission. You can take control in your own hands by expressing what you are and are not comfortable with. For example, you may not want interns or residents to be a part of your appointments and procedures, may not want to be touched in certain places, or may request a provider of a certain gender, if available. Ideally your providers should be asking permission before touching you and will be explaining procedures anyway, and you can also articulate how important this is to you as a survivor of trauma.

• You may have difficulty with breastfeeding/chestfeeding, pelvic exams, or other aspects of reproductive care that you can talk to your providers about in advance. You have a voice and are learning how to practice using it, even if it's challenging to do so. Working with a therapist on this can be tremendously beneficial to explore what you need and learn how to express your needs.

As we talked about some ideas for working with healthcare providers moving forward, what are some options that stand out to you? What could you see yourself incorporating now when interacting with providers, or what has inspired you to utilize later on at some point?

_____

_____

_____

Let's turn our focus now on some of the mental health treatment options available to help you continue your healing journey.

Professional mental health treatment options for reproductive trauma

You may already be working with a mental health professional and are using this book as a supplement to your care. Or, perhaps you have been inspired by some of the information you are learning here and want to continue your healing with some additional support. Let's review some options available to you in your stage of recovery (or active traumatization). Again, this is by no means an exhaustive list, as trauma therapists tend to incorporate a number of different therapeutic skills in their work with clients. Resources are found in the next chapter to help you locate some of these options.

EMDR therapy:

EMDR (Eye Movement Desensitization and Reprocessing) therapy is an evidence-based psychotherapy extensively studied specifically for trauma since its origins in the 1980s. It has been shown to be safe and effective for both pregnant and postpartum people for the treatment of reproductive trauma.[9] Studies have shown that pregnant women with PTSD had a significant reduction in PTSD symptoms, fear of childbirth, and anxiety symptoms following EMDR.[10] Those who had prior traumatic birth experiences felt more prepared for their upcoming deliveries and had resolution (or reduction) of their PTSD symptoms. And this part is really important: studies show that pregnant people who had EMDR therapy looked back at their first (traumatic) birth experience with new, more positive feelings and had more feelings of capability with their second birth experience, even when they had delivery complications the second time around![11] Additionally, postpartum women who have had EMDR therapy after traumatic birth experiences had significant reductions in flashbacks, PTSD, anxiety, and depression symptoms, and noticed overall improvements in their social functioning, even years after treatment.[12]

EMDR therapy helps correct the way the brain stores a traumatic memory so it is no longer stuck in _trauma time_ in the fragmented way you may have experienced. EMDR has been transformative for my practice, as I have seen countless survivors of reproductive trauma and loss heal from unimaginable events. What I find powerful about EMDR is that it is your own brain doing the healing. It's inspiring to watch a client spontaneously shift from having negatively held beliefs about their experience ("I'm permanently damaged," "I failed," "I'm a bad mother," etc.) to more positive and adaptive ones ("I'm alive now," "I'm capable," "I'm a protective mom," etc.) The concepts of negative and positive beliefs may be familiar to you from previous chapters; we have referenced important EMDR tenets throughout this book.

What happens during EMDR therapy?

During sessions of EMDR therapy, as the name implies, client's memories don't just become *desensitized* (less intense); they are also *reprocessed* with spontaneous new thoughts and beliefs about themselves and their experience. It's an honor as the therapist, to stay out of the way and witness my clients' brains doing the healing.

EMDR therapy essentially connects the mind and body using bilateral stimulation as you recall a traumatic memory (your therapist might use little tappers, eye movements, sounds, or other options). You do not constantly talk about what you went through.

Because it is a mind/body therapy, or a "bottom-up" approach, trauma is no longer stuck in the body, and the person does not feel they have to talk themselves out of their thoughts or purposefully change their behaviors.

Dialectical Behavioral Therapy (DBT):

DBT essentially helps you deal with overwhelming emotions.[13] The core areas of focus with DBT are learning emotional regulation skills, skills for managing distress and crisis, interpersonal effectiveness skills (communication and relationships), and mindfulness. You have been introduced to a number of DBT skills throughout this workbook. These skills are all profoundly helpful for people experiencing trauma symptoms, and DBT can be helpful in conjunction with other trauma therapies to treat PTSD.[14]

Cognitive Behavioral Therapy (CBT):

Cognitive Behavioral Therapy models of PTSD suggest that unhelpful coping strategies, disjointed trauma memories, and negative beliefs maintain PTSD.[15] There are typically two main types of CBT typically used to treat trauma: Trauma Focused Cognitive Behavioral Therapy (TF-CBT) and Prolonged Exposure Therapy (PET). Some promising case studies have shown that CBT is an effective treatment for postnatal PTSD.[16] TF-CBT research has also shown a decrease in self-reported PTSD with pregnant survivors of abuse from low-income backgrounds who identify as minorities.[17] You have also been taught some CBT skills in this workbook, such as using the hierarchy ladder to manage overwhelming situations, and thinking about how you would talk to a friend, and applying that same compassion to yourself.

Interpersonal Psychotherapy (IPT):

IPT has been shown to be effective for perinatal mental health symptoms and addressing many of the core themes that change during parenthood.[18] Role changes, interpersonal conflicts (including how to learn how to communicate more effectively), and building support are addressed. IPT has been shown to be an effective intervention for treatment of distress for people during their pregnancy and postpartum period, reducing symptoms of depression and anxiety, and helping them improve their support.[19] You learned some important IPT skills and concepts in Chapters 8 and 9.

We just discussed several options for therapy so you can be an informed consumer. As you are choosing a mental health provider for your trauma treatment, it is helpful to ask about their experience with what you went through. If they have had years of experience and a robust training background, then the hope would be that they would have the discernment to suggest what treatment methods might be the most helpful for you. A trauma therapist can also empower you to feel involved throughout your treatment. Part of trauma treatment is ensuring you are an active part of your care. You can keep collaborating with your therapist about what is and what is not working. You can find your way by partnering with professionals and educating yourself.

Are you in therapy now? Have you been considering therapy to address your reproductive trauma? Is there anything currently holding you back from starting therapy?

_____

_____

_____

Additional options

Intensive Outpatient Programs (IOPs):

You might be finding that you are white-knuckling it in between your sessions, or needing more glue to keep it all together. For people needing more frequent appointments, or finding that they need more structured support, IOPs can be tremendously beneficial. Sessions usually occur between three to five times a week and typically last for several hours. A number of IOPs began offering virtual options during the pandemic, and some have continued offering this choice. These programs tend to offer a mix of individual psychotherapy and support groups, and some also provide medication management by a psychiatrist if needed. These programs are structured and supportive, and often last for several weeks with the goal of stabilizing the person until they feel able to step back down into individual outpatient therapy.

Pregnant or postpartum people might join an IOP when they are struggling with their mental health symptoms so significantly that they are having difficulty functioning or attending to much else. The structure and frequency of IOP sessions is helpful when someone's symptoms take center stage. Examples of why a pregnant or new parent may attend an IOP include:

- being overwhelmed with the intensity of their PTSD or anxiety symptoms

- experiencing OCD, and/or having frequent intrusive and racing thoughts

- struggling with a lack of motivation

- having a difficult time getting through the day (or not able to easily care for themselves or the baby)

- having suicidal thoughts

If this option appeals to you, there are some IOPs that welcome and encourage babies to attend with their parents as part of the program.

Trauma support groups:

As we were talking earlier in Chapter 8, sometimes it can be hard to find safety in the telling of your story. It can be such a corrective experience when you can tell your story to safe people and have a contained space to be heard and believed. This is especially the case when those people have been through something similar. Perhaps you have already found an online support group helpful if you were going through infertility treatments, or joined an in-person breastfeeding support group to help you through your feeding struggles. Support groups can be incredibly beneficial on the journey of parenthood, in general, and this is particularly the case when you are experiencing challenges or finding that your own network cannot relate to what you have gone through.

Trauma support groups, in particular, can be very helpful for survivors of reproductive trauma. These groups tend to be structured in a way that they may pair any sharing with learning skills to manage the symptoms of PTSD. These trauma groups are typically led by trained therapists so that any potential triggers can be managed, and people can feel safe to share when they are activated. A number of groups are being offered via virtual means which helps with flexibility and accessibility. Some groups tend to focus more on skill building and minimize sharing for the purpose of not activating the attendees. Rather than feeling like you have to find the perfect fit right away, here's the bottom line: if you do attend a group that does not feel like a good fit for any reason, it's absolutely okay to try another group. Part of trauma recovery is learning how to find what works for you, and finding your safe people.

There are two basic types of support groups:

Process Support Groups	Skill Building Support Groups
• May be fairly informal, or may have a semi-structured format, (an agenda, everyone given time to share, etc.) depending on the focus of the group • May or may not have skill building as part of the group • These may be led by a professional, or instead, by a peer (someone who has experienced what you have)	• Tend to be more structured with less (or no) sharing time with the intention of preventing triggering of attendees • Attendees learn about the issues they are experiencing (e.g. trauma) and learn skills to manage their symptoms • These tend to be led by mental health professionals

Have you ever attended a support group? If so, what was your experience? If not, have there been any hesitations about joining a group before?

_____

_____

What might be the pros and cons of attending a support group now?

_____

_____

_____

Journaling:

As a survivor of reproductive trauma, it can be common to remember some parts of your past in fragmented bits and pieces, so journaling about your experience(s) can be helpful, whether or not you decide to share it with others. People who journal about their trauma can find validation from others, if the journal entry is shared, and it helps organize their experience and distance themselves from it.[20] Others find that keeping their journals private, instead, helps them find the freedom to express themselves and their innermost thoughts. Sometimes new insights are gained, and themes may emerge that you otherwise would not have discovered if you were just stuck in your head thinking about it. Journaling can help distance you from the story because expressive writing can have a desensitization aspect to it (meaning, as you write about your story, it may no longer have the emotional punch it once did). For example, some people found that as they used expressive writing after their babies went to the NICU, or as they recovered from their traumatic births, their PTSD symptoms reduced.[21]

Journaling can take many different forms, and can be unscripted and free-flowing, or more structured, with a themed focus, and prompts.

If you do use journaling, pay attention to how you feel before, during, and after you write. As a survivor of trauma, this can be a practice of attunement, to ensure you are staying within your *window of tolerance.*

If writing about your experience feels too overwhelming for you, or it's difficult to do this without getting triggered or going down a spiral of despair, it's okay. Please remember that there is no one way to heal. Sometimes people find that as they journal, it can be difficult to feel contained, and they may feel more triggered, like the wheels are falling off the bus. However, if you're finding that writing is both useful AND challenging, doing this with a therapist's help can be useful because they can provide you with some journaling prompts.

What has it been like for you to use the journal prompts throughout this workbook? Have you found that you prefer more of a free-flow type of journal entry, and to do this on your own? Or, do you prefer it when there are journal prompts and examples to help you "stay within the lines"?

_____

_____

_____

_____

_____

Medication support:

Sometimes, people who are pregnant or nursing worry about taking medication out of concern for how it may impact the baby. I understand this can be a complex and nuanced decision for many people; I regularly hold space for clients who are recognizing they are suffering and are wanting help but are also worried about their choices. It is very important as you weigh your options that you are informing yourself with reliable information. A prescriber (psychiatrist, psychiatric nurse practitioner, ObGyn, primary care physician, etc.) who has trained experience in prescribing medication for pregnant and postpartum people (and trauma!) can help address your questions and share any up-to-date relevant studies with you. Even if you still feel undecided about the choice, it can be useful to attend an appointment so you can ask questions and empower yourself with knowledge. It can be helpful to think about how you are currently impacted by your symptoms, and the impact if you were not to receive treatment. Questions like "How am I functioning on a daily basis?", "How long have I been feeling this way?", "What are the downsides of not taking meds?", "How bad does it get sometimes?", and "What is the impact on my ability to parent?" can be prompts to check in with yourself as you consider your options. Because indecisiveness can be a challenging aspect of trauma recovery, this can add on to what might already be a difficult decision, so this can be a good time to practice self-compassion. Sometimes giving yourself timelines might be helpful, like if you have not noticed significant improvement in *x* amount of months that you will consider a medication evaluation, or if you are nervous about the psychiatrist's recommendation but are desperate for relief, giving yourself 2 months to try it out and then re-evaluating your progress.

Couples therapy and/or parenting workshops:

As we talked a lot about in Chapters 8 and 9, your relationships have likely changed since you have become a parent, and particularly since being impacted by trauma. If your partner is also experiencing their own mental health symptoms and/or healing from their own trauma, there may be some significant stressors and conflict in your relationship right now. Going to couples therapy together can be a tremendous gift for your relationship and each other. Learning communication skills can help strengthen your bond and help you navigate through this challenging time. You can learn how to voice your needs more directly to each other, and learn how to be more empathetic. Working on your relationship can help you feel like healing is an issue you share together and are able to then conquer together. Remember that having your partner's support can also have a positive impact on your treatment, your healing, and your symptoms.[22] As you are looking for a couples' therapist, finding one that specializes in parenting, attachment, and trauma can be beneficial (and/or sex and intimacy if this is needed). Some couples' therapists are open to having the baby in session with you, and may offer virtual sessions for flexibility. Similarly, there are parenting workshops and other resources to address both your relationship and your growing bond with your baby. If you do not have the bandwidth to address your relationship right now, you can consider this option in the future as well.

Mind/body work:

From mindfulness, meditation, breath work, self-compassion, mindful movement, yoga, and beyond, you have learned a number of mind/body techniques and skills. I hope you have found a few to regularly practice to manage some of your symptoms. You can now continue your practice by downloading apps, signing up for classes, or exploring more trauma-informed options that resonate with you.

Go back and review some of the skills you learned in Chapters 5, 6, and 7. **What were some of your favorite mind/body skills that you want to keep practicing?**

_____
_____
_____
_____
_____

Now let's think about something that does not necessarily fall under mental health treatment, but is something that some parents have found to be an important part of their healing journeys. Some people find that by following up with their providers for a scheduled debrief, they can address aspects of their trauma that feel unresolved, get answers to their lingering questions, or speak up about aspects of their care they found problematic.

Debriefing with your provider

I've noticed that some people want, and can have healing and repairing conversations with a provider after their trauma. They feel heard and supported and their questions are answered. They find clarity about what happened, and even though what happened to them was still traumatic, they find some sense of validation. Certainly the opposite can be true as well, where people do not get the support, answers, or validation they are needing from their provider during the debrief, which can cause even more pain. I have found that my clients instinctively know whether or not they need this, and suspect whether or not their provider may be a helpful part of their healing. It's complicated, isn't it? Some people have providers they may want to thank for providing comfort and safety during what was otherwise one of the worst days of their lives, while others felt harmed by some of their providers. As you know yourself best and what you need, my hope is that you can determine whether this may be helpful.

I want to reassure you that if this does not sound like something you want or need, (or are recognizing that it would not feel safe to see your provider again), that is okay. Every person will need different things. Besides, both the research and my own anecdotal observation on this one are quite mixed. Some studies show that a debrief with the provider after a reproductive trauma can be beneficial in reducing a fear of future childbirth.[23] Other studies show that critical incident stress debriefing was not effective in preventing any postnatal distress.[24] I suspect part of the reason why there are such mixed results with debriefing is because this concept is not standardized across providers, meaning providers are humans, and debriefing is likely taking place in very different ways in each office.

> If you do not receive the response you were hoping for from your provider, please know that it has nothing to do with your worth, your deservingness of support, or your ability to heal.
>
> Instead, it may have to do with your provider's own "stuff" (fears, defensiveness, emotional limitations, systemic barriers, etc.).

As you think about what you went through, is there anything you have been thinking about that would be helpful to communicate or clarify with your providers?

_____

_____

Some survivors of reproductive trauma have a difficult time speaking up to their providers afterward for a multitude of reasons. Perhaps you had a negative interaction, were mistreated, or feel triggered around that person or some of the people involved in your care. Maybe the thought of returning to the hospital or clinic feels overwhelming. Yet, it's also possible that you may want to ask some questions and seek clarity about what happened during your experiences, your hospitalization, or the procedures you went through. I've found this can be the case for some survivors, particularly if there are some missing gaps of time in memory, or confusion when events happened so quickly.

If it feels uncomfortable or unsafe in any way to be with your provider, then you do not have to meet with them again, even if you would like to follow up and discuss your care, or if you have questions. Depending on where you are located in the world, your options will be different considering your patient rights and options. Options might include transferring your care to another provider, requesting your records yourself, speaking with a hospital representative, filing a grievance, or going over your medical records with another provider, if you choose.

> ### What are your options if you faced harm at the hands of your provider?
>
> It depends on where you are in the world, and what you are needing/wanting. There are some resources at the end of the book to learn about your rights and what options you might have.
>
> You may have many options such as writing a letter, asking for a meeting to review your records, filing grievances, or exploring legal options.

Some survivors have also found healing from writing a letter to their provider or hospital to express themselves, even if they did not end up sending it. Whatever choices you end up making, it's okay (and preferrable) to take your time and this is not a necessary step in your healing if this option does not appeal to you. This can be an activating process for some, and it's important you do this (or any healing work) in a way that is not further traumatizing to your system. As such, you might want to do this with a therapist who specializes in reproductive trauma, and there are other trauma-informed birth workers who also offer these services. You deserve support.

If the idea of writing a letter to your provider appeals to you, think about what you might want to include. What would you wish them to know about your experience? What would you have preferred happen instead? What questions might you write down, or what emotions might you express? What support might you need in order to tolerate this exercise?

_____
_____
_____
_____

What's next for you? Final reflections:

You are learning a lot about yourself during or after what might essentially be an existential crisis. You may have lost so much, both literally and figuratively. You may have had the rug pulled out from underneath you and your entire worldview may have been shaken. As you are now rising from the ashes and learning to find safety in your body again, you may be finding clarity in aspects of your life that you never had before. You may be reappraising so much of your world and seeing a preciousness to life and your health that is even more important to you now. Or, your journey may have just begun.

As you read through this chapter and learned about some of the treatment options that can help you continue to heal, what options stand out for you? Which treatment options do you see yourself pursuing now, or shortly?

_____
_____
_____
_____
_____

Of the treatment options and choices you read about, which sound interesting but may be something that you would rather consider at some point in the future?

_____
_____
_____
_____
_____

What are some of the biggest takeaways you have learned as you have worked through this book? Is it a specific skill? Is it learning something that you never learned before about trauma, like the way your mind and body have responded to what you went through? Did you learn more about the way that you hold trauma in your body? Or perhaps, are you feeling more empowered by focusing on what is within your control (such as concentrating on strengthening your bond with your baby)?

_____

_____

_____

_____

This part may be difficult and you may not be ready for it yet, so please return to this prompt when you're able. Is there anything that you are grateful for right now, no matter how small? It might be gratitude in your ability to take care of yourself in new ways, your support network that you're cultivating, the resiliency you did not even know you had, etc.

_____

_____

_____

_____

_____

What have you learned about yourself along the way?

_____

_____

_____

_____

_____

Thank you for being here and for doing this work. It's been an honor to imagine us working through your journey together, and I wish you ongoing support, strength and peace as you continue on through your healing.

Chapter highlights

- Everyone's healing journey may look different, and healing is possible.

- Posttraumatic growth can look like having a transformed experience, and feeling like a changing person following a traumatic experience.

- Resiliency, or learning how to cope with difficult experiences, can be taught and practiced.

- There are numerous treatment options to continue your healing journey, and finding the right choice for you can be part of regaining control.

- You have worked really hard to build some new skills throughout this book. This chapter has given you some ideas of how you can continue your healing journey.

Notes

1 Tedeschi, R.G., & Calhoun, L.G. (1996). The posttraumatic growth inventory: measuring the positive legacy of trauma. *Journal of Traumatic Stress*, 9(3), 455–471. https://doi.org/10.1007/BF02103658; Tedeschi, R.G., & Calhoun, L.G. (2004). Posttraumatic growth: conceptual foundations and empirical evidence. *Psychological Inquiry*, 15(1), 1–18. http://www.jstor.org/stable/20447194

2 Ayers, S. (2017). Birth trauma and post-traumatic stress disorder: the importance of risk and resilience. *Journal of Reproductive and Infant Psychology*, 35(5), 427–430. doi:10.1080/02646838.2017.1386874; Beck, C.T., Watson, S., & Gable, R.K. (2018). Traumatic childbirth and its aftermath: is there anything positive? *The Journal of Perinatal Education*, 27(3), 175–184. https://doi.org/10.1891/1058-1243.27.3.175; Sawyer, A., & Ayers, S. (2009). Post-traumatic growth in women after childbirth. *Psychology & Health*, 24(4), 457–471; Sawyer, A., Ayers, S., Young, D., Bradley, R., & Smith, H. (2012). Posttraumatic growth after childbirth: a prospective study. *Psychology & Health*, 27(3), 362–377. https://doi.org/10.1080/08870446.2011.578745

3 Pagnoni, G. (2012). Dynamical properties of BOLD activity from the ventral posteromedial cortex associated with meditation and attentional skills. *Journal of Neuroscience*, 32(15) 5242–5249. https://doi.org/10.1523/JNEUROSCI.4135-11.2012; Yang, C.C., Barrós-Loscertales, A., Li, M., Pinazo, D., Borchardt, V., Avila, C., & Walter, M. (2019). Alterations in brain structure and amplitude of low-frequency after 8 weeks of mindfulness meditation training in meditation-naïve subjects. *Scientific Reports*, 9(10977). https://www.nature.com/articles/s41598-019-47470-4

4 Beck, C.T., Eaton, C.M., & Gable, R.K. (2016). Vicarious posttraumatic growth in labor and delivery nurses. *Journal of Obstetric, Gynecologic, and Neonatal Nursing*, 45(6), 801–812. https://doi.org/10.1016/j.jogn.2016.07.008

5 Sippel, L.M., Pietrzak, R.H., Charney, D.S., Mayes, L.C., & Southwick, S.M. (2015). How does social support enhance resilience in the trauma-exposed individual? *Ecology and Society*, 20(4), 10.

6 Southwick, S.M., & Charney, D.S. (2012). *Resilience: the Science of Mastering Life's Greatest Challenges*. Cambridge University Press. https://doi.org/10.1017/CBO9781139013857

7 Rothschild, B. (2010). *8 Keys to Safe Trauma Recovery: Take Charge Strategies to Empower Your Healing*. Norton.

8 Adapted from M. Harris and R. Fallot (Eds.) (2001). Using trauma theory to design service systems. *New Directions for Mental Health Services*, 89.

9 Baas, M., van Pampus, M.G., Braam, L., Stramrood, C., & de Jongh, A. (2020). The effects of PTSD treatment during pregnancy: systematic review and case study. *European Journal of Psychotraumatology*, 11(1), 1762310. https://doi.org/10.1080/20008198.2020.1762310

10 Baas, M.A.M., van Pampus, M.G., Stramrood, C.A.I., Dijksman, L.M., Vanhommerig, J.W., & de Jongh, A. (2022). Treatment of pregnant women with fear of childbirth using EMDR therapy: results of a multi-center randomized controlled trial. *Frontiers in Psychiatry*, 12, 798249. doi:10.3389/fpsyt.2021.798249

11 Stramrood, C., van der Velde, J., Weijmar Schultz, W.C.M., & van Pampus, M. (2011, March). A new application of EMDR: treatment of posttraumatic stress following childbirth. Poster presentation at the American Psychosomatic Society 69th Annual Scientific Meeting, San Antonio, TX; Stramrood, C., Paarlberg, K.M., Vingerhoets, A.J., van den Berg, P.P., & van Pampus, M.G. (2012, March). Posttraumatic stress following childbirth: diagnosis, treatment and prevention. Poster presented at the 70th annual scientific meeting of the American Psychomatic Society, Athens, Greece; Stramrood, C.A.I., van der Velde, J., Doornbos, B., Paarlberg, K.M., Weijmar Schultz, W.C.M., & van Pampus, M.G. (2012). The patient observer: eye-movement desensitization and reprocessing for the treatment of posttraumatic stress following childbirth. *Birth: Issues in Perinatal Care*, 39(1), 70–76. https://doi.org/(...)23-536X.2011.00517.x

12 Beck, C.T. (2004). Birth trauma: in the eye of the beholder. *Nursing Research*, 53, 28–35; Chiorino, V., Cattaneo, M.C., Macchi, E.A., Salerno, R., Roveraro, S., Bertolucci, G.G., Mosca, F., Fumagalli, M., Cortinovis, I., Carletto, S., & Fernandez, I. (2020). The EMDR recent birth trauma protocol: a pilot randomised clinical trial after traumatic childbirth. *Psychology & Health*, 35(7), 795–810. https://doi.org/10.1080/08870446.2019.1699088; Sandström, M., Wiberg, B., Wikman, M., Willman, A.K., & Högberg, U. (2008). A pilot study of eye movement desensitisation and reprocessing treatment (EMDR) for post-traumatic stress after childbirth. *Midwifery*, 24(1), 62–73. https://doi.org/10.1016/j.midw.2006.07.008; van Deursen-Gelderloos, M., & Bakker, E. (2015). Is EMDR effective for women with posttraumatic stress symptoms after childbirth? *European Health Psychologist*, 17(S), 873.

13 Linehan, M.M. (1993). *Cognitive-behavioral Treatment of Borderline Personality Disorder*. Guilford Press.

14 Snoek, A., Beekman, A.T.F., Dekker, J., et al. (2020) A randomized controlled trial comparing the clinical efficacy and cost-effectiveness of Eye Movement Desensitization and Reprocessing (EMDR) and integrated EMDR-Dialectical Behavioural Therapy (DBT) in the treatment of patients with post-traumatic stress disorder and comorbid (Sub)clinical borderline personality disorder: study design. *BMC Psychiatry*, 20, 396. https://doi.org/10.1186/s12888-020-02713-x; Steil, R., Dittmann, C., Müller-Engelmann, M., Dyer, A., Maasch, A.M., & Priebe, K. (2018). Dialectical behaviour therapy for posttraumatic stress disorder related to childhood sexual abuse: a pilot study in an outpatient treatment setting. *European Journal of Psychotraumatology*, 9(1), 1423832. https://doi.org/10.1080/20008198.2018.1423832

15 Beierl, E.T., Böllinghaus, I., Clark, D.M., Glucksman, E., & Ehlers, A. (2020). Cognitive paths from trauma to posttraumatic stress disorder: a prospective study of Ehlers and Clark's model in survivors of assaults or road traffic collisions. *Psychological Medicine*, 50(13), 2172–2181. https://doi.org/10.1017/S0033291719002253; Kar, N. (2011). Cognitive behavioral therapy for the treatment of post-traumatic stress disorder: a review. *Neuropsychiatric Disease and Treatment*, 7, 167–181. doi:10.2147/NDT.S10389

16 Ayers, S., McKenzie-McHarg, K., & Eagle, A. (2007). Cognitive behavior therapy for postnatal post-traumatic stress disorder: case studies. *Journal of Psychosomatic Obstetrics & Gynecology*, 28, 177–184.
17 Stevens, N.R., Lillis, T.A., Wagner, L., Tirone, V., Hobfoll, S.E., Lillis, T.A., ... Hobfoll, S.E. (2019). A feasibility study of trauma-sensitive obstetric care for low-income, ethno-racial minority pregnant abuse survivors. *Journal of Psychosomatic Obstetrics & Gynecology*, 40(1), 66–74.
18 Grigoriadis, S., & Ravitz, P. (2007). An approach to interpersonal psychotherapy for postpartum depression focusing on interpersonal changes. *Can Fam Physician*, 53(9), 1469–1475.
19 Bright, K.S., Charrois, E.M., Mughal, M.K., Wajid, A., McNeil, D., Stuart, S., Hayden, K.A., & Kingston, D. (2020). Interpersonal psychotherapy to reduce psychological distress in perinatal women: a systematic review. *International Journal of Environmental Research and Public Health*, 17(22), 8421. https://doi.org/10.3390/ijerph17228421
20 Blainey, S.H., & Slade, P. (2015). Exploring the process of writing about and sharing traumatic birth experiences online. *British Journal of Health Psychology*, 20(20), 243–260; Colton, A.B. (2004). Sharing birth stories with others and receiving validating was helpful in healing. *From Trauma to (Re)Birth: The Birth Story as a Site of Transformation*, 24(3), 679–704.
21 Furuta, M., Horsch, A., Ng, E.S.W., Bick, D., Spain, D., & Sin, J. (2018). Effectiveness of trauma-focused psychological therapies for treating post-traumatic stress disorder symptoms in women following childbirth: a systematic review and meta-analysis. *Frontiers in Psychiatry*, 9, 591. https://doi.org/10.3389/fpsyt.2018.00591
22 Ganz, M.B., Rasmussen, H.F., McDougall, T.V., Corner, G.W., Black, T.T., & De Los Santos, H.F. (2022). Emotionally focused couple therapy within VA healthcare: reductions in relationship distress, PTSD, and depressive symptoms as a function of attachment-based couple treatment. *Couple and Family Psychology: Research and Practice*, 11(1), 15–32. https://doi.org/10.1037/cfp0000210; Misri, S., Kostaras, X., Fox, D., & Kostaras, D. (2000). The impact of partner support in the treatment of postpartum depression. *Can J Psychiatry*, 45(6), 554–558; Shnaider, P., Sijercic, I., Wanklyn, S.G., Suvak, M.K., & Monson, C.M. (2017). The role of social support in cognitive-behavioral conjoint therapy for posttraumatic stress disorder. *Behavior Therapy*, 48(3), 285–294. https://doi.org/10.1016/j.beth.2016.05.003
23 Kershaw, K., Jolly, J., Bhabra, K., & Ford, J. (2005). Randomised controlled trial of community debriefing following operative delivery. *BJOG: An International Journal of Obstetrics And Gynaecology*, 112(11), 1504–1509. https://doi.org/10.1111/j.1471-0528.2005.00723.x
24 Priest, S.R., Henderson, J., Evans, S.F., & Hagan, R. (2003). Stress debriefing after childbirth: a randomised controlled trial. *The Medical Journal of Australia*, 178(11), 542–545. https://doi.org/10.5694/j.1326-5377.2003.tb05355.x; Selkirk, R., McLaren, S., Ollerenshaw, A., McLachlan, A.J., & Moten, J. (2006) The longitudinal effects of midwife-led postnatal debriefing on the psychological health of mothers. *Journal of Reproductive and Infant Psychology*, 24, 133–147.

Chapter 13

Resources and support

The resources in this chapter represent some of the concepts covered throughout this workbook and I hope they inspire and support you on your healing journey. These resources are up to date at the time of publishing. This list is not exhaustive by any means but represents some viable options to look for support.

Websites

Attachment/bonding/relationships:

- Circle of Security: circleofsecurityinternational.com

    o Videos and other info to learn ways to enhance your connection with your child

- The Gottman Institute: Gottman.com

    o Find a Gottman-trained therapist and "Bringing Home Baby" parents workshop

Birth advocacy/reproductive justice:

- Birth Equity: birthequity.org

    o Advocating for change with the Black maternal health and infant mortality crisis, providing training, research, and advocacy work

- Birth Monopoly: birthmonopoly.com

    o Info on healthcare rights, filing grievances with a hospital or state board

- Black Mamas Matter Alliance: blackmamasmatter.org

    o Resources, advocacy for Black mothers, Black Maternal Health week

- Every Mother Counts: everymothercounts.org

    o Addressing maternal health and equitable, respectful, and accessible maternity care

- Improving Birth: improvingbirth.org

    o Info about improving birth experiences, education about filing grievances, resources for birth trauma survivors

DOI: 10.4324/9781003379973-16

- Shades of Blue Project: shadesofblueproject.org
  - o Breaking cultural barriers in maternal mental health

Birth trauma:

- Birth Trauma Association: birthtraumaassociation.org.uk
  - o Support, resources, info for parents, partners, and providers. UK-based
- Make Birth Better: makebirthbetter.org
  - o Support for survivors of traumatic births and trainings for professionals. UK-based
- Prevention and Treatment of Traumatic Birth: pattch.org
  - o Education to prevent or reduce reproductive PTSD, resources for survivors and providers

Dads and partners:

- Music Football Fatherhood: musicfootballfatherhood.com
  - o Conversations around fatherhood and mental health. UK-based
- Postpartum Support International: postpartum.net
  - o Support for fathers, partners, queer and trans parents via free info, support groups, and online chat forums
- Prepare Foundation: prepare.org.au
  - o Supporting fathers throughout the pregnancy and postpartum period. Australia-based

EMDR therapy:

- EMDR International Association: emdria.org
  - o Info about EMDR therapy, find a therapist by specialty type and geographic area (you can filter by "birth trauma and pregnancy loss")

Emergency resources:

- Crisis Text Lines: crisistextline.org
  - o Text HOME to 741741 to connect with a crisis counselor in the US and Canada, text SHOUT to 85258 in the UK, and HELLO to 50808 in Ireland
- US National Suicide Prevention Lifeline: 988lifeline.org Dial 988
  - o Lifeline available 24/7 for referrals and support. US nationwide
- SAMHSA: Substance Abuse and Mental Health Services Administration samhsa.gov
  - o 1-800-662-4357 helpline available for referrals and information. US nationwide

Infertility:

- Infertility IQ: fertilityiq.com
  - o Provider reviews, educational video content including mental health info
- Resolve: Resolve.org
  - o Advocacy, support, info

Intensive outpatient programs:

- To find a list of Inpatient and Intensive Outpatient Perinatal Psychiatric Programs, go to Postpartum Support International: postpartum.net

Grief/loss:

- Postpartum Support International: postpartum.net
  - Free online support groups
- Return to Zero H.O.P.E.: rtzhope.org
  - Info for friends and family, online support groups, retreats

Medication:

- Mother to Baby: mothertobaby.org/
  - Medications during pregnancy and breastfeeding
- Postpartum Support International Directory: postpartum.net
  - Find a Perinatal Psychiatrist, Nurse Practitioner, or other prescriber in your area

Meditation and mindfulness:

- Self-Compassion: self-compassion.org
  - Free self-compassion guided practices and research
- Dr. Arielle Schwartz: drarielleschwartz.com
  - Free videos on trauma-informed yoga and self-compassion practices
- Tara Brach: tarabrach.com
  - Guided meditations including trauma-informed practices

OCD:

- International OCD Foundation: iocdf.org
  - Includes info about Perinatal OCD
- Maternal OCD: maternalocd.org
  - Resources for mothers and professionals, helpline for support, articles, and research. UK-based

Perinatal mental health resources:

- Action on Postpartum Psychosis: app-network.org
  - Peer support, training, and research. UK-based
- Gidget Foundation: gidgetfoundation.org.au
  - Info and support for PMADs. Australia-based
- MGH Center for Women's Mental Health: womensmentalhealth.org
  - Info about medication, studies/research, PMADs, treatment resources, etc.

- PANDAS: pandasfoundation.org.uk

  o Postnatal depression awareness, support groups, free hotline. UK-based

- Perinatal Anxiety and Depression Aotearoa: pada.nz

  o Support, information, and access to treatment. New Zealand-based.

- Perinatal Mental Health Project: pmhp.za.org

  o Support, info, and access to treatment, free helplines in English and Afrikaans. South Africa-based.

- Postpartum Stress Center: postpartumstress.com

  o Education, support, trainings. Pennsylvania-based.

- Postpartum Health Alliance: postpartumhealthalliance.org

  o Resources, support groups, educational and training events, free warmline. San Diego, California-based.

- Postpartum Support International: postpartum.net

  o Online support groups, referrals to providers worldwide who specialize in perinatal mental health, info, free helpline

- Postpartum Support Network Africa: postpartumafrica.org/

  o Support, awareness, and connections to treatment. Africa-based.

Books

Attachment:

- *Attached* by Amir Levin, M.D. and Rachel Heller, M.A.

- *Healing Your Attachment Wounds* by Diane Poole Heller, Ph.D.

Infertility:

- *Infertility and PTSD: The Unchartered Storm* by Joanna Flemons, LCSW

Mindfulness:

- *Trauma Sensitive Mindfulness: Practices for Safe and Transformative Healing* by David A. Treleaven

- *Self-Compassion: How Women Can Harness Kindness to Speak Up, Claim Their Power and Thrive* by Kristin Neff, Ph.D.

Perinatal mental health:

- *Beyond the Blues* by Shoshana S. Bennett, Ph.D. and Pec Indman, Ed.D., MFT

- *Dropping the Baby and Other Scary Thoughts* by Karen Kleiman and Amy Wenzel

- *Good Moms Have Scary Thoughts: A Healing Guide to the Secret Fears of New Mothers* by Karen Kleiman, MSW

- *Parental Mental Health: Factoring in Fathers* by Jane I. Honikman and Daniel B. Singley

- *The Postpartum Husband* by Karen Kleiman, MSW

- *The Pregnancy and Postpartum Anxiety Workbook: Practical Skills to Help You Overcome Anxiety, Worry, Panic Attacks, Obsessions, and Compulsions* by Pamela S. Weigartz, Ph.D. and Kevin L. Gyoerkoe, Psy.D.

- *The Pregnancy and Postpartum Mood Workbook: The Guide to Surviving Your Emotions When Having a Baby* by Bethany Warren, LCSW, PMH-C and Beth Creager Berger, Ph.D.

- *The Pregnancy Workbook: Manage Anxiety and Worry with CBT and Mindfulness Techniques* by Katayune Kaeni, Psy.D., PMH-C

Relationships:

- *And Baby Makes Three: The Six-Step Plan for Preserving Marital Intimacy and Rekindling Romance After Baby Arrives* by John Gottman, Ph.D. and Julie Schwartz Gottman, Ph.D.

- *Hold Me Tight* by Dr. Sue Johnson (and workbook by the same name)

- *What About Us? A New Parents Guide to Safeguarding Your Over-Anxious, Over-Extended, Sleep-Deprived Relationship* by Karen Kleiman, MSW

Reproductive Justice:

- *Birthing Justice: Black Women, Pregnancy and Childbirth* edited by Julia Chinyere Oparah and Alicia Bonaparte

- *Reproductive Justice: An Introduction* by Loretta Ross and Rickie Solinger

- *Reproductive Justice and Sexual Rights: Transnational Perspectives* by Tanya Saroj Bakhru

Yoga:

- *Trauma-Informed Yoga for Survivors of Sexual Assault: Practices for Healing and Teaching with Compassion* (and companion card deck of affirmations) by Zahabiyah Yamasaki, M.Ed., RYT

- *Yoga for Trauma Recovery: Theory, Philosophy and Practice* by Lisa Danylchuk

Apps

Perinatal and postpartum:

- Believe Her: believeherapp.com

  o Black Maternal Support

- MGH Perinatal Depression Scale: MGHPDS

  o Edinburgh Postnatal Depression Scale, info, and resources

Meditation/relaxation/breathing:

- Calm: www.calm.com

  o Meditation and guided relaxation exercises including sleep

- Headspace: headspace.com
  - o Meditation exercises
- Insight Timer: insighttimer.com
  - o Free relaxation and guided meditation exercises including trauma informed options and sleep

Podcasts

I love podcasts and there are simply too many great ones for me to name here. These are a few that might be helpful on your healing journey, and those that hit some of the major themes we've covered in this book.

- The Birth Trauma Mama Podcast:
  - o Personal stories and professional guests
- Good Inside: goodinside.podcast.com
  - o Parenting podcast with themes of attachment and connection
- Mom and Mind: momandmind.com
  - o Various Perinatal Mental Health topics including reproductive trauma, pregnancy loss, EMDR therapy, etc.

INDEX